TRAVELER
New York

NATIONAL GEOGRAPHIC

TRAVELER
New York

Michael S. Durham

Contents

How to use this guide 6–7 About the author 8
New York areas 47–225 Excursions 227–234 Travelwise 235–264
Index 265–269 Credits 270–271

Page 1: Taxicabs
Pages 2–3: Manhattan's
sparkling skyline
Left: The Chrysler
Building

How to use this guide

See back flap for keys to text and map symbols

The *National Geographic Traveler* brings you the best of New York in text, pictures, and maps. Divided into three sections, the guide begins with an overview of history and culture. Following are ten area chapters with featured sites chosen by the author for their particular interest and treated in depth. Each chapter opens with its own contents list for easy reference. A final chapter suggests possible excursions from the city.

A pictorial map introduces each area of the city, highlighting the featured sites and locating other places of interest. Walks, plotted on their own maps, suggest routes for discovering the most about an area. Features and sidebars offer intriguing detail on history, culture, or contemporary life.

The final section, Travelwise, lists essential information for the traveler—pre-trip planning, getting around, and survival—plus a selection of hotels and restaurants arranged by area, shops, and entertainment possibilities.

To the best of our knowledge, site information is accurate as of the press date. However, it's always advisable to call ahead whenever possible.

66

Color coding

Each area of the city is color coded for easy reference. Find the area you want on the map on the front flap, and look for the color flash at the top of the pages of the relevant chapter. Information in **Travelwise** is also color coded to each area.

South Street Seaport Museum & Marketplace
- 🅰 Map p. 48
- ✉ 12 Fulton St.
- ☎ 212/748-8600
- 🕐 Closed Tues. in winter
- 💲 $$
- 🚇 Subway: 2, 3, 4, 5 to Fulton St.

Visitor information

Practical information is given in the side column next to each major site (see key to symbols on back flap). The map reference gives the page number where the site is shown on a map. Further details include the site's address, telephone number, days closed, entrance fee ranging from $ (under $4) to $$$$$ (over $25), and the nearest subway stop. Visitor information for smaller sites is provided in parentheses within the text.

TRAVELWISE

- Color-coded area name
- Category name
- Hotel name, price range
- Address, telephone, & fax numbers
- Brief description of hotel
- Hotel facilities & credit card details
- Category name
- Restaurant name & price range
- Address & telephone number
- Brief description of restaurant
- Restaurant facilities & credit card details

Hotel & restaurant prices

An explanation of the price ranges used in entries is given in the Hotels & Restaurants section beginning on p. 238.

AREA MAPS

Important featured site

Point of interest

- A locator map accompanies each area map and shows the location of that area in the city.

WALKING TOURS

Featured site (in bold) on walk route

Direction of route

Walk route

Start point

Building outline

Red numbered bullets link sites on map to descriptions in the text

Point of interest not on walk route

- An information box gives the starting and ending points, time and length of walk, and places not to miss along the route.

EXCURSION MAPS

Town containing point of interest

State

Point of interest

- Towns and cities described in the Excursions chapter (pp. 227–34) are highlighted in yellow on the map. Other suggested places to visit are also highlighted and are shown with a red diamond symbol.

TRAVELER
New York

About the author

Michael S. Durham, born and raised in New York City, now lives far from those streets in rural upstate New York. His continuing interest in the city is reflected in his writings, particularly the Mid-Atlantic volume of the *Smithsonian Guides to Historic America*. He has been an editor at the American Heritage Publishing Company and a correspondent, writer, and editor for *Life* magazine in both Paris and New York City.

His books include *Desert Between the Mountains* (Henry Holt, 1997); *Miracles of Mary* (HarperCollins, 1995); and *Powerful Days* (Stewart, Tabori & Chang, 1991), based on his coverage of the Civil Rights movement in the 1960s.

From experience he knows that New York City is not only a fine place to visit but a great place to live as well.

With contributions by:
Mary Ann Lynch, contributing editor and author of New York today
Lauren McGrath, compiler of Travelwise

History
& culture

Times Square

New York today

NEW YORK CITY, THE TURN OF THE 21ST CENTURY. TIMES SQUARE GLEAMS from its spectacular high-tech makeover. Harlem pulses to the beat of an all-out economic renaissance. Throughout Manhattan and the boroughs, museums and galleries play musical chairs, and many are expanding. But the events of Sept. 11, 2001, have tested the city's fiber as never before in its 400-year history. The World Trade Center destruction and aftermath galvanized the world's attention. No better tribute could be paid to the lives destroyed than by the city's response, memorializing the tragedy while continuing forward with confidence and resolve.

The global nexus of creativity and commerce, the Big Apple is now more than ever the nation's heartbeat. Countless millions trace their ancestry to New York. People from all corners of the world keep coming, to seek a better life or realize a personal dream. Immigrants and itinerants, dreamers and schemers, students and professionals, these and more transplant themselves "beside the golden door." This ever expanding cultural mix propels change and creativity, making the city endlessly fascinating.

The question is not who lives in New York City, but rather, who does not? Whether you are Old World Italian, Chinese, Jamaican, Greek, Islamic, Slavic, or Iroquois Indian, you can find a neighborhood waiting for you, or you can start one up. In one sense, the essence of New York is its ever changing population base, but there is tremendous stability within all that change. People come here with their traditions intact. They find niches in the workplace, settle, and assimilate, but they do not forget or discard their backgrounds.

Parades honoring various ethnic groups are as regular as the daily papers. Major ones such as the Puerto Rico Day Parade and St. Patrick's Day Parade sweep along Manhattan's wide thoroughfares. Other more intimate celebrations, such as the Italian processions with saints carried aloft offer an authentic version of old-time traditions.

All over town, institutions are renovating, adding on, improving their offerings and facilities. Characteristically, the city hangs onto what works and adds to, modulates, and sometimes even miraculously resurrects, what has not. Thus Times Square, for a while on a downward slide, was transformed. Another crossroads, Columbus Circle, will soon have a megacomplex that will bring new jobs and house a jazz center. Elsewhere, commercial development is rescuing underused space. Renovated large lofts around Chelsea and the Meatpacking District are new havens for galleries and artists. The future relocation of a SoHo museum to the Lower East Side will enrich the vibrant scene already there.

Entertainment-wise, the future promises terrific excitement. TriBeCa staged its first Annual film Festival in 2002, a sign of Lower Manhattan's continuing comeback after 9/11. The IRT No. 7 subway to Queens, where a new arts and culture scene flourishes, has been designated part of the National Millennium Trail. The city is on the short list to host the 2012 Olympic Games. The Grammy Awards are back for the first time in years, and the city is working on getting the Oscar awards or some part of the program, plus the Super Bowl in 2007 or 2008. Meanwhile, well-organized civic and public groups vigilantly keep watch that growth and preservation are balanced.

At times the city may seem to be a chaotic jumble of worn infrastructure, bickering politicians, gridlocked traffic from Macy's to the Holland Tunnel, and garbage piled up high during strikes. And in some respects, that it is. But whatever its problems or defeats, its victories are of such magnitude, its achievements so grand, its sheer human spectacle so astonishing, that nothing ever makes it stop. As for those who choose to make New York their home, or those who find they just have to visit again, the chances are they will have discovered that New York City might really be the

A gift of friendship from the French in 1886, the Statue of Liberty still shines in New York Harbor.

world's most unique metropolis. It is without question the city that never sleeps, a place where at any time of day or night it is possible to find food, entertainment, drugstores, transportation, and architectural spectacle all around—and that's just for starters.

Maybe this is the kicker that separates a New Yorker from those who find the city is not for them: To survive in New York City, one must actually be aware of one's surroundings, ready to adapt, eager to excel, willing to be constantly tested in every possible way, and—

most importantly—in the know. About anything and everything. If New Yorkers are anything, they are "up to speed." In New York you can have a fascinating conversation with anyone you meet, from the street panhandler trying to sell you an original poem to the person seated next to you in the subway or Shea Stadium, from your waiter or—it goes without saying—your cab driver. And not only are they all in the know, but they know they are in the know, and they are strongly opinionated about what they know.

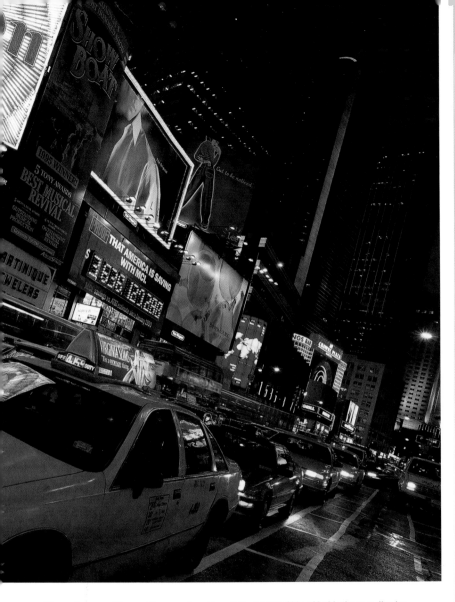

Times Square, ablaze with neon signs, lies at the heart of New York's theater district.

NEW YORK, NEW YORK

Who might be New York's power players today? Wall Street traders, yes, celebrities, sometimes. Donald Trump, George Steinbrenner, Whoopi Goldberg, former Mayor Rudy Giuliani, Beverly Sills—we can make a very long list. But power players are also the subway conductor on your trip uptown to the zoo, the park ranger at Ellis Island who brings history to life, the baker who makes those bagels that you seek out on your every trip to New York. And power players are firemen, policemen, and emergency workers who put themselves in harm's way.

Power players can be musicians, writers, actors, and artists, forging inspiring works. In *Gangs of New York* (2002), Martin Scorsese cinematically re-creates New York's bloody Draft Riots of 1863, dramatizing their spark in the conflict between an Irish immigrant and a "nativist" American, and their followers. Remove the men and the story changes. Remove their followers and the story changes, too.

The point is that each and every resident has been, and is, vital to the New York mix, part of its incredible, unfolding destiny. Eight million people live in New York. It takes all of them to light up the metropolis to a voltage that casts its light upon the rest of the world. New Yorkers crammed together are the phenomenon that makes the city.

EATING OUT IN NEW YORK

No city in the country comes close to being New York's culinary equal. Nowhere can you find so many different things to eat and places to eat them. You can buy a hot pretzel—or a hot dog—from a street vendor. You can sit at a sushi bar and dine on raw fish. You can sample the cooking of some of the world's greatest chefs. New York has seafood and soul food—and Chinese, Japanese, Korean, and Thai restaurants galore. You can even have coffee in the Caffé Vivaldi where Woody Allen filmed

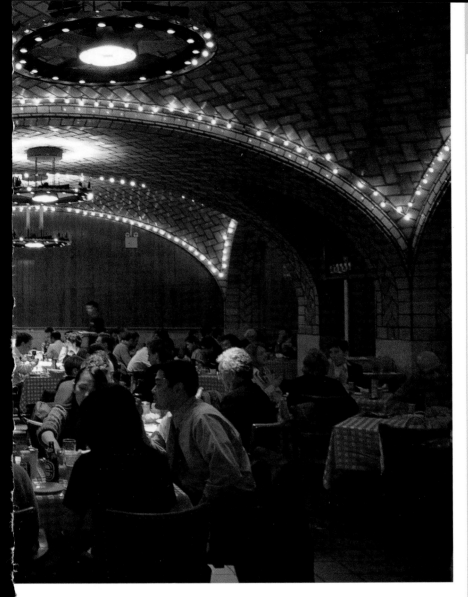

You can find some of New York's fine seafood beneath the vaulted ceilings of Grand Central's Oyster Bar.

Bullets over Broadway. But smokers be warned: 2002 restrictions ban smoking completely in many cafés, restaurants, and bars.

New York's taste in food has been shaped by its immigrant population. Here, plain down-home American cooking is considered exotic, and the city's few genuine diners are chic. Many foods and drinks familiar to the rest of the country originated here. The recipe for the round doughy bagel, which is boiled, then baked, was a closely held secret in the Jewish community. In the 1960s the rest of the country discovered bagels, but somehow they still taste better in New York.

Vichysoisse, another all-American favorite with a French name, was invented at the now-extinct Ritz-Carlton Hotel. The egg cream is a blending of seltzer, chocolate syrup, and milk

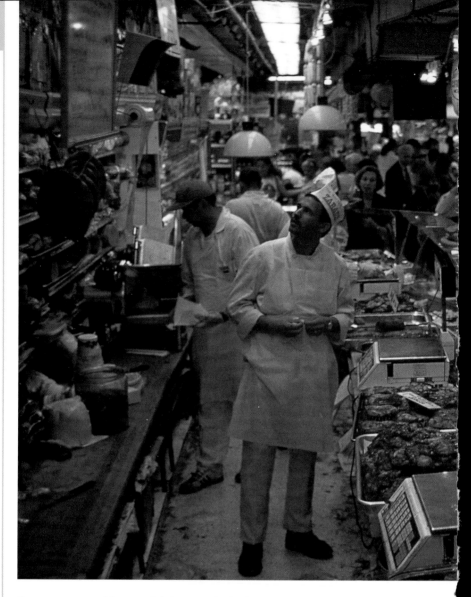

(but no eggs or cream) known only in New York. On the other hand, the Reuben sandwich—a daunting combination of corned beef, swiss cheese, and sauerkraut (on New York rye, of course)—has a national following.

Delmonico's restaurant (*56 Beaver St.*) claims to have invented lobster Newburg and baked Alaska and gave its name to the Delmonico steak. Until Delmonico's opened in 1831, fine Parisian restaurants did not exist in the United States. The first restaurant to print its menu in French or allow women in the dining room, it is still at the downtown location it has occupied since 1891.

No culinary tour of New York would be complete without a meal in a delicatessen and a coffee shop. Here the food is hearty, the service brusque, and the amenities few. The delicatessen came with immigrants from Germany and central Europe. Some are strictly kosher and their specialties—pastrami, whitefish, matzo-ball soup—might be exotic to some palates, but their huge menus have something for every taste. Try Katz's Delicatessen or

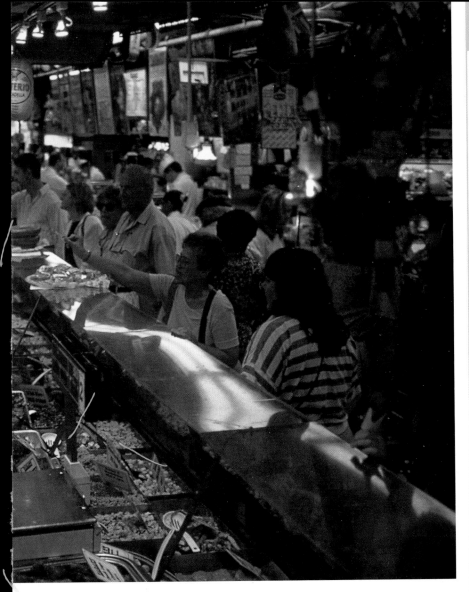

Zabar's delicatessan and food shop on the Upper West Side serves up a stunning variety of comestibles.

the celebrity-struck Stage Delicatessen.

Coffee shops fill a need for quick and inexpensive restaurants. They offer delicatessenlike specialties—lox, cream cheese, and bagels for Sunday brunch—with ethnic touches depending on the owner (today probably a Greek). In recent years, the coffee shop, which never made much fuss about its coffee, has been under siege from coffee bars operated by chains such as Starbucks. And trendy restaurants open and close with lightning speed in SoHo, though the many operated by restaurateur Drew Nieporent in TriBeCa, including Nobu, seem longer lived, and excellent restaurants can be found in hotels such as the Trump International Hotel and Towers at Columbus Circle, home to the four-star restaurant, Jean Georges. ■

History of New York

IN 1998 NEW YORK CITY MARKED ITS "CENTENNIAL." COMPARED WITH THE gusto the city brought to other recent anniversaries—the centennials of the Brooklyn Bridge and the Statue of Liberty, for example—it was a lackluster affair. For one thing, almost everyone realized that the city was much, much older. For another, what was actually being commemorated was not a founding or a discovery, but the 100th anniversary of an administrative act: the incorporation of the city within its present boundaries.

zThe consolidation added the boroughs of Brooklyn, the Bronx, Staten Island, and Queens to Manhattan, greatly increasing the tax base; it also increased the city's population from two million to nearly three million, making Greater New York in 1898 the second largest city in the world—next only to London, with four million people. But it has never been the city's size that distinguishes it. It is the spirit that possesses the city and its residents. New Yorkers dramatically demonstrated their proud resilience in the recovery after the terrorist attack on the World Trade Center on Sept. 11, 2001.

A 1664 map of New Amsterdam shows the area that is today Lower Manhattan.

t' Fort nieuw Amsterdam op de Manhatans

There are many other dates worthy of note. For example: 1609, when English explorer Henry Hudson passed Manhattan Island on his way up the river that now bears his name; 1625, when the first permanent settlement was established on Manhattan; 1639 (for Bronx residents), when a Dane, Johannes Bronck, settled just north of Manhattan. Anglophiles might celebrate 1674, the year the English took control of the city away from the Dutch, but patriots surely prefer November 25, 1783, when the British left New York City for good after the Revolutionary War. For more than a century, Evacuation Day, as it was called, was celebrated with enthusiasm in New York City.

Of course, Manhattan and the surrounding region was "discovered"—if that's the right word—by Paleo-Indians about 11,500 years ago. Their descendants were living in the region when Giovanni da Verrazano became the first European to sail into New York Harbor in 1524, a year the city's many Italians honor, although da Verrazano was sailing for France. Other groups relate to other dates. Africans came to New Amsterdam as slaves in 1626, the year Peter Minuit purchased the island of Manhattan from the Indians. There would not be a serious attempt to free them until 1799, when the state legislature passed the Gradual Emancipation Act. Jews might well honor the year 1654, when 23 Sephardic refugees from Brazil arrived in New York and formed Shearith Israel—the first Jewish congregation in the city and America.

DUTCH NEW AMSTERDAM

The first Europeans to spend any time on Manhattan Island were Adraien Block, a Dutch navigator, and his crew, who passed the winter of 1613 there after their ship burned offshore. Over the winter and with the help of Indians, Block built another ship and set sail for home. On the way out, Block sailed through the tricky strait in the East River that he named Hellegat (Hell's Gate) into the body of water he called Long Island Sound and on to Block Island, which he named for himself.

The same year, 1614, the colony called New Netherland was formed, with most of its activity centered up the Hudson River near Albany. In 1625, some Dutch families from elsewhere in the colony were ordered to Manhattan Island, and the next year their leader, Peter Minuit, purchased it from the Indians with trinkets, blankets, cloth, and metal goods said to be worth about $24. The Indians had no concept of property and could not have imagined they were selling their land rights. And though Minuit is remembered as one of history's great bargainers, some might say that $24 would not have been a bad price for an island that was—except for the southern tip where the settlers were eking out a miserable existence—mostly wilderness. The earliest view of New Amsterdam, the future New York City by Joost Hartgers, based on drawings made in 1625–26, shows about 30 simple houses, a windmill, a fortification called Fort Amsterdam, and ships offshore.

Trade in beaver furs—to be made into

popular felt hats back in Holland—was the colony's one and only reason for existence. The number of pelts obtained from the Indians for export went from 7,520 in 1629 to almost 30,000 thirty years later. In 1628, when the first Dutch Reformed minister, Jonas Michaëlius, arrived from Holland, he was appalled by the ungodly state of the city's 270 residents, but the church he founded continues today as the Marble Collegiate Reformed Church (*29th St. at 5th Ave.*).

As the colony grew, its devotion to business and easygoing ways attracted such religious dissenters as Anne Hutchinson. Driven from Puritan New England, she came to New York in 1642, only to be killed by Indians the next year. In 1644 the 11 slaves who had come with the first settlers were declared to be "half free." That is, they were free and could own land, but their children remained in bondage.

English Quakers, who arrived in New Netherland in 1657, were made less welcome by Governor Peter Stuyvesant. When Stuyvesant ordered Quaker John Bowne arrested in 1662, Bowne appealed to the Dutch West India Company, whose directors ordered Stuyvesant to stop. Religious persecution, they sensibly believed, was bad for business. In other ways, Stuyvesant was an effective administrator: He encouraged trade, established a municipal government, and made and kept peace with the Indians. When threatened by the English presence, he built a wall stretching 2,340 feet, from the East River to the Hudson River, to protect New Amsterdam from invasion from the north.

ENGLISH NEW YORK

When the English came, however, they came from the sea. On August 26, 1664, Col. Richard Nicolls, acting on behalf of the king's brother, James, the Duke of York, landed 450 soldiers in Brooklyn and placed the remainder of his force aboard ships anchored strategically around Manhattan. Stuyvesant, with a handful of soldiers, made a brave show of resisting, but leading citizens persuaded him to surrender. Nicolls became the first English governor, naming the town after his patron, but the settlement was to change hands once more. Warring with the French and the English in 1673, the Dutch took New York

back, then sued for peace the following year and returned it to England.

Under the English, New York shed its vestiges as a trading post and grew into a city, though not initially a prosperous one. British restrictions and ill-advised actions, such as paring away New Jersey as a separate colony, hindered commerce and growth. In 1683, under the new English governor, Thomas Dongan, a provincial assembly drew up a Charter of Liberties and Privileges, which included the freedom of religion and a right of self-government. By the time it reached England for approval, however, James, who as the Duke of York had charged Dongan with loosening the reins on New York, had become King James II. From his kingly perspective, the Charter of Liberties gave the colonists entirely too much liberty—so he nullified it.

The Glorious Revolution of 1688, which deposed the Roman Catholic King James, caused confusion about who was running New York. A German-born merchant and militia officer, Jacob Leisler, seized Fort George (Fort Amsterdam's English name) in May 1689, and proceeded to rule for most of the next two years. Leisler, an ardent member of the Dutch Reformed Church, ordered the arrest of "papists," dissolved the provincial assembly, and in 1690 attempted an unsuccessful invasion of Canada. When the new king, William of Orange, sent a governor, Leisler was arrested for treason and hanged on May 16, 1691.

In 1734, another test of colonists' rights occurred when John Peter Zenger, publisher of the *New-York Weekly Journal*, was arrested and jailed for libeling the British governor, William Cosby, with merciless parodies and diatribes. At his trial, Zenger's lawyer, 80-year-old Andrew Hamilton, persuaded the jury that Zenger's articles were not libelous because they were true. It was a milestone case that established the principle of a free press in America. Hamilton told the jury: "The question before the court … is not of small or private concern. It is not the cause of a poor printer, nor of New York alone, which you are trying. No! It may in its consequences affect every freeman that lives under British government on the main of America! It is the best cause. It is the cause of liberty!"

The cause of liberty continued to be an

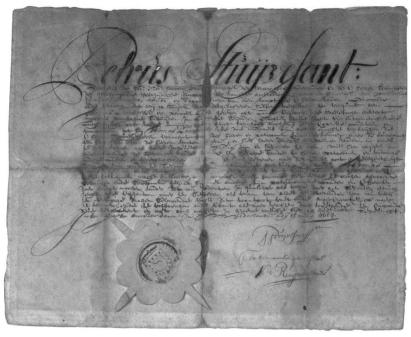

A deed signed by Peter Stuyvesant on May 15, 1664

undercurrent of this period, even infusing controversy into seemingly nonpartisan events like the founding of King's College (today's Columbia University) in 1754. After Britain emerged victorious from the French and Indian Wars, New Yorkers were rankled by having to support English troops headquartered in the city. To raise revenue for this purpose, Parliament passed the Sugar Act of 1764, which imposed strictly enforced duties on New York's molasses trade, and the Stamp Act of 1765, which required stamps for commercial transactions. In resistance, on October 7, 1765, New York convened a Stamp Act Congress in the city and sent a message to Parliament denying its right to tax the Colonies without their consent.

Mobs protesting the Stamp Act, led by the violently inclined Sons of Liberty, attacked the homes and property of British officials. When the Sons erected a liberty pole in the Fields (now City Hall Park), the redcoats cut it down, starting a sequence of semi-comic events that kept both sides busy putting up and cutting down liberty poles. Tension eased early in 1766, when Parliament repealed the Stamp Act and lowered duties on sugar and molasses. Suddenly King George III was a hero, and a statue lionizing the monarch as a Roman emperor was erected in Bowling Green.

The goodwill was short-lived. In 1767 Parliament's Townshend taxes on a variety of goods ignited more protests. Early in 1770, following a liberty pole incident, citizens and soldiers fought with bayonets, fists, and brickbats on a rise near John Street called Golden Hill, a clash that has been called by some the first blood of the Revolution. Then came the duties on tea, which led to the famous Boston Tea Party in December 1773 and less well-remembered New York Tea Party, April 22, 1774. The New York tea dumping by Sons of Liberty dressed like Indians, as their Boston counterparts had been, took place before a cheering crowd.

In the two years that followed, there were lulls amid the tension as New Yorkers sorted out their loyalties in preparation for war. City merchants, believing prosperity depended on peace and stability, were reluctant to carry the conflict further. And New Yorkers were aware that their city would be a strategic prize and battleground in a war. George Washington, commander of the Continental Army, understood this, too, writing that British control of New York would "stop the intercourse between the northern and southern Colonies, upon which depends the Safety of America."

REVOLUTION

With war on the way, Washington moved to reinforce the city. When the Declaration of Independence reached the city on July 9, 1776, Washington had it read to his men. Once dismissed, they tore down the statue of George III in Bowling Green and melted it down to make bullets. By that time, New York was practically under siege. Nearly 500 British ships carrying 32,000 troops, commanded by Gen. William Howe, had arrived off New York and started disembarking soldiers on Staten Island.

On August 27, five days after Howe began moving men across the Narrows to Brooklyn, the British met the Americans defending Brooklyn Heights and, in the Battle of Long Island, drove them back to their entrenchment, taking some 1,000 prisoners in the process. Fortunately for the Americans, Howe hesitated. During the night of August 29–30, Washington ferried his entire force across the East River to Manhattan. Howe bided his time, waiting for an unsuccessful peace conference with the Americans on Staten Island to take place, before landing on Manhattan at Kip's Bay (near today's 34th Street) on September 15. When the green and outnumbered American troops broke ranks and fled, Washington in a rage tried to rally them and had to be pulled out of the line of enemy fire by an aide.

Although the Americans were in flight and divided between the northern and southern ends of the island, Howe did not press his advantage. Legend has it that Mrs. Robert Murray, a patriotic woman residing near present-day 34th Street and Park Avenue, intentionally delayed him with an invitation to tea. More likely, the visit took place while Howe was waiting for his forces to land on Manhattan. The delay allowed the Americans in the south to sneak up the west side to rejoin Washington. The next day they drove back the British at about 125th Street in a two-hour battle that boosted morale, though it was clear the Americans could not hold the city. On October 16, Washington withdrew from

Dwarfed by office buildings, Fraunces Tavern, now a museum and restaurant, evokes colonial days.

Manhattan, leaving nearly 3,000 men to defend Fort Washington, which fell a month later.

The British occupied New York City for the rest of the war, from 1776 to 1783; during this time two serious fires destroyed some 600 buildings. Many Loyalists left at the outbreak of war, and during the frenzied summer of

Alexander Hamilton (1755–1804), influential shaper of an emerging New York

1783, some 60,000 more left the country through New York. The city became the holding pen for American prisoners of war, with many kept in appalling conditions on prison ships in the harbor, where an estimated 11,000 prisoners died—far exceeding the 6,824 Americans killed in battle throughout the country.

The tide turned in favor of the Americans after Lord Cornwallis surrendered at Yorktown, Virginia, in 1781. New York City would not be liberated until after the Treaty of Paris, signed on September 3, 1783, ended the hostilities and recognized American independence. The British occupation ended with an orderly withdrawal on November 25, as Washington led his troops into the city. On the evening of December 4, Washington took leave of his officers in an emotional parting at Fraunces Tavern (see pp. 54, 55). He returned to be sworn in as the nation's first President in

Hand-painted lithograph of an aerial view of Manhattan and Brooklyn by Léon-Auguste Asselineau (circa 1850)

1789. By that time, New York City was the capital of both New York State and the United States of America.

RECOVERY & RECOGNITION

Although New York would not be a capital city for long—the federal government moved to Philadelphia in 1790, the state to Albany in 1797—the city charged with characteristic energy into the 19th century. In a mere 30 years—from 1790, the year of the first federal census, to 1820—the city's population grew from 33,000 to 123,706, making it the largest city in the nation. This post-revolutionary period is the first from which many buildings survive. Castle Clinton (see p. 53) was built in preparation for the war with Great Britain in 1812. Commerce from the China and

California trades caused the rise of the South Street Seaport (see pp. 64–65). City Hall was completed in 1812. Federal Hall, built on the site where Washington was inaugurated, dates from 1842. Trinity Church, its steeple now dwarfed by skyscrapers, was completed in 1846.

This period also saw the rise of such institutions as the New York Stock Exchange, which began after the American Revolution but started trading in earnest after the War of 1812. As early as 1784, Alexander Hamilton helped found the Bank of New York, today one of the country's largest financial institutions (located at 48 Wall Street since 1797); later, as the country's first secretary of the treasury, Hamilton pursued policies that aided the growth of business and commerce in the city. (He died in the nation's most famous duel— with Aaron Burr on July 11, 1804.) Under Mayor and Governor De Witt Clinton, New York became the country's leading commercial center, when the 1825 opening of the Erie Canal connected the Great Lakes with the Hudson River and thus with the city.

COMMISSIONERS' PLAN OF 1811

In 1811 the city took steps to order its future growth by imposing a strict grid on the largely undeveloped region between 14th and 155th Streets. For a city that had grown haphazardly for almost three centuries, the Commissioners' Plan of 1811, as the grid was called, was remarkably forward looking.

A traditional ticker tape parade—this one in 1969 marked the return of the first astronauts to land on the moon.

Running north and south were 12 numbered, widely spaced (920 feet in the interior of the island) avenues. The 155 cross streets stretching from the East to the Hudson Rivers were considerably closer together—200 feet. This purposeful configuration created long, rectangular blocks ideally suited, the planners believed, for "straight-sided and right-angled houses [which] are the most cheap to build, and the most convenient to live in."

Broadway, then called Bloomingdale Road, was the only thoroughfare allowed to cut across the grid. In doing so it created Manhattan's unusual triangular "squares"— Times Square, Herald Square, and the like. At the time, no one anticipated how fast the city would grow. Even the commissioners thought it would take time—"possibly centuries"—for the city to reach 155th Street.

The Commissioners' Plan, with its long, straight avenues and side streets, did accomplish its stated purpose of providing for the "free and abundant circulation of air" and controlling growth. Otherwise, it has been criticized for its monotony, for not providing enough parks, for requiring that much of the natural topography of Manhattan be leveled, and for the narrow side streets, which became a problem when the automobile came on the scene.

19TH-CENTURY SETBACKS: EPIDEMICS & WARS

There were setbacks along the way to preeminence. The yellow fever epidemic of 1798 took more than 2,000 lives. The Great Fire of 1835 destroyed more than 600 buildings in the heart of the city. The embargoes and blockades of the War of 1812 were hard on New York. When the British fleet threatened to invade in 1814, the city mobilized to strengthen its defenses and the mayor, De Witt Clinton, announced he would prefer to "die in a ditch than tamely and cowardly surrender this delightful city." After the war, from which the city escaped unscathed, there were severe losses in the financial panics of 1837 and 1857.

New Yorkers were less militant during the Civil War, particularly merchants who had profited doing business with the southern states. Although New Yorkers had responded to the initial call for troops, by the summer of 1863, when President Lincoln instituted the first draft, that fervor had dimmed. Immigrant Irish laborers were outraged by the draft, particularly the provision that allowed a man to buy an exemption for $300, a sum way beyond their means. In general, they felt that the War Between the States was not their war.

July 11, the first day of the lottery, was quiet. On July 13, when a second lottery was scheduled, the city exploded. A rampaging mob attacked police officers, wrecked draft offices, and ransacked the homes and offices of prominent Republicans and abolitionists. Then the violence turned against blacks: The Colored Orphan Asylum on Fifth Avenue at West 43rd Street was burned, and black men were brutally killed along Bleecker Street, then a black neighborhood. It took the combined efforts of police, politicians, Archbishop John Hughes, and five regiments of the Union Army to restore order. Over three days of

Helium-filled balloons in all shapes and sizes float high above Macy's Thanksgiving Day Parade.

rioting, some 105 people were killed and immense amounts of property destroyed in what is considered the most violent urban riot ever to occur in the country.

AFTER THE CIVIL WAR

The city boomed in the post-Civil War era, in spite of a city government, increasingly con-trolled by "Boss" Tweed and his Tammany Hall henchmen, which took municipal corruption and inefficiency to dazzling new heights. The addition of such enduring institutions as the American Museum of Natural History (1869), the Metropolitan Museum of Art (1870), and, in 1891, Carnegie Hall and the New York Botanical Garden, gave the city the cultural dominance it had always longed for. The dedication of the Statue of Liberty in 1886 came in the midst of one of the greatest migrations in history. Of an estimated 23 million Europeans who came to America between 1880 and 1919, 17 million were processed through New York. Most of these settled in the city.

The city would never look the same after

its first skyscraper, the Tower Building, was erected on lower Broadway between 1888 and 1889. This ushered in one of the most remarkable building booms in history, which lasted until the onset of the Great Depression of the 1930s. Characteristically—in a city that has often torn down as easily as it builds—the Tower Building did not last past 1913. But many steel-framed buildings from that era still stand: the triangular Flatiron Building; the 1904 New York Times Building, which marked the beginnings of Times Square; the grandiose Woolworth Building; and two art deco masterpieces, the Chrysler and Empire State Buildings, each a symbol of the city.

Like all great cities, New York is subject to cycles, the ebb and flow of time and change. New Yorkers cannot count on continuity; the city changes even as words about it are written or read. No one could have predicted that one morning hijacked planes would crash into the Twin Towers. The city and nation reeled. Just over a year later, on Nov. 2, 2002, NYC's Olympic proposal won it the national bid as the U.S. candidate for the 2012 Games.

At the start of the 21st century, the sparkle at the center of the city is as intense as it ever has been. Two cherished public spaces, the New York Public Library and Grand Central Terminal, have been restored; the Museum of Modern Art is expanding; the Hayden Planetarium is getting a major face-lift. No urban rejuvenation has been more spectacular than that of Times Square, for decades a somewhat depressed and dangerous place, which now gleams with bright new signs and shops and glamorous, restored theaters.

In Times Square, as throughout the city and its history, economics and commerce have been the driving forces for change. All great cities are subject to cycles. Those that endure, like New York City, do so through imagination, courage, and readiness to adapt, without sacrificing their essential nature. In the words of essayist E. B. White, written in 1949: "New York is nothing like Paris; it is nothing like London; and it is not Spokane multiplied by sixty, or Detroit by four."

New York is, and always will be, uniquely New York. ■

Celebrating the Feast of San Gennaro in Little Italy

The arts

NEW YORK CAN FAIRLY BE CONSIDERED THE ART CENTER OF THE entire world. Why? Is it the artists who live here? Or the city's lively galleries and museums? Is it because the money, patrons, and collectors are here? Or critics and commentators? Is it because New York itself—wild, diverse, unpredictable—nurtures creativity and is such a good subject for art? All of these factors and undoubtedly more—those intangibles of place, spirit, and tradition—have contributed to New York's preeminence in the arts.

ART

In colonial times, portraiture occupied such successful New York artists as Gerardus Duyckinck (1723–1797). New York-born Abraham Delanoy (1742–1795) studied portraiture with Benjamin West in London, and, on returning to the city, painted members of the Livingston, Beekman, and Stuyvesant families. In the early republic, Robert Fulton and Samuel F.B. Morse were both accomplished painters before they turned to other pursuits—steamboats and the telegraph—that made them famous. John Vanderlyn returned from Paris to do a panoramic painting of Versailles, which he displayed in a rotunda in City Hall Park; it now hangs in the Metropolitan Museum of Art.

The Hudson River school, led by Thomas Cole and Asher B. Durand, believed it could capture the country's divine essence in glorious landscapes. Two of its members, John Frederick Kensett and Thomas Worthington Whittredge, were among the founders of the Metropolitan Museum of Art in 1870, a time when no work by an American artist was considered museum worthy.

Throughout the 19th century, New York artists banded together—and contentiously disbanded. In 1826 Morse and other younger artists rebelled against the conservative American Academy of Fine Arts and its president, historical painter John Trumbull, to found the National Academy of Design (see p. 151), now on Fifth Avenue. When the National Academy became stodgy, younger artists such as John La Farge and Albert Pinkham Ryder founded the American Society of Artists in 1877. This organization helped establish the Art Students League, the distinguished art school where Robert Henri, William Merritt Chase, and Thomas Hart

Benton taught and had as pupils George Bellows, Rockwell Kent, and Edward Hopper. The school still operates from its 1892 building (*215 West 57th St.*).

A group of New York-based impressionists known as The Ten also broke away from the National Academy of Design and set up their own gallery in 1898. Early in the 20th century, a different group, called The Eight, declared independence, and in 1908 put on a famous exhibit at the Macbeth Gallery; the paintings of William Glackens, George Luks, Everett Shinn, and John Sloan included realistic scenes of New York. The Macbeth Gallery show spawned the popular Exhibition of Independent Artists in 1910 and, in 1913, the Armory Show (see pp. 82–83), which exhibited the work of younger New York artists such as Stuart Davis, Marsden Hartley, John Marin, Joseph Stella (known for his evocation of Coney Island and the Brooklyn Bridge), and Edward Hopper, whose vision of New York is lonely, alienated, and melancholy.

Photographer Alfred Stieglitz was another influential figure of the era. In his gallery at 291 Fifth Avenue, he exhibited John Marin, Max Weber, and others, and during the 1920s and '30s he promoted the work of Arthur Dove, Charles Demuth, and Georgia O'Keeffe, whom he married in 1924. To gain attention for their work, other New York painters formed the American Abstract Artists in 1936. Its members—among them Mark Rothko, Willem de Kooning, Robert Motherwell, and Jackson Pollock—went on to experiment with a form of art that grew into the New York school, also called action painting, but best

The spiraling interior of the Solomon R. Guggenheim Museum, Frank Lloyd Wright's only New York building

known as abstract expressionism. Starting in the mid-1960s, abstract art veered in new, realistic directions with Robert Rauschenberg and Jasper Johns. This led into pop art and the works of Roy Lichtenstein, Andy Warhol, and James Rosenquist, with their vivid use of advertising and popular images. Most of these artists used New York as a subject, but as a group, the action painters expressed the city best, and none better than Jackson Pollock. His wild canvases—with paint slopped directly on canvas to pull beauty out of chaos—could serve as a painterly metaphor for New York City as a whole.

CLASSICAL MUSIC

Talent from abroad has always bolstered the New York music scene. In 1833 Lorenzo Da Ponte, librettist for Mozart's *Don Giovanni* and a New Yorker since 1805, founded the Italian Opera House, one in a succession of halls that followed the city as it moved uptown. In 1850, P.T. Barnum brought the Swedish soprano Jenny Lind to New York to perform at Castle Clinton. Antonin Dvořák was music director of the National Conservatory of Music on East 17th Street from 1892 to 1895; Tchaikovsky conducted at the opening of Carnegie Hall in 1891. Kurt Masur was director of a symphony orchestra in Leipzig before he took over the New York Philharmonic in 1991.

Wealthy New Yorkers have patronized the musical arts, sometimes as a path to social status. In 1825, John Jacob Astor, a music shop owner before he became one of the richest men in America, arranged the production of Rossini's *Il Barbiere di Siviglia,* the first full-length Italian opera performed in the city. The original 3,700-seat Metropolitan Opera House at Broadway and 39th Street was founded in 1883 by wealthy New Yorkers who were denied boxes at the Academy of Music (built in 1854) on 14th Street. In 1891, Carnegie Hall on West 57th Street opened. Built by Andrew Carnegie, it became home to one of the world's greatest orchestras, the New York Philharmonic, founded in 1842. Although other halls were built, the Metropolitan and Carnegie Hall reigned supreme until 1961, when Lincoln Center for the Performing Arts (see pp. 176–78), opened on the Upper West Side.

Robert Moses, the city's master planner, had chosen the site in the 1950s as part of a slum-clearance program.

In the mid-19th century, diarist George Templeton Strong noted that he could attend a concert most nights of the year. Had he lived today, it would have been several concerts every night. Classical music pervades the city; it is performed in large halls and in intimate spaces—museums, schools, churches—and unique venues such as Symphony Space, a converted movie theater at Broadway and 95th Street, or outdoors at Lincoln Center. You can hear a musician scratching out a Beethoven sonata on the street or listen to the New York Philharmonic perform under "the stars" (rarely visible in the city) in Central Park.

THEATER

"The Broadway theater is dead!" "Long live the Broadway theater!" Variations of these two cries have been heard, together and separately, ever since there has been theater in New York City. And yet the Broadway theater persists, even thrives, much changed over the years but still with us nonetheless. Of all the institutions identified with New York, the theater is perhaps the most prominent. "To see a show" is the main reason many people come to the city. And to act in the theater, or to write for it, or to play some other role connected with it, is still a dream that brings many young people to New York.

The theater has always been a fragile institution, vulnerable to all sorts of pressures, such as the American Revolution, the Great Depression, and World War II. Motion pictures (especially "talkies"), radio and television, the spread of regional theater, and the current phenomenon known as home entertainment have all caused doomsayers to predict the New York theater's demise. Financially, the theater always seems to be on shaky footing. Today's cost of staging a production runs into millions of dollars, and as a result a single ticket can cost more than $100.

The dearth of serious or innovative new plays on Broadway is another recurring complaint, but the fact is that Broadway's essential conservatism provides an opportunity for theaters elsewhere in the city. Ever since the 1950s, when Tennessee Williams's *Summer and*

Frequent outdoor concerts and plays in Central Park are major summertime events.

Smoke opened at the Circle in the Square Theatre in Greenwich Village, the alternative theater known as Off Broadway has been a major theatrical force, frequently producing plays that wind up on Broadway. Off Broadway dates from 1951, when producer/director Theodore Mann and director Jose Quintero founded the Circle in the Square as a nonprofit theater. Jason Robards, George C. Scott, and Geraldine Page all began their careers there. In 1971 the theater moved to larger premises on 1633 Broadway between 49th & 50th Sts. As Off-Broadway theater became more main-stream, another phenomenon, Off-off Broadway, burgeoned in the turbulent 1960s as a testing ground for experimental theater. Playwright Sam Shepard is one of several who first had works performed at the Caffe Cino, a coffeehouse on Cornelia Street, where Off-off Broadway supposedly started in 1958.

The theater has been a cultural force in New York City since the mid-18th century; the first known professional production was *Richard III*, staged in 1750 by an English company at a Nassau Street theater. The versatile William Dunlap—manager, producer, playwright—was the city's leading impresario in the beginning of the 19th century. He ran the dominant Park Theater on Park Row, importing popular actors from England. From Lower Manhattan, the city's theater district moved to lower Broadway and then, in the 1870s, to Union Square. There vaudeville got its start at Tony Pastor's New 14th Street Theater, and grand opera was performed at the Academy of Music. By 1900, the final shift to Longacre Square, as Times Square was origi-nally called, had taken place.

The legitimate theater thrived in the 1920s. Eugene O'Neill and other American

Jerome Robbins' Broadway, a medley of the choreographer's works, opened in 1989.

dramatists—Maxwell Anderson, Marc Connelly, Robert E. Sherwood, among them—were produced regularly on Broadway. The American musical began its shift from gaudy revue to more dramatic and serious forms such as *Show Boat,* Jerome Kern's and Oscar Hammerstein II's 1927 hit. Today, lavish productions such as *The Lion King* attract new family audiences. Broadway theater thrives.

The restoration of venerated buildings introduced a new magic to Broadway. Even more remarkable has been the biggest Off-Broadway theater redevelopment in the city's history, along 42nd Street's western stretch. Where intimate rundown theaters once stood, a new 39-story residential tower houses the Theater Row complex *(410-412 W. 42nd St.),* with five new theaters under one roof. The 12-million-dollar Little Shubert Theater at No. 422 stages larger productions.

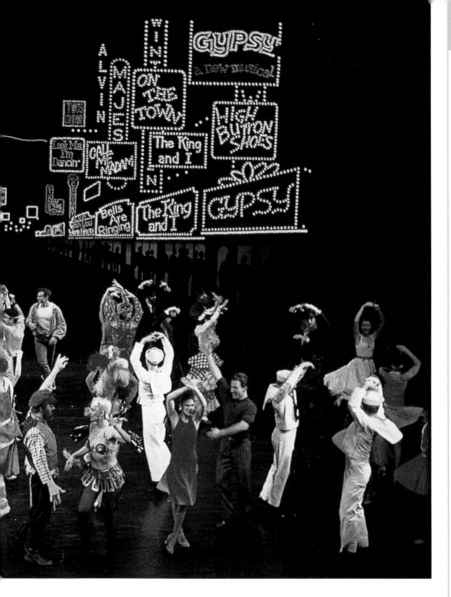

WRITERS & NEW YORK

New York is a rich backdrop for literature. In 1791, Susanna Rowson published *Charlotte Temple, a Tale of Truth,* a lurid novel about a fallen woman. Edgar Allan Poe was inspired by a New York murder to write *The Mystery of Marie Roget* (1845). After coming to New York in 1866, Horatio Alger wrote inspirational novels chronicling the rise of street urchins to success through hard work. In *Leaves of Grass* (1855), poet Walt Whitman celebrated the city as "the no more beyond of the western world."

In the 1950s, Jack Kerouac and the Beats made poetry out of city life. About Times Square, Allen Ginsberg wrote, "There all the apocalyptic hipsters in New York eventually stopped, fascinated by the timeless room." Today, resident authors Jay McInerney (*Bright Lights, Big City*), Grace Paley (*Enormous Changes at the Last Moment*), and Stanley Crouch (*Adventures in the Skin Trade*) often make the city their subject matter.

New York has given other writers the perspective to write brilliantly about where they came from. For Willa Cather, 40 years a New Yorker, it was the Nebraska of her childhood. Thomas Wolfe described his youth in North Carolina in the semiautobiographical novel he wrote in New York, *Look Homeward, Angel* (1929).

Washington Irving was one of the first city-born writers. His satirical *Knickerbocker's*

Walt Whitman (1819–1892) sang the praises of Manhattan and Brooklyn Bridge.

History of New York was published in 1809. Herman Melville was born at 6 Pearl Street in 1819. He left to go to sea and returned to write such works as *Typee*. Novelist Henry James used his grandmother's Greenwich Village house as the setting for his 1881 novel *Washington Square*. His neighbor Edith Wharton wrote *The Age of Innocence* (1920) about the city's elite. Novelist Nathanael West was born Nathan Weinstein in 1903 on East 81st Street. Brooklyn-raised Norman Mailer is still a prominent New York literary figure.

Harlem has produced such important writers as James Baldwin, who wrote about black New York in his 1953 novel, *Go Tell It on the Mountain*. Although they were born elsewhere, Richard Wright, Ralph Ellison, and Langston Hughes drew on their Harlem experience in their writings. In the 1920s, the

movement known as the Harlem Renaissance (see pp. 200–201) attracted black writers from all over the country, including Zora Neale Hurston, author of *Their Eyes Were Watching God* (1937).

New York writers have always gathered in literary groups, clubs, salons, or in association with publications. In the 1820s, Irving was a leader of the Knickerbockers, gentlemen who wrote "for no other earthly purpose but to please ourselves." A few years later, James Fenimore Cooper founded the Bread and Cheese Club. Herman Melville gravitated toward the Young Americans, dedicated to encouraging a national literature. At the turn of the 20th century, Greenwich Village was a hotbed of literary activity, centered around the *New Masses* and other journals, theater groups, and salons. While some Village writers struggled, others, like Mark Twain, lived in patrician comfort in a town house near Washington Square.

In the 1920s, critics, editors, and intellectuals became recognizable figures on the literary scene—names such as Mark Van Doren, Lionel Trilling, Malcolm Cowley, and Brooklyn-born Alfred Kazin. The Algonquin Round Table was a lunch group of writers and artists that met during the 1920s at the Algonquin Hotel. Its members—among them Dorothy Parker, *New Yorker* editor Harold Ross, drama critic Alexander Woolcott—were known for witty barbs and quips. In the East Village today, St. Mark's Poetry Project, long identified with such writers as Ed Sanders and Ann Waldman, fosters poetry as performance. A community of writers is also alive today in New York via television talk shows and on the worldwide web, where one can engage in an on-line dialogue with a writer.

Even with the advent of the digital age and new ways to publish and market on-line, New York's foothold as the center of the world's publishing industry is certain. This is the place the industry began. The publishing houses, the publishers, editors, agents, lawyers, press agents, reading venues, groups that give awards, media that publicize them—and all the other elements encircling the process of writing are entrenched here to stay. As for writers themselves, the next Philip Roth or Tom Wolfe (both New Yorkers, by the way) will sooner or later make the trek to mecca, hoping for a deal over lunch at the Four Seasons, or Surya, or the latest spot. To be followed, of course, by an appearance on all the morning shows, live from New York.

NEW YORK IN SONG, FILM, & TELEVISION

Question: What do "Take the A Train," *Taxi Driver,* and *Seinfeld* have in common? Answer: They are by New Yorkers, about New York, and products of New York's creative industries— popular music, film, and television. "A Train" is a jazz composition by the great Harlem musician Duke Ellington. *Taxi Driver* is a quintessential New York movie, directed by New Yorker Martin Scorsese, starring a New York actor, Robert De Niro, and filmed on the city's mean streets (the title of yet another Scorsese film). *Seinfeld* was a phenomenally successful 1990s situation comedy that featured a self-absorbed collection of characters only found in New York.

Anyone wandering around New York will encounter, sooner or later, a street blocked by a crew in the process of making a film, television episode, or commercial. There will be cameras, trailers, lights, dozens of busy people, and occasionally a star or two. Both film and television started in New York City, shifted to Hollywood, but have never really abandoned the city. The film industry, in particular, has a number of producers and directors who, by choice, do most of their work in New York, among them Scorsese, Sidney Lumet, Spike Lee, and Woody Allen. In Woody Allen's films, the anxiety level of the neurotic characters rises whenever the plot requires them to leave Manhattan.

From the turn of the 20th century, when filmmakers associated with Thomas Edison started in the city, to World War I, New York was the moviemaking center of the country. Even in 1920, as the industry began moving to Hollywood, Famous Players–Lasky Productions, the production company that would become Paramount, opened Astoria Studios in Queens and continued to produce features there until 1937. The studio was taken over by the military during World War II and closed in the 1960s. In 1975 it reopened; Bob Fosse's *All That Jazz* (1979) and Woody Allen's

Radio Days (1987) were among the features made there. In 1988 the American Museum of the Moving Image (see p. 225), which documents New York's film history, took over part of the facilities.

Television also came of age in New York City. In 1927, an image of then-Secretary of Commerce Herbert Hoover was beamed from the AT&T labs in New York to a receiver in Washington, D.C. The first CBS broadcast, in 1931, featured New York Mayor Jimmy Walker and composer George Gershwin. By the late 1940s, New York had four networks and about two-thirds of the nation's television sets. In the early 1950s, situation comedies such as *I Love Lucy* and *The Honeymooners* were all New York produced. Soon afterward, the entertainment end of the business shifted to the West Coast.

Still, New York remains a force in television. The network news is produced here, and such shows as *60 Minutes, Saturday Night Live,* and David Letterman's *Late Show* rely on a biting brand of humor that has its roots in New York. *Seinfeld* was so New York-oriented that it still brings out-of-towners to the Upper West Side in search of Tom's restaurant, where the characters hung out; while such police and legal dramas as *NYPD Blue* and *Law & Order* present a grittier side of city life.

Hundreds of songs have featured the city since "New York, Oh What a Charming City," and other 19th-century ditties, products of Tin Pan Alley, the country's songwriting capital, which moved from Union Square to West 28th Street to Times Square. Many songs, such as "New York, New York," written by Betty Comden, Adolph Green, and Leonard Bernstein, celebrate the city, and some are geographically specific: Bob Dylan's 1965 "Positively 4th Street," for example. Certain writers vent hostility, including Hank Williams, Jr., who wrote "I Hate New York" in 1983; while other contemporary songs are socially conscious, such as Lou Reed's "Halloween Parade," with its AIDS theme. But of all New York songs and singers, Frank Sinatra belting out "New York, New York" is a universal favorite, and its oft-quoted line, "If I can make it here, I'll make it anywhere," is the heart of the New York City frame of mind.

ARCHITECTURE

Architecturally, New York is a proud but restless city. It is the city's nature to build, tear down, and build again, though in recent years preservation efforts have increased—and for good reason. New York today has only a handful of buildings left from the colonial era. Most are remotely located in the outer boroughs—at Historic Richmond Town on Staten Island, for example.

Buildings from the years after independence are better represented, with many surviving examples of the row house and its cousin, the brownstone, New Jersey sandstone over a brick frame. Those years also saw the construction of the Astor House (1836)—forerunner of the modern hotel—and A.T. Stewart (1846), the department store. The Gothic Revival style in church architecture was introduced with the completion of the third Trinity Church (see p. 57) in 1846.

In 1857, Richard M. Hunt, Leopold Eidlitz, and Richard Upjohn and his son, Richard M., and others founded the American Institute of Architects, to put the practice of architecture on a professional footing. Cast-iron buildings were introduced in the city around 1850 by the inventive James Bogardus, and the world's first passenger elevator—the innovation that would make the city's later skyward growth possible—began its vertical journey in the Haughwout Building in 1857.

In the post-Civil War years, the luxury apartment was introduced as a living alternative for the wealthy. One of the first was Richard Morris Hunt's Stuyvesant, constructed on East 18th Street in 1869. On the Upper West Side, the still fashionable Dakota Apartments were completed in 1884. For the poor, there was the tenement with windowless flats, a housing type preserved today in the Lower East Side Tenement Museum (see p. 69). The postwar years also saw the construction of magnificent beaux arts public buildings—the Metropolitan Museum of Art, the New York Public Library, Audubon Terrace, and the Brooklyn Museum. And during this time, the millionaires' freestanding mansions on Fifth Avenue were built, including James B. Duke's 1912 mansion at Fifth Avenue and 78th Street, designed by Julian Abele, one of the city's first African-American architects.

SKYLINE TRANSFORMED

Then came the skyscraper, a word coined in the 1890s to describe an iron-framed building on which masonry was hung like a "curtain." The skyscraper, which transformed the city's skyline into one of the world's wonders, was born in Chicago but came to full flower in New York. In 1889 architect Bradford Gilbert built New York's first skyscraper, the Tower Building, a structure so thin and tall that New Yorkers thought it would blow over. In the ensuing race to build the world's tallest building, early record-holders included architect H.H. Richardson's Park Row Building (1896–1897, 30 stories), Ernest Flagg's Singer Tower (1906–1908, 47 stories), Napoleon LeBrun's Metropolitan Life Insurance Tower (1907–1909, 50 stories), and Cass Gilbert's Woolworth Building (1910–1913, 60 stories).

D. H. Burnham's triangular, 21-story Flatiron Building, when built in 1901–1903 the tallest building north of the financial district, remains a favorite with the public. The 1915 Equitable Building on lower Broadway blocked out so much sunlight that the city changed the zoning regulations to require setbacks—creating the so-called wedding-cake profile—on tall buildings. The race for height culminated in 1930 with the art deco Chrysler and the Empire State Buildings; the last, with 102 stories, was the city's record holder until eclipsed by the World Trade Center's twin towers in the 1970s. Both towers were demolished in the terrorist attack of Sept. 11, 2001.

After World War II, form rather than height became the prime architectural concern. The unadorned, boxy international style is reflected in the UN Secretariat Building, Lever House, and the bronze-clad Seagram Building, the last designed by Ludwig Mies van der Rohe, whose work is considered the epitome of the international style. Philip Johnson's AT&T Building (1984, now the Sony Building) brought postmodernism to New York City. Other landmarks of modern architecture are Frank Lloyd Wright's Guggenheim

Noted for its gleaming stainless-steel spire, the Chrysler Building was for a few months in 1930 the world's tallest building.

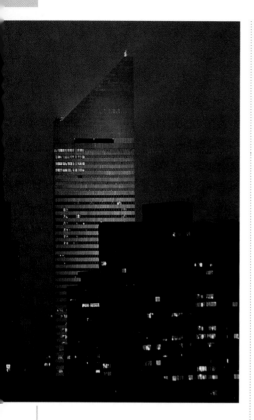

Citicorp Center's sloping pinnacle rises above older rectilinear Midtown buildings.

(1959), Marcel Breuer's Whitney Museum of American Art (1966), and the Citicorp Center (1978)—with its slanted roof a distinctive addition to the city's skyline.

The heyday of the skyscrapers may be over, but New York continues to both redesign existing structures and build anew. The cleanup after the World Trade Center disaster took more than a year, but the site now stands ready for renewal once a suitable architectural plan is approved. One can also expect future major construction on the city's east and west sides as waterfront areas are reclaimed. The 15-story Jacob K. Javits Convention Center (see p. 97), designed for the city by I. M. Pei, is already an established landmark against the West Side skyline. Opened in 1986 and busy ever since, the center features an elaborate glass-paned modern facade and Galleria River Pavilion (added in 1989), with outdoor terraces overlooking the Hudson River. These are popular for fashion and movie shoots.

In the next few years, Columbus Circle will be transformed by its new business/entertainment complex; the addition to the Museum of Modern Art will be nearing completion; and construction around 42nd Street will have completed several entertainment complexes, theater restorations, and guaranteed-to-be-impressive architectural light structures. And never one to let go of the past—witness the resurrection of the Times Square theater district—the city has plans for a major renovation that will move some of the train service out of Penn Station into the U.S. Post Office, a structure strongly reminiscent of the grandeur of the old Penn Station that was demolished (see below). Although buildings may disappear in the city, they are never forgotten, and often they live on—their grace and spirit echoed in creations blending old and new. And thus the city grows and endures.

PRESERVING & TEARING DOWN NEW YORK

Imbued with what Walt Whitman called "the pull-down-and-build-over-again spirit," early New Yorkers were not concerned about historic preservation. Particularly on Manhattan. Land is too scarce and valuable there to permit sentimentality over something as ephemeral as an old building.

So New York has done a lot of tearing down. The hope always is, of course, that the replacement will be better than what is lost. Sometimes that happens. In 1899–1900, the 45-foot-high granite walls around the reservoir at Fifth Avenue and 42nd Street—a sterling example of "Egyptian architecture"—were torn down to make way for the New York Public Library, one of the city's most beloved buildings.

The demolition of the majestic first Waldorf-Astoria Hotel is unlamented today because it made way for the incomparable Empire State Building. There was grumbling, however, in 1939, when opulent brownstone residences on West 53rd Street were torn down to make way for the Museum of Modern Art, an international-style building

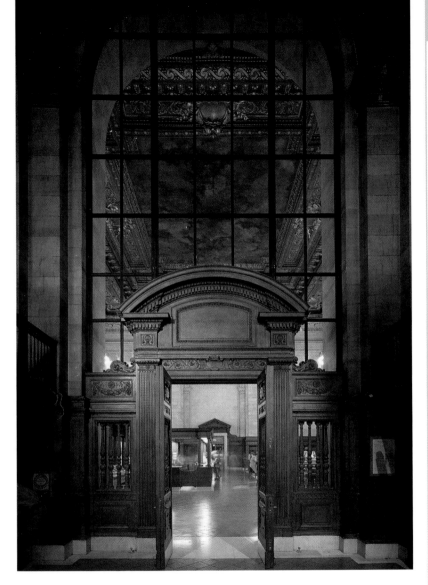

The New York Public Library's opulent interior

that became a landmark in its own right—a worthwhile trade-off by anyone's standards.

There are certain buildings whose demise New Yorkers now regret. Ernest Flagg's great Singer Tower, at 47 stories, is now remembered as the tallest building ever demolished. The Brokaw mansions that once stood at Fifth Avenue and 79th Street were emblems of wealth that are irreplaceable today. But the loss that shocked New York was the demolition in 1963–64 of Pennsylvania Station, a "monumental act of vandalism," as the *New York Times* called it.

HISTORIC PRESERVATION

Penn Station's demolition marked the beginning of the historic preservation movement in New York City. In 1965, the city created the Landmarks Preservation Commission to identify and protect landmark buildings and

Where the city began—today's Battery Park and financial district at the southern tip of Manhattan

districts—and public interiors and scenic vistas—based on aesthetic, cultural, architectural, and historic criteria. Brooklyn Heights was one of the first neighborhoods to gain landmark status as a historic district. Today there are over 1,000 individual landmarks, 9 scenic landmarks, and 82 historic districts, encompassing nearly 21,000 buildings.

There have been several tests of the com-

mission's considerable powers. When it rejected proposals to build a 54-story office tower over Grand Central or to squeeze in one adjacent to St. Bartholomew's Church on Park Avenue, opponents' appeals went to the Supreme Court. In both cases, the court upheld the landmark legislation and the city's right to protect its architectural heritage.

In other battles, the Edgar Rice mansion at

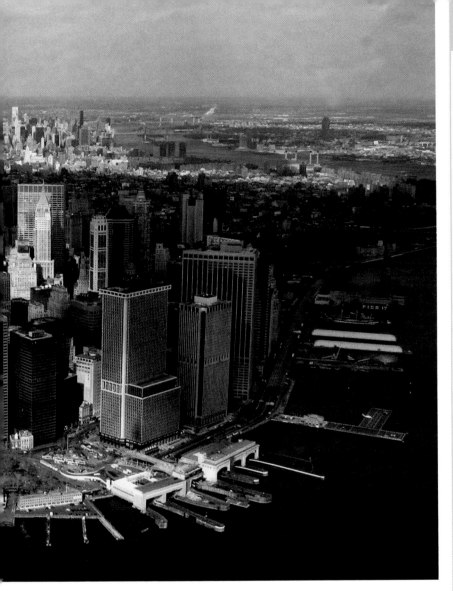

the corner of 89th Street and Riverside Drive, owned by a Jewish religious school, was saved after a battle involving charges of discrimination. Even Park Avenue's first glass tower, the Lever House, only 30 years old at the time, had to be landmarked to save it from destruction. There have also been compromises: One allowed the New York Palace Hotel to be tacked onto the rear of the Villard Houses on Madison Avenue.

And there have been defeats. There is no way, ever, to replace such New York fixtures as Luchow's, the ornate German restaurant on 14th Street, or the low-slung art deco Airlines Terminal Building at 42nd Street and Park Avenue South, or the Hotel Biltmore on Madison Avenue, or the crenelated 71st Regiment Armory on East 34th Street, or ....

Today's preservationist forces might have saved some of those monuments; going forward, the new civic vigilance—which saved Grand Central and rescued Times Square's historic theaters—bodes well for the future of New York's architectural treasures. ■

Entrances

Fly in or drive in, take a car, bus, train, ocean liner, or ferry, ride a bike or walk the Brooklyn Bridge: Any way you reach New York is dramatic. The city's exuberant etching of the skyline is exhilarating. By day the Chrysler Building gleams, and by night, lights of bridges, traffic, and skyscrapers cut the darkness. Fighting commuter traffic or rushing shoulder to shoulder with thousands in Grand Central Terminal, the excitement builds. You are entering the Big Apple.

TUNNELS

It is impossible to drive into Manhattan without negotiating a bridge or a tunnel. For those being taken somewhere by bus or taxi, it helps to understand where you are going. The Holland and Lincoln Tunnels, on the west side, go under the Hudson to New Jersey. The Brooklyn-Battery and Queens-Midtown Tunnels, on the east side, lead to the boroughs.

New York City has made important contributions to the evolution of tunnels. When the Holland Tunnel opened in 1927, it was the city's first vehicular tunnel and the world's longest. Its ventilation system was an engineering triumph. The 1950 Brooklyn-Battery Tunnel, at 9,117 feet, is North America's longest continuous vehicular tunnel. The Lincoln Tunnel, built between 1937 and 1957, is at 40 million vehicles a year, the world's busiest tunnel. The Queens-Midtown Tunnel, stretching a mere 6,300 feet, holds no titles, but is a frequent route to La Guardia and Kennedy airports.

BRIDGES

To drivers, the tunnels can be terrifying, but the bridges are distracting. Some of them are beautiful; form and function marry so well in their spans that motorists can find it difficult to keep their eyes on the road. The beauty of the city's major spans is best appreciated from above, maybe from a circling plane or a skyscraper's observation deck. Here you will certainly hear the question, "Which bridge is that?"

The primary bridges, from Manhattan's tip and going uptown, are the Brooklyn Bridge, the Manhattan Bridge, the Williamsburg Bridge, the Queensboro Bridge, and the Triborough Bridge (125th Street). High on the west side, the George Washington Bridge connects to New Jersey.

The age of the great New York bridges began with the opening of the Brooklyn Bridge in 1883, joining Manhattan to what was then one of the world's largest cities. Measuring some 3,580 feet, with a central span of 1,595.5 feet between the two massive stone towers, the bridge was for years the world's longest, and it was the world's first steel suspension bridge.

In 1867 a steel suspension bridge was a radical idea, but this was John Augustus Roebling's plan. When the German-born engineer died, his son, Washington Roebling, saw the project through. Washington was crippled by the bends while working underwater in 1872, but he supervised the construction from a distance, using a telescope and passing instructions through his wife.

Today, the Brooklyn Bridge is still a marvel and a symbol of the city. Walk across the pedestrian walkway for a close-up view of the structure and harbor views; looking uptown, you will see the main bridges. On the Brooklyn side, the riverfront promenade provides spectacular views of lower Manhattan.

The city today has 2,027 bridges, 76 of which cross water. New York's first bridge, the King's Bridge, was built by Frederick Philipse across Spuyten Duvil Creek between Manhattan and the Bronx in 1693 and lasted until 1917. The city's oldest surviving bridge is High Bridge, constructed between 1837 and 1848 to carry water into Manhattan via the Croton Aqueduct system. The 1964 Verrazano Narrows Bridge between Staten Island and Brooklyn provides a spectacular starting point for the New York City Marathon. It is also the last bridge designed by the city's master bridge-builder, Swiss-born Othmar H. Ammann, whose other projects include the George Washington Bridge (1931), the Triborough Bridge (1936), the Bronx-Whitestone Bridge (1939), and the Throgs Neck Bridge (1961). The stately Queensboro

Top: The Brooklyn Bridge's architectural grace   Bottom: The Acela Express, North America's first high-speed passenger train, at Penn Station

Bridge will always be identified with F. Scott Fitzgerald's evocative words in *The Great Gatsby*: "The city seen from the Queensboro Bridge is always the city seen for the first time, in its first wild promise of all the mystery and the beauty in the world."

NEW YORK HARBOR

Go out into New York Harbor any way you can: There is no better view of New York than from its beckoning waters. Odds are slim that you will arrive in Manhattan as the immigrants did, crowding the rail of a ship to watch the city rise gradually from the horizon. But once you are on the water, the excitement will build, whether you are on a Circle Line cruise around Manhattan, a ferry, or a speedboat thrill ride; whether passing the Statue of Liberty or en route to Ellis Island—where millions of immigrants first touched American soil.

The Dutch settlers were quick to recognize the virtues of New York Harbor. It was wide, close to open ocean, and deep, providing easy passage around the island. This natural harbor became a magnet for commercial enterprise, beginning with the trade in furs. Peter Stuyvesant built the first wharf on the East River in 1648. The American Revolution, the War of 1812, the steamship, the industrial revolution, and the 1912 completion of the Ambrose Channel—which allowed ocean liner access from the East River—all contributed to the growth of the Port of New York. For the first 50 years of the 20th century, it was the world's busiest port.

Today, container ships go to facilities in Brooklyn and New Jersey, and the era of the transatlantic ocean liners is over. Nonetheless, the harbor remains a precious resource. Parts have been imaginatively restored, such as the South Street Seaport Museum (see pp. 64–65) near Manhattan's tip. This "living" historic district on the site of the original Port of New York includes 18th- and 19th-century buildings and a marina. Along the Hudson is Chelsea Piers, once a port of call and now a sports-entertainment complex at the beautifully restored piers 59 to 62. *Titanic* was en route to Chelsea Piers when it sank in 1912.

Revitalization under way includes a state-legislated 325-million-dollar waterfront park, along the Hudson from Battery City to 59th Street; and plans for revamping the East River waterfront from Governors Island to Randalls Island, including areas along Manhattan, Brooklyn, and Queens.

AIRPORTS

You can dream about steaming into New York Harbor aboard a passenger liner, but if you are coming from any distance, you will probably fly. From a plane you get a view of the city in its entirety; it brings home the fact that New York is a city of islands and waterways. You can reach New York via three major airports: La Guardia handles domestic carriers; John F. Kennedy (JFK) International, and Newark in New Jersey, are gateways for overseas flights.

Through the 1930s, Newark was the only airport serving the city. This so galled New York's feisty mayor, Fiorello La Guardia, that he once refused to get off a plane at Newark because his ticket read New York. The city got the point. Shortly thereafter, in December 1939, La Guardia Airport in north-central Queens opened.

John F. Kennedy International Airport opened in 1948 on Jamaica Bay, 15 miles from Manhattan. Then the largest airport in the world, it was named Idlewild until 1963. At JFK, airlines were allowed to design their own terminals, a decision that brought leading architects into airport design and produced such notable buildings as Eero Saarinen's TWA Terminal A (1956–1962), a winged masterpiece of curved concrete and glass, intended, in Saarinen's words, "to interpret the sensation of flying."

New York has played an important role in the history of flight. As early as 1830, 30,000 people watched a hot-air balloon launch from Castle Clinton. It flew an astounding 30 miles. The first international air races, sponsored by the *New York Herald,* were held in New York in 1907. In 1927, Charles Lindbergh left from Roosevelt Field on Long Island on his transatlantic flight. By then, important names in flight—Curtiss, Wright, Fairchild, and Sikorsky—had made New York and Long Island a center for airplane manufacturing. In the modern era, commercial jet service began in New York City in 1958; Pan Am inaugurated the first jumbo jet service from JFK in 1969. ■

S tart near the harbor and
follow the city's growth
north, from where George
Washington was sworn in as
president, through the fast-
paced financial district, to the
ever changing ethnic and
artsy neighborhoods.

Lower Manhattan

The stern face of Liberty

Lower Manhattan

FROM ANYWHERE ELSE IN Manhattan, go south, to the heart of Lower Manhattan. For it is here that you start to understand the changes the city has undergone: from fortification to thriving colony to seat of government to place of entry for immigrants to busy seaport to what it is today—the financial nerve center of the entire world.

Manhattan

Area of map detail

Though the aftermath of the attack on the World Trade Center on Sept. 11, 2001, left a devastated area north of Trinity Church, the area south to the harbor was untouched. A memorial wall on Church Street provides detailed information on the history of the World Trade Center, the attack, and restoration plans, and gives viewing access to the site, ground zero. In contrast, beginning a visit near the harbor is like a modern-day immigration experience, with family and school groups and sightseers from far and wide. In fair weather, vendors, performers, and foodstands create a carnival-like atmosphere. The federal-style James Watson House *(7 State St. bet. Pearl and Whitehall Sts.)* stands proudly nearby, dwarfed by skyscrapers. The lone survivor of the elegant houses that were once all around, it is now the Rectory of the Shrine of the Blessed Elizabeth Ann Seton (1774–1821), canonized in 1975 as the first American-born saint.

Some may feel drawn to a historic walk up Broadway, guided by Heritage Trail markers and signage. Others will head to the Battery for tickets to Liberty Island or Ellis Island (see pp. 50–52) or the always-free Staten Island Ferry.

The neighborhoods of Lower Manhattan from the Brooklyn Bridge to Houston Street—Chinatown, Little Italy, the Lower East Side, SoHo, and TriBeCa—are evocative of earlier times and foreign ways. Traditionally this is where immigrants lived and worked, but now these areas are as likely to be inhabited by American-born artists or stockbrokers. At the turn of the 20th century, about three-quarters of the residents of the Lower East Side were Jewish; today Hispanics and Asians make up the majority of the population in this neighborhood south of Houston Street and east of the Bowery.

Youth-oriented boutiques, galleries, restaurants, and bars contemporize the flavor here, but Orchard Street, New York's old-time shopping district, remains the same. Where immigrants once shopped at pushcarts and small stores, clothes and bargains on tables and racks still clog the sidewalks, typifying the neighborhood's vibrant street life. ■

LOWER MANHATTAN

❶ Castle Clinton ❷ Bowling Green
❸ U.S. Custom House ❹ Fraunces
Tavern ❺ Ground Zero ❻ TriBeCa
❼ African Burial Ground ❽ SoHo
❾ Chinatown ❿ Shearith Israel
Graveyard ⓫ Little Italy ⓬ St. Patrick's
Old Cathedral ⓭ Lower East Side
Tenement Museum ⓮ Lower East Side

Statue of Liberty National Monument

Statue of Liberty National Monument
www.nps.gov/stli

⬛ Map p. 48

✉ Liberty Island, New York Harbor

☎ 212/363-3200

$ $$ (Tickets at Castle Clinton)

🚇 Subway: 1, 9 to South Ferry

⛴ Ferry from Battery Park at 30-min. intervals

Note: The statue is closed; the island grounds are open.

View from the torch

BECAUSE SHE IS LOCATED FAR OUT IN UPPER NEW YORK BAY, the Statue of Liberty is rarely seen by many New Yorkers. Perhaps for that reason, even the most jaded have never tired of her. Nor have the words of Emma Lazarus's famous poem—"Give me your tired, your poor, your huddled masses yearning to be free"—which are inscribed on a bronze tablet on the base, lost their power. The Statue of Liberty, dedicated in 1886, was a gift to America from the people of France to celebrate the alliance of the two nations in achieving the independence of the United States of America.

Sculptor Frédéric Bartholdi modeled the statue on the ancient wonder, the Colossus of Rhodes. The statue's torch symbolizes enlightenment; her seven-pointed headdress denotes the continents.

She holds a tablet representing the Declaration of Independence. Lady Liberty is 151 feet tall, weighs 2,225 tons, and has a 35-foot waistline. Her index finger is eight feet long.

French engineer Gustave Eiffel,

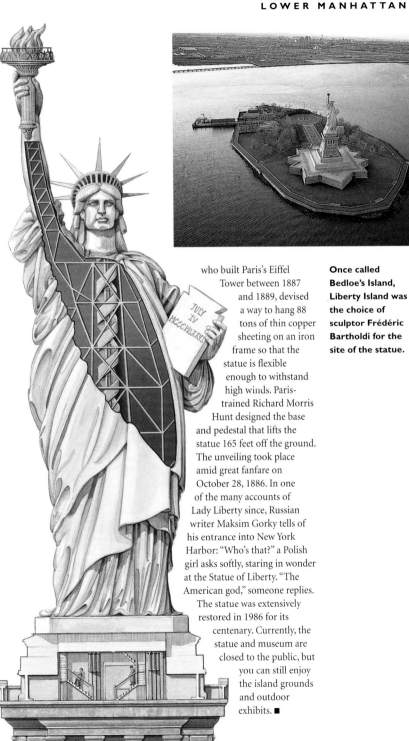

who built Paris's Eiffel Tower between 1887 and 1889, devised a way to hang 88 tons of thin copper sheeting on an iron frame so that the statue is flexible enough to withstand high winds. Paris-trained Richard Morris Hunt designed the base and pedestal that lifts the statue 165 feet off the ground. The unveiling took place amid great fanfare on October 28, 1886. In one of the many accounts of Lady Liberty since, Russian writer Maksim Gorky tells of his entrance into New York Harbor: "Who's that?" a Polish girl asks softly, staring in wonder at the Statue of Liberty. "The American god," someone replies. The statue was extensively restored in 1986 for its centenary. Currently, the statue and museum are closed to the public, but you can still enjoy the island grounds and outdoor exhibits. ■

Once called Bedloe's Island, Liberty Island was the choice of sculptor Frédéric Bartholdi for the site of the statue.

Ellis Island National Monument

SOME 100 MILLION AMERICANS AND MANY FROM OTHER countries have ancestors who passed through Ellis Island as immigrants. If you are one of them, or even if you are not, a visit to the restored processing center, the Ellis Island National Monument, is a moving experience. It begins with a ferry ride, a small-scale simulation of those immigrant landings long ago. Inside, stand in the Great Registry—a room 200 feet long, 100 feet wide, and 56 feet high—and imagine the lines of anxious arrivals waiting to be processed. One-third of the 16 million who arrived here between 1892 and 1924 ventured no farther than New York.

Ellis Island National Monument
www.nps.gov/elis
- Map p. 48
- New York Harbor
- 212/269-5755
- $$ (includes ferry)
- Subway: 1, 9 to South Ferry
- Circle Line ferry from Battery Park

The island is named for Samuel Ellis, who purchased it in 1785. Over the years it grew, with landfill, from 3 to more than 27 acres. In 1892, the federal government

The Great Registry where anxious immigrants were once processed

opened an immigration processing facility on the island. After it burned in 1897, it was replaced with the existing huge French Renaissance-style building of brick and limestone, which opened in

1900. During 1907, its busiest year, 1,285,349 immigrants entered the country through Ellis Island; 75 percent of them were from Italy, Russia, and Austria-Hungary, and the rest from northern Europe and countries all over the world, including China, Japan, Canada, and Mexico.

In 1924 Congress set strict quotas on immigration. From then on, the numbers passing through dwindled. The facility closed in 1954, a 160-million-dollar restoration began in 1984, and the Ellis Island Museum of Immigration opened in 1990. Exhibits on three floors re-create the experience of the immigrants on Ellis Island and celebrate their contribution to America. Follow their journey through the entry inspections and health checks, see the dormitory and dining hall, and hear the voices of immigrants telling their stories. The Wall of Honor outside is engraved with the names of thousands of immigrants; relatives can still add a name to the wall. On the island's south side are 29 medical buildings, untouched and deteriorating— listed by the National Trust for Historic Preservation as some of the nation's most endangered historic places. ■

Manhattan's historic tip

BATTERY PARK IS A 21-ACRE SWATH OF GREENERY—AND
a place of refuge for the financial district's many office workers—at
the southernmost tip of Manhattan Island. It is dotted with
memorials honoring, among others, early Dutch and Jewish settlers,
the Coast Guard, and the explorer Giovanni da Verrazano, who first
sighted the Battery's shore. To the north of it, the winding streets of
the oldest part of the city disappear into canyons of skyscrapers. To
the south, open water beckons. You can smell salt water and feel the
pull of one of the most famous harbors in the world.

The Battery's principal building,
Castle Clinton, is Manhattan's
only existing fort. The circular
structure was actually on an island
100 yards offshore when it was built
in the days leading up to the War of
1812 with Great Britain. It took
successive landfills to create the terrain that is Battery Park today. The
fortification was named for DeWitt
Clinton, a famous New York figure
who, as mayor, was responsible for
reinforcing the harbor defenses.

Castle Clinton, whose 28 guns
never fired at an enemy, has had a
varied history. In 1823 it was
renamed Castle Garden and
converted into an entertainment
arena. From 1855 to 1890 (before
Ellis Island opened) it was the city's
immigration center. Luis Sanguino's
statue, "The Immigrants" (1973),
pays tribute to the 7.7 million new
arrivals who passed through Castle
Clinton. In 1896 the building was
transformed into the New York
Aquarium, and so it remained until
1940. After a battle over its fate,
Castle Clinton was restored in the
1970s and opened as a historic site
with a small museum. Concerts and
events are held here in the summer.

Castle Clinton
www.nps.gov/cacl
- Map p. 48
- Battery Park
- 212/344-7220
- Subway: 4, 5 to
  Bowling Green; 1, 9
  to South Ferry

**Castle Clinton
in Battery Park
is a reminder that
Lower Manhattan
began as a
walled fortress.**

A bull in bronze, sculptured by Arturo Di Modica, is a symbol of a Wall Street stock market on its way up.

The 1907 Cass Gilbert-designed **U.S. Custom House** (*corner of Broad & Wall Sts.*) stands on the site of Fort Amsterdam (later Fort George), built by the Dutch in 1625. The highlight of the monumental exterior is Daniel Chester French's "The Four Continents," four allegorical sculpture groupings, each dominated by a female figure. Asia appears serene; America radiates vigor; Europe is regal; and Africa slumbers. The **National Museum of the American Indian** (see p. 56) is located within.

Just north of the National Museum of the American Indian is tiny **Bowling Green,** with benches and a picturesque fountain. Once used for cattle, this became the city's first public park in 1733, when it was rented to

Washington's farewell

On December 4, 1783, following his victory over the British, George Washington gave a farewell dinner at Fraunces Tavern (see opposite) for his officers. The general was unusually eloquent on this emotional occasion: "With a heart full of love and gratitude I now take my leave of you. I most devoutly wish that your latter days may be as prosperous and happy as your former ones have been glorious and honorable." ■

three citizens for lawn bowling, at the yearly rent of one peppercorn. In 1770, the British erected a gilded statue of George III on the green. Revolutionary patriots later pulled it down and, legend has it, melted it into ammunition.

An unusual attraction north of Bowling Green is the massive bronze bull statue. The gift of a city sculptor, it arrived unexpectedly at the New York Stock Exchange one evening in the 1980s. It was later moved and it has become a favorite picture-taking spot.

Wherever you wander, note the history preserved in street names: Wall Street takes its name from the wooden barricade the Dutch erected in 1653 to protect the colony's northern flank. Bowling Green was actually used for lawn bowling.

Rector Street is a tribute to the rectors of Trinity Church. Beaver Street was at one time rich in beaver, while Pearl Street once marked the shore and was named for the gleam of shells. Battery Park is named after the gun battery the British mounted there in the 1700s to defend the harbor.

Entering the historic block that includes **Fraunces Tavern** is a time warp back to colonial times. The tavern dates from 1719 and is today one of the financial district's better and more atmospheric restaurants. Samuel Fraunces, a West Indian who, tradition says, was black, purchased the brick building in 1763 and opened it as a tavern. It was saved for patriotic reasons—George Washington dined here (see box p. 54)—and, miraculously, the whole block has survived.

After deteriorating throughout the 19th century, Fraunces Tavern was reconstructed in 1907 in authentic Georgian style. Only the west brick wall is from the original building. It opened in 1910 as a restaurant and museum, which includes the Long Room, a re-creation of the site of Washington's farewell speech, and the Clinton Room, decorated with federal furnishings and 1834 wallpaper.

FRAUNCES TAVERN HISTORIC DISTRICT
Today the block by the tavern—bounded by Pearl, Broad, and Water Streets, and Coenties Slip—is a designated historic district with a number of early 19th-century buildings in the federal and Greek Revival styles. Coenties Slip, once a wharf created by landfill, is now landlocked. The adjacent plaza (55 Water St.) holds the **New York Vietnam Veterans Memorial,** a 14-foot-high rectangular glass prism, commemorating those who died in the war. ■

Fraunces Tavern Museum
www.frauncestavernmuseum
.org
▲ Map p. 48
✉ 54 Pearl St.
☎ 212/425-1778
$ $
🚇 4, 5 to Bowling Green; 1, 9 to South Ferry

National Museum of the American Indian

National Museum of the American Indian: The George Gustav Heye Center

www.nmai.si.edu/heye

🅰 Map p. 48

✉ 1 Bowling Green

☎ 212/514-3888

🚇 Subway: 4, 5 to Bowling Green; 1, 9 to South Ferry

ONE MILLION ARTIFACTS COLLECTED BY WEALTHY NEW Yorker George Gustav Heye (1874–1957) during his journeys throughout the Americas form the cornerstone of this fascinating museum.

Displayed on a rotating basis in the sprawling beaux-arts U.S. Custom House, the artifacts represent significant Native American places, from the American Southwest and Hawaii, to Canada, to South and Central America. They include stone and wood carvings from the Pacific Northwest; feather bonnets and quilled hides from the North American plains; Navajo weavings; ceramics from Costa Rica, central Mexico, and Peru; Mayan carved jade; featherwork from the Amazon; and the list goes on. One current exhibit focuses on contemporary Native American artists, including Rick Bartow, Joe Feddersen, Harry Fonseca, Jaune Quick-to-See-Smith, and Kay WalkingStick. Another details the history of the Native American cowboy through clothing, saddles, blankets, hunting tools, and pow-wow regalia.

Since it opened in 1994, the museum has become a popular attraction—3.7 million visitors through 2002. It comes under the auspices of the Smithsonian Institution, which plans to open an adjunct museum on the National Mall in 2004. ■

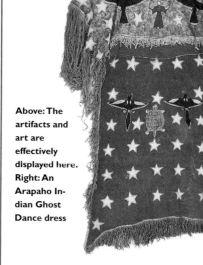

Above: The artifacts and art are effectively displayed here. Right: An Arapaho Indian Ghost Dance dress

Trinity Church,
a spiritual oasis
amid skyscrapers
devoted to the
pursuit of business
and profit

Trinity Church

IN ITS 300 YEARS AT THE HEAD OF WALL STREET, Trinity Church has earned a prominent place in the life of the financial community. A good time to visit this lovely church is during the week at midday, when—during services or concerts or on strolls through the historic graveyard—you can join Wall Streeters as they shake off the tensions of their fast-moving jobs.

Trinity is a very wealthy church, thanks to a land grant from Queen Anne in 1705 that gave it a huge chunk of Manhattan Island. The present building is actually the third church on the site. The first, completed in 1698, burned in the Great Fire of 1776. It was rebuilt in 1787. Two years later a service was held honoring George Washington's inauguration as President. After this building was razed, Richard Upjohn designed the present church in the Gothic Revival style, using New Jersey brownstone.

The 280-foot steeple was, until the 1860s, the highest point in the city and a landmark for ships at sea. Richard Morris Hunt designed the three sculptured bronze doors as a memorial to a wealthy parishioner, John Jacob Astor.

The church's museum displays newspapers, burial records, maps, and other documents and artifacts. The graveyard contains the remains of many prominent New Yorkers, among them Alexander Hamilton (see pp. 23 and 25) and Robert Fulton, developer of the steamboat. ■

Trinity Church
www.trinitywallstreet.org
⬛ Map p. 48
✉ Broadway
at Wall St.
☎ 212/602-0800 for information on concerts and services

Trinity Church Museum
☎ 212/602-0872
🕐 Closed p.m. Sun.
💲 Donation
🚇 Subway: 2, 3 to Wall St.; 1, 9 to Rector St.; 4, 5 to Wall St.

New York Stock Exchange

After a bell is rung to open trading, the floor of the stock exchange is abuzz with the buying and selling of shares.

AT THE NEW YORK STOCK EXCHANGE (NYSE) PANDEMONI-um reigns; people are invariably astonished that the business of trading securities, despite the mass of tickers, computers, and monitors, is still conducted by traders waving arms and shouting orders. It wasn't always this disorderly. In the early days members were assigned chairs. Today's traders are too busy to sit down, but a membership is still called a seat on the exchange.

New York Stock Exchange

www.nyse.com

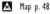 Map p. 48

✉ 20 Broad St.

☎ 212/656-5168 (for group tours)

🚇 Subway: 2, 3, 4, 5 to Wall St.

Note: The Stock Exchange is currently closed to visitors.

The NYSE is the world's largest equities marketplace, home to nearly 2,800 companies valued at about 15 trillion dollars in global market capitalization. It is, in short, the center of the global economy. No one could have imagined such magnitude when, in 1792, 24 investors gathered under a buttonwood tree. There, at Wall and William Streets, they agreed to buy and sell stocks and bonds only among themselves.

In 1903 the institution moved into its current two-million-dollar neoclassic building. The pediment sculpture, grandly titled "Integrity Protecting the Works of Man," was designed by J.Q.A. Ward. Although the exchange is now strictly regulated, "integrity" has not always universally applied.

Low points include the crash of October 1929 and the conviction and imprisonment of its president, Richard Whitney, in 1938 for bilking customers.

The NYSE is currently closed to visitors. ∎

Federal Hall

From its pedestal, Federal Hall's statue of George Washington gazes at the columned facade of the New York Stock Exchange.

FEDERAL HALL, POSSIBLY THE CITY'S FIRST GREEK REVIVAL building, stands at the heart of the busiest financial district in the world. Every business day, hordes of Wall Streeters stream past a location rich in colonial history. The financiers probably know that the statue in front is George Washington, but many of them—even those who spend their lunch hours lounging on the steps—may not realize that this is where he took the oath as the country's first President.

The present Federal Hall, erected in 1842, was designed by Ithiel Town and Alexander Jackson Davis. Eight Doric columns, 32 feet high, line the front and rear, on Pine Street. The statue of Washington, sculptured in 1883 by John Quincy Adams Ward, shows him lifting his hand from a Bible. Federal Hall housed the U.S. Customs Service for 20 years, then other agencies until it became a national monument in 1955. Browse the interior exhibits, featuring mementos of the first inauguration, and pick up Heritage Trail maps of the area at the information center.

Nearby, the Bank of Manhattan Building, now the **Trump Building** (*40 Wall St.*), at 927 feet was the world's tallest in 1929 until the Chrysler Building surpassed it in 1930. First National City Bank Building, now **Citibank,** at No. 55 was built in 1840; it took 40 teams of oxen to haul its 16 Ionic granite columns up Wall Street. It was remodeled and enlarged in 1907. ■

Federal Hall National Monument
www.nps.gov/feha
- Map p. 48
- 26 Wall St.
- 212/825-6888
- Closed Sat.–Sun.
- Subway: 2, 3, 4, 5 to Wall St.

Walk up Broadway

If you would rather avoid fast-paced crowds, try this tour on a weekend, when the streets are quieter. It begins at the foot of Broadway, near Battery Park, going from the financial district to City Hall, convenient to shopping and restaurants.

Your stroll begins in front of the **National Museum of the American Indian** (see p. 56) ❶; be sure to take a peek inside. Then proceed to the Renaissance-style **Cunard Building** ❷ by Benjamin Morris, located at 25 Broadway. Constructed in 1921 as the Cunard Line's New York headquarters, it now houses a post office. You can buy stamps in the Great Hall, one of the city's best interior spaces. This room is where tickets for the *Titanic, Lusitania,* and other famous ocean liners were sold; its murals and decorated domed ceiling were based on Raphael's Villa Madama in Rome. Across from Bowling Green on Broadway is the **Museum of American Financial History** (see p. 74). Continue up Broadway. The building at No. 26, designed by Carrère and Hastings, has a pyramidlike tower; it was once the Standard Oil Building.

Just north of **Trinity Church** (see p. 57) and the head of Wall Street, the hulking 1915 **Equitable Building** ❸ (*120 Broadway*) rises straight up for 40 stories. The protests of critics who feared that such buildings would make the city a sunless canyon led to zoning laws in 1916 requiring setbacks (in which upper stories are stepped back to allow more light to reach street level). Just beyond the Equitable Building, the sleek **Marine Midland Building** ❹ (*140 Broadway*), built in 1967 by Skidmore, Owings & Merrill, has one of Lower Manhattan's nicer plazas, set off by Isamu Noguchi's red cube sculpture (1973). Turn right on Liberty Street.

Ahead, the **Federal Reserve Bank** ❺ (*33 Liberty St., tel 212/720-6130 for free tours with advance reservation*), in the style of a Renaissance palace, holds the cash reserves of many banks plus gold bullion from countries throughout the world. The four-story Vermont marble building at No. 65, fronted by Ionic columns, was built in 1901 for the Chamber of Commerce of the State of New York. The organization was founded by 20 city

merchants meeting at Fraunces Tavern in 1768. Turn left on Nassau Street, then right on John Street. The austere **John Street United Methodist Church** ❻ (*44 John St., tel 212/269-0014*), built in 1841, replaced the 1768 Wesley Chapel, the first Methodist church in the United States. An early sexton was a slave who purchased his freedom from the chapel's trustees. He later founded the country's first black Methodist church.

Turn left on William Street. On the southwest corner of Fulton Street is the site of writer Washington Irving's birthplace (*131 William St.*). Turn left on Fulton, and right on Broadway. **St. Paul's Chapel** and its churchyard ❼ (*Tel 212/602-0874*), between Fulton and Vesey Streets, has been in continuous use since it opened in 1766 as an adjunct of Trinity Church. George Washington worshiped here; his pew is marked by a plaque. It is on St. Paul's iron fence that, in the aftermath of the Sept. 11, 2001, terrorist attack, thousands of people created a spontaneous memorial to the victims by stringing signed T-shirts, banners, posters, baseball caps, photos, and teddy bears.

Just beyond St. Paul's is the **ground zero site;** a viewing area, accessed at Liberty Street and Broadway, overlooks the enormous pit where the Twin Towers fell.

Proceed up Broadway. Number 233, between Park Place and Barclay Street, is the 60-story **Woolworth Building** ❽. Topped

Ⓜ	Map inside front cover
►	National Museum of the American Indian
⟷	1.25 miles
⏱	2.5 hours
►	City Hall, City Hall Park

NOT TO BE MISSED
- Cunard Building
- Federal Reserve Bank
- Woolworth Building

by a golden crown, it was the world's tallest until 1929, when the tower at 40 Wall Street outdid it. Its architect, Cass Gilbert, described it as a steel frame covered with masonry and terra-cotta. The building's lobby—decorated with murals, a vaulted, mosaic-studded ceiling, and a stained-glass skylight—includes a whimsical statue showing F. W. Woolworth, founder of the five-and-ten chain that bears his name, counting money. Cut across City Hall Park to **City Hall** (see p. 62) to end the tour. You can go back to Broadway or swing over to **South Street Seaport** (see pp. 64–65) for refreshments or more sight-seeing. ■

The Gothic beauty of the Woolworth Building made it an instant landmark in 1913.

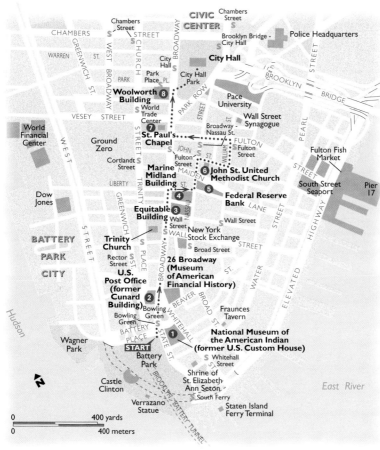

City Hall & beyond

CITY HALL PARK, ONCE A DUTCH COW PASTURE AND NOW pleasantly landscaped, surrounds the magnificent, federal-style City Hall. Frederick MacMonnies' bronze statue of patriot Nathan Hale on the green is a reminder that Americans once protested British rule here. For a liberating experience, stroll across the street to the imposing Brooklyn Bridge, with its wide wooden walkways and spectacular views north and south.

City Hall
- Map p. 48
- City Hall Park
- 212/788-6865
- Closed Sat.–Sun. Tour reservations required.
- Subway: 4, 5, 6 to Brooklyn Bridge; 2, 3 to Park Place

City Hall's soaring rotunda, reached by twin spiral staircases, is the centerpiece of the 1812 building.

Even if you are a stranger to New York, chances are you will recognize City Hall. It is on these steps that the mayor greets visiting heroes and dignitaries and hands over the keys to the city, a scene captured countless times in news footage. City Hall has also been the center of numerous celebrations and demonstrations. Here is where ticker-tape parades up Broadway from the Battery generally end, a tradition that started spontaneously in 1886 when office workers threw ticker tape out of windows during a parade celebrating the dedication of the Statue of Liberty. Although City Hall is congenially sited in the middle of City Hall Park, you might wonder why its architects, John McComb, Jr., and Joseph Francois Mangin, faced the building south. Answer: When City Hall was built in 1812, no one thought the city would extend much farther north.

Venture inside where you will see, in the lobby, a bronze copy of a statue of George Washington, done from life by the French sculptor Jean-Antoine Houdon.

The **Governor's Room,** once used by the governor on visits to the city, is now a museum with George Washington's writing table on display. The painting collection includes a portrait of Washington on Evacuation Day 1783, by John Trumbull, a leading historical painter, as well as works by John Wesley Jarvis, who painted the heroes of the War of 1812; Samuel F. B. Morse, inventor of the telegraph, whose painting of Lafayette was done during the marquis's triumphal return to this country in 1824; and George Catlin, later known for Western paintings, who did the portrait of DeWitt Clinton.

Northeast of City Hall, near Park Row, which borders the park, J.Q.A. Ward's statue of Horace Greeley shows the disheveled publisher seated with an open newspaper over his right knee. For years Park Row was the center of Manhattan's newspaper publishing. Greeley's Tribune Building on Park Row was torn down in 1966. The *New York Times* was published at 41 Park Row from 1858 until the paper moved to Times Square in 1904.

OTHER SIGHTS
Nearby at 31 Chambers Street is the **Surrogate's Court** or Hall of Records. Completed in 1911, this beaux arts building is adorned with sculpture. Philip Martiny did the facade carvings, including a row of city mayors below the Chambers Street cornice, and the two groupings flanking the main entrance, "New York in Its Infancy" and "New York in Revolutionary Times." The wedding-cake tower of the 1914 **Municipal Building** *(Centre and Chambers Sts.)* is topped by Adolph Weinman's 25-foot-tall copper statue, "Civic

Fame," the largest statue in Manhattan.

Head two blocks north on Elk Street to reach the **African Burial Ground** *(Duane and Elk Sts.)*. Human remains dug up in 1991 by workers excavating at Broadway and Duane turned out to have come from a five-acre graveyard, where upward of 20,000 African Americans were buried between 1712 and 1794. The find drew attention to the large number of African slaves and freed men in the city in the 18th century. Slave revolts in 1714 and 1741 were brutally suppressed, the leaders executed and then presumably buried here. ■

A fountain spouts in City Hall Park, in existence since 1730 as The Common. The Municipal Building rises behind.

Tweed Courthouse

At the north end of City Hall Park is a three-story marble courthouse that is often confused for City Hall. Today the building, officially named the Old New York County Courthouse, is held in high esteem, and its interiors are among the finest of middle 19th-century New York. But when it was finished in 1878, the assessments were not so generous, and it was known as the Tweed Courthouse after the man who went down in history as a corrupt politician. One account described the building as "a gloomy meandering mess of unattractive rooms." The unfavorable review probably reflected the public's frustration, as the courthouse had taken 20 years to build and cost almost 13 million dollars, 50 times the original estimate. Two-thirds of that amount is believed to have been diverted into the sizable pockets of William M. "Boss" Tweed and his cronies. ■

South Street Seaport Museum & Marketplace

South Street Seaport Museum & Marketplace
www.southstreetseaport.org

🅰 Map p. 48

Ⓜ Fulton St at South St.

🕒 Closed Tues. Oct.–March

💲 $$

🚇 Subway: 2, 3, 4, 5, J, Z, M to Fulton St.

Visitor center

✉ 209 Water St.

☎ 212/748-8786

This tall ship is part of the fleet on display at Piers 15 and 16.

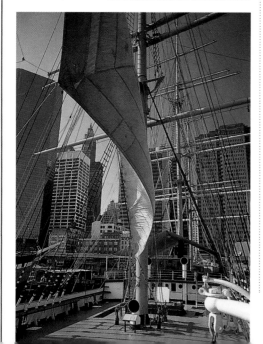

FOR A TRIP BACK TO THE DAYS WHEN NEW YORK HARBOR was the world's busiest port, visit the 11-square-block historic district around the East River at South and Fulton Streets. Here is the South Street Seaport Museum & Marketplace, a restoration of the early 19th-century waterfront. Developed in the 1980s, the seaport offers a mix of historic preservation and entertainment, cobblestone streets, and live open-air fish trading.

Titanic Memorial Lighthouse at the intersection of Pearl, Water, and Fulton Streets marks your introduction to the seaport. Do not let crowds obscure the fact that the seaport surrounding the market is an outstanding maritime museum, in and among important 18th- and 19th-century buildings.

The seaport divides into two areas ahead of you, with F.D.R. Drive perpendicular to Fulton Street in between. West of the drive, in front of the lighthouse, are complexes of joined buildings. These house the seaport's museums, exhibits, offices, and small stores. East of F.D.R. Drive

is the pier, where there are historic ships and where tickets for harbor excursions can be purchased. **Pier 17** also has a multilevel shopping center, including a food court. For spectacular river and Brooklyn Bridge views, go to the area outside the food court where there are complimentary lounges.

EXPLORING THE SEAPORT

Orienting yourself at the visitor center is advisable. There you can find out about special events, purchase tickets for all attractions and seaport Liberty Line harbor cruises, and pick up a free map. To get to the center, walk past the large information sign (worth reading) and go down Fulton Street. The Visitors' Center is in the middle of Schermerhorn Row, the complex on the right.

Schermerhorn Row dates from 1812 and comprises 12 federal-style brick buildings. Walking around the building brings you to John Street. This was once Burlington Slip, a water entrance for ships from China that unloaded their wares into the countinghouse of the **A. A. Low Building** (171 John St.). The building was constructed in 1850 by a trader whose clipper ships dominated the mid-century China trade. It now houses galleries. There is also the **Children's Center** (165 John St.).

The buildings at Fulton and Water Streets contain four interesting places. **Bowne & Co. Stationers** (*211 Water St., tel 212/ 748-8651*) is a working restoration of a 19th-century printing shop. Ship models and ocean liner memorabilia are on display at the **Whitman Gallery** (*209 Water St., tel 212/748-8600*), and the **Melville Gallery** (*213 Water St., tel 212/748-8600*) has visual art exhibits. The **Museum Library** above the Melville Gallery is open by appointment.

Be sure to stroll **Piers 15** and **16,** where you can choose among an authentic schooner; music cruises; Circle Line tours around the island; a speedboat thrill ride; and even seasonal tugboat rides (*information, tel 212/748-8786*). Included in the fleet here are the **Ambrose** (1908), a lightship that marked the entrance to New York harbor; the **Peking,** a four-masted ship built in 1911 in Hamburg, Germany; and **Pioneer** (1885), a former cargo schooner popular for its twilight sails. ■

Eateries and shops fill the three-story Pier 17 building, a 1983 addition to the seaport's complex.

Fulton Fish Market: It's the real thing

Since Dutch colonial times, New York's store and restaurant owners have bought their fish at the Fulton market. Once the country's largest fresh fish market, it is named for Robert Fulton, developer of the steamboat. From 1814 he ran a Manhattan-to-Brooklyn ferry, whose building stood on the market site. While much of the "selling" has moved to the Bronx, pungent smells and fishing paraphernalia—from hand-painted signage to massive scales—plus haggling clientele and family-run businesses still make a visit unforgettable.

The only way to see the market is by guided tour, offered by the South Street Seaport Museum April through October (212/748-8786). ■

The neighborhoods

MOST IMMIGRANTS HISTORICALLY BEGAN THEIR NEW American lives in the neighborhoods, an area—especially SoHo and TriBeCa—that more recently has become hip and trendy.

Museum of Chinese in the Americas

www.moca-nyc.org

✉ 70 Mulberry St. at Bayard St.

☎ 212/619-4785

🕑 Closed Mon.

💲 $

🚇 Subway: B, D, Q to Grand St.; J, M, N, R, Z, 6 to Canal St.

CHINATOWN

For the center of Chinatown, head for Mott and Pell Streets below Canal Street. New York's first Chinese settlement developed in the mid-1870s along Mott Street, and today the area is filled with good restaurants, cafés, curio and antique shops, and bookstores. Try one of the many fine restaurants and then explore and enjoy the mix of old and new.

Quong Yuen Shing & Co. (*32 Mott St.*), established in 1892 as a grocery store, sells figurines and ceramics. The 1801 **Church of the Transfiguration** (*29 Mott St., tel 212/962-5157*) was built for English Lutherans, sold to an Irish Roman Catholic congregation in 1853, and attracted an Italian community before becoming primarily Chinese.

The most visible symbols of Chinatown are the Chinese shop signs and the pagoda-style roofs that top anything from banks to telephone booths. At 41 Mott Street stands the only wooden pagoda roof left in Chinatown. The **Eastern States Buddhist Temple** (*64 Mott St., tel 212/966-6229*) is filled with candles and offerings to more than a hundred gold Buddhas, while the small **Museum of Chinese in the Americas** holds fascinating exhibits.

You may seek out enclaves such as Doyers Street, once a dead-end alley known as Bloody Alley, where warring tongs (similar to gangs today) ambushed one another. Confucius Plaza at Chatham Square is graced by a bronze statue of the ancient philosopher.

Newspapers and brochures about current affairs in China are posted on the **Wall of Democracy** on Bayard Street. Chinatown today is expanding—into Little Italy. Canal Street, once the division between Chinatown and Little Italy, has a bustling sidewalk market and Chinese groceries stocked with curious roots, herbs, and vegetables, but it is no substitute for the atmosphere of the cramped and winding interior streets around Mott Street.

Historic sites

Structures such as the **Edward Mooney House** (circa 1785–89), at 18 Bowery, recall an era when the area was known for its fine residences. Stanford White designed the Bowery Savings Bank (1895), now the Greenpoint Bank at 130 Bowery, in the classical style of a Roman temple. **St. James Roman Catholic Church** (*32 James St.*) is the city's second oldest Roman Catholic church. Nearby, the **First Shearith Israel Graveyard** (*55–57 St. James Place*) is the burial ground of the first Jewish congregation in North America, formed in 1654 by Sephardim from Brazil.

LITTLE ITALY

Unlike Chinatown, Little Italy has shrunk over the years; Mulberry Street north of Canal is the pulse of what remains. Here there are good Italian restaurants, cafés, delis, private clubs, and legendary Mafia sites. You might start off with a cappuccino and a treat on Mulberry or at **Ferrara's** (*195*

Opposite: On Chinatown's busy Mott Street signs are in English and Cantonese—and tourists mix with residents.

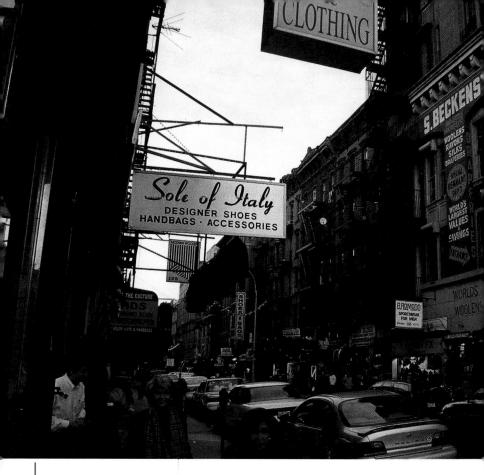

Grand St.), a hundred-year-old
pastry shop just around the corner.

Little Italy's annual gala is the
Feast of San Gennaro, held for ten
days around September 19. A statue
is paraded through the streets and
there are food stalls, music, and dancing, with activity centered around the
courtyard of the **Church of the
Most Precious Blood** *(109
Mulberry St.).* Mulberry Street is also
connected to organized crime. Before
being jailed, mobster boss John Gotti
frequented the Ravenite Social
Club at No. 247. Gangster Joey Gallo
was shot to death in 1972, while
celebrating his birthday at No. 129,
Umberto's Clam House.

Some historic sites have little
original connection with Italian
residents. Gothic **St. Patrick's**

Old Cathedral *(263 Mulberry
St., tel 212/226-8075)* is one of the
city's oldest churches (1809–1815),
largely rebuilt after a fire in the
1860s. Its first congregation was
Irish; a smaller Italian congregation
developed in the 1880s. The
**Stephen Van Rensselaer
House** *(149 Mulberry St.),* with
its brickwork front, gambrel roof,
and dormer windows, was built
about 1816. The baroque-style
1909 New York City Police
Headquarters *(1 Police Plaza),*
once a proud symbol of the city's
modern police force, was converted
into luxury apartments in the 1980s.

LOWER EAST SIDE

Street names are all that remain of
the Lower East Side's rural, colonial

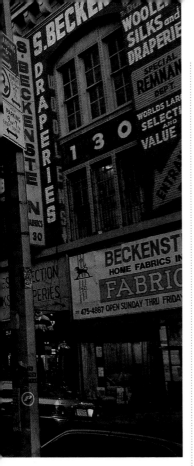

past. Orchard Street ran through fruit trees. The Bowery, a principal north–south thoroughfare, once led to Peter Stuyvesant's bouwerie, or farm. Some of the city's finest houses were on the Bowery, but once the immigrants arrived—Irish in the 1830s, then Germans, and, in the 1880s, thousands of eastern European Jews, Poles, Italians, Romanians, Russians, and Greeks—the Lower East Side became a place of tenements and slums.

For an orientation to the general area, visit the **Lower East Side Tenement Museum.** This unusual museum represents the first attempt to preserve and restore a tenement building. Purchased by the museum in 1988, the six-story brownstone was built in 1863

before housing laws. Living conditions were appalling—tiny, windowless rooms, without electricity or plumbing. Some 10,000 people are estimated to have lived in the building until it was condemned in 1935. Visitors can see immigrants' apartments and educational displays, as well as pick up informative pamphlets. The small shop sells gifts and books on immigrant life.

The **Henry Street Settlement** (263–267 Henry St., tel 212/766-9200) was founded in 1893 by Lillian Wald, a German Jew from Rochester, New York. An educational organization, it still helps immigrants adjust to American life. The settlement owns three landmark buildings: Federal-style Nos. 263 and 265 were built in 1827; No. 267, a Greek Revival building, in 1900. Across the street at No. 152 is a Buddhist temple that until 1990 was a social center for retired rabbis.

The recently restored **Eldridge Street Synagogue** belies the belief that the entire Lower East Side was impoverished. Completed in 1887, the Moorish Revival building cost $100,000, a stupendous sum at the time.

As the population changed, synagogues took over churches. The 1826 **Bialystoker Synagogue** (7–13 Bialystoker Pl.,

Lower East Side Tenement Museum
www.tenement.org
✉ 97 Orchard St.
Museum Visitor Center
✉ 90 Orchard St.
☎ 212/431-0233
🕐 Closed Mon.
💲 $–$$
🚇 Subway: F to Delancey St.; B, D, Q to Grand St.; J, M, Z to Essex St.

Eldridge Street Synagogue
✉ 12–16 Eldridge St. at Canal St.
☎ 212/219-0888
🚇 Subway: B, D, Q to Grand St.

Brightly painted murals cover a boarded-up building on Rivington Street.

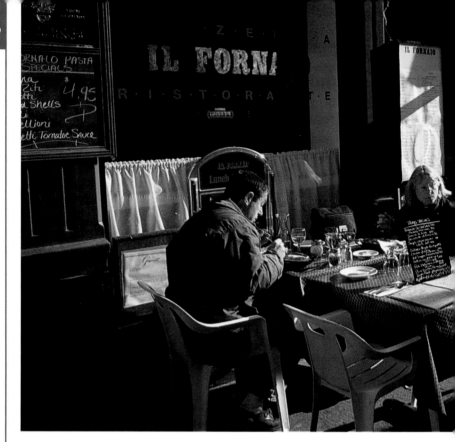

tel 212/475-0165) was built in 1826 as the Willett Street Methodist Episcopal Church and it became a synagogue in 1905. The **Forward Building** *(173 E. Broadway),* a ten-story classical revival structure that now houses a Chinese church, was completed in 1912 for the *Jewish Daily Forward,* a widely read Yiddish newspaper. The building is decorated with flaming torches, symbols of the socialist causes the paper supported. Nearby, the Educational Alliance at No. 197 was founded in 1897 to ease the process of Americanization. Comedian Eddie Cantor, sculptor Chaim Gross, and broadcasting pioneer David Sarnoff studied here; they are just a few of the talented people from Lower East.

Traditional Jewish shops bring former residents back to the "old neighborhood" for religious items—and especially for food. The **Essex Street Market,** filled with a vibrant mix of food merchants, originally housed pushcart peddlars. Other cherished institutions are Streit's Matzoh Company *(150 Rivington St.),* where you can watch the freshly baked unleavened bread slide from conveyor belts; Guss Pickles *(35 Essex St.);* Kossar's Bialys *(367 Grand);* and Katz's, the popular delicatessen *(205 E. Houston St.).* Meg Ryan's memorable moment in the 1989 film *When Harry Met Sally* was filmed at the latter, and yes, the food is that good.

SOHO & TRIBECA

SoHo, an acronym for South of Houston (Street), lies between Houston and Canal Streets, West Broadway, and Lafayette Street.

Famous for its concentration of fine cast-iron buildings (see pp. 72–73), its main thoroughfare, West Broadway, is lined with art galleries, antiques stores, and trendy restaurants.

In the 1970s SoHo's lofts and low rents attracted young artists. As the area was "discovered," rents soared, and artists sought affordable space elsewhere. Many moved to an industrial section, bordered by Canal and Chambers Streets, and West and Church Streets.

The area acquired a chic new name, TriBeCa ("triangle below Canal"), and the SoHo phenomenon began to repeat itself, with building conversions and an influx of shops, galleries, restaurants, and nightclubs.

Into the 1990s, the transformation of TriBeCa picked up speed, led by Robert DeNiro's 1989 reno-vation of a warehouse into the TriBeCa Film Center and the TriBeCa Grill *(375 Greenwich, tel 212/941-3900)*. From Sixth Avenue to Hudson Street there are now upscale furniture stores, unusual shops, and restaurants in all price ranges, from Drew Nieporent's establishments to Bubby's *(120 Hudson)*, where brunch is an insti-tution. The TriBeCa Grand Hotel *(2 Avenue of the Americas, tel 212/519-6600)* caters to the entertainment industry, offering state-of-the-art screening facilities and a public lounge frequented by young celebs. In 2002 DeNiro and others estab-lished the TriBeCa Film Festival. As the neighborhood's vigorous evolu-tion continues, it guards its archi-tectural treasures, including the federal-style Harrison Street Houses *(25–41 Harrison St.)*. ■

Outside an Italian restaurant in SoHo, tables spill onto the narrow sidewalk.

Walk: Cast iron in SoHo

This walk takes you through SoHo's historic cast-iron district. It begins in the heart of SoHo on West Broadway, goes south, then briefly touches on Canal Street before swinging back north, ending along Broadway. Along the way you will see some of the country's most outstanding examples of the cast-iron style, which were prefabricated in factories, then shipped to the building site and bolted onto the structures. The result was instant and highly ornate architecture with the appearance of stone carving.

Start on West Broadway, between Prince and Spring Streets. You can pick up a free gallery guide at any gallery nearby and head west on Prince Street for a coffeehouse treat. Then it's on to 429 West Broadway, the **Nancy Hoffman Gallery** ❶ *(Tel 212/966-6676)* for contemporary art. One of the first on the SoHo art scene in the 1970s, this is one of the few majors not to have relocated. Across the street No. 420 was home to the famed Leo Castelli Gallery until 1999. Just before you enter the cast-iron district, stop by **Cipriani Downtown** *(376 W. Broadway, tel 212/343-0999)*, a French bistro offering cozy tables indoor or out, with heated lamps for winter.

Turn left (east) at Broome Street. The building at No. 489 was built in 1873, as indicated by the date on it. The brick-and-brownstone building at No. 484 is not cast iron, but it has lovely gargoyles and facade decorations. Turn right (south) on Wooster Street to No. 33, the **Performing Garage** *(Tel 212/966-9796)*, home of the avant-garde Wooster Group of actors. Alumni members Spalding Gray and Willem Dafoe still appear here. Staying on Wooster, cross Grand Street. Look back at the Grecian-style Nos. 72 and 74 and 68–70 Grand Street, designed by George da Cunha. The streets become grittier as you go south a short block to Canal Street, where you turn left. Artists may want to visit **Pearl Paint** *(308 Canal St., tel 212/431-7932)*, just across the street, the world's largest art supply store. Otherwise, turn left from Canal Street onto Greene Street, heading uptown.

This is SoHo's premier cast-iron district, with an unbroken expanse of ten buildings, No. 8 through Nos. 32–34. Mostly Italianate, these are by some of cast iron's best architects. Isaac F. Duckworth designed the imposing, Empire-style building at Nos. 28–30. Known as the **Queen of Greene Street** ❷ its

mansard roof is a fitting crown. The true cast-iron king, however, is the ubiquitous Henry Fernbach, who designed most of this block, including Nos. 60, 62, 67, 69, 71, 75, 77, and 81. Note the many variations in the exterior staircases, columns, and windows, with the repetitive identical elements that suggest their origin in a cast-iron mold. One of the most extravagant structures, also by Duckworth, and aptly dubbed the **King of Greene Street** ❸, is Nos. 72–76, with stacked porches supported by Corinthian pillars—five stories high.

Turn right (east) on Spring Street, then right (south) on Mercer. If you need a break, Bar 89 at No. 89 has a skylight view of the surrounding buildings. Turn left (east) on Broome Street. Vaux and Withers, designers of the Jefferson Market Courthouse (see p. 80), designed No. 488 in 1872. Turn left (north) on Broadway. The 1857 **Haughwout Building** ❹ *(488 Broadway at Broome St.)* is the oldest and best preserved cast-iron building in the city, and the first to have a passenger elevator, designed and installed by Elisha Otis. John P. Gaynor designed the building, known for its harmonious arches, for a china and glass business.

On the left, between Broome and Spring Streets, 521–523 Broadway is all that remains of the larger, elegant thousand-bed St. Nicholas Hotel (1854), which closed in the 1870s. Alfred Zucker built 555 Broadway in 1889 for wholesaler Charles Rouss, a real-life Horatio Alger story. A sign on the construction site read: "He who builds, owns, and will occupy this marvel of brick, iron, and granite, thirteen years ago walked these streets penniless and $50,000 in debt." Stand across the street to read the lettering on the building, and stop in at No. 560, loaded with galleries. The dark green structure at 561 Broadway is known as the **Little Singer Building** ⑤, designed in 1903 by Ernest Flagg for the Singer Manufacturing Company. Note the terra-cotta facade and intricate wrought-iron balconies. In its emphasis on windows, the building is often cited as a precursor to the glass-curtain walls of 1950s skyscrapers.

At Prince Street, bibliophiles will want to turn right and then a quick left to 126 Crosby Street, **Housing Works Used Book Café** (*Tel 212/334-3324*); eclectic lectures and readings, and live music shows are offered. Back on Broadway, find No. 583, the **New Museum of Contemporary Art** ⑥ (*583 Broadway, tel 212/219-1222*). Dating from 1977, it has featured such innovative exhibits as living paintings, in which the artists are part of the art and talk to (and even insult) the viewers. Pamper yourself at one of the trendy boutiques or cosmetics salons that have replaced museums along this stretch.

The tour ends just below Houston Street. Check to see what's showing at the **Angelika** (*18 W. Houston St., 212/995-2000*), one of the city's best independent cinemas, to the west. ■

Ⓜ Map inside front cover
▶ West Broadway
⟷ 1.1 miles
🕐 1.5 hours
▶ Below Houston Street

NOT TO BE MISSED
- Queen of Greene Street
- King of Greene Street
- Haughwout Building
- Little Singer Building

Renovated cast-iron-fronted buildings along Greene Street

An exhibit of sacred works at the Museum of the Jewish Heritage

Museums off the beaten track

THE DRAWING CENTER

Founded to promote drawing as an art, the center's excellent contemporary and historical exhibits feature everyone from Picasso to contemporary cartoonists and street artists.
✉ 35 Wooster St. ☎ 212/219-2166
🕐 Closed Sun. 🚇 Subway: A, C, E to Canal St.; N, R to Prince St.

MUSEUM OF AMERICAN FINANCIAL HISTORY

This display is based on the personal collection of founder John E. Herzog. The collection includes an 1880 stock ticker invented by Thomas Edison.
✉ 26 Broadway ☎ 212/908-4110 🕐 Closed Sun.–Mon. 🚇 Subway: 1, 9 to South St.; 4, 5 to Bowling Green

MUSEUM OF JEWISH HERITAGE

A living memorial to the Holocaust, the museum opened in 1997, with a new wing debuting in 2003. Kevin Roche designed the hexagonal granite structure.
✉ 18 1st Pl., Battery Park City ☎ 212/968-1800 🕐 Closed Sat. & Jewish holidays 💲 $$
🚇 Subway: 1, 9 to Rector St.

NEW YORK CITY FIRE MUSEUM

This rich collection of historic fire-fighting equipment and memorabilia, housed in a former fire station in SoHo, includes fire engines dating back to 1765.
✉ 278 Spring St. between Hudson and Varick Sts. ☎ 212/691-1303 🕐 Closed Mon. 💲 $
🚇 Subway: 1, 9 to Spring St.

NEW YORK UNEARTHED

This museum preserves and exhibits archaeological objects dug up as the city expanded. A glassed-in laboratory area lets you see archaeologists analyze their finds, and a video display simulates a descent into an excavation site.
✉ 17 State St. at Battery Park ☎ 212/748-8628 🕐 Closed weekends 🚇 Subway: 1, 9 to South Ferry; 4, 5 to Bowling Green ∎

The streets are refreshingly narrow; the buildings are quaint and low-rise. Greenwich Village and its East Village neighbor have been home to New York's finest families, its immigrants, and some of America's best artists and writers.

The Villages

Old Glory on an East Village tenement

The Villages

GREENWICH VILLAGE IS ONE OF NEW YORK'S MOST LEGENDARY neighborhoods. Centered around and west of Washington Square Park, it extends from Houston Street north to 14th Street and from Broadway west to the Hudson River. Today it is often called the West Village to distinguish it from its neighbor, the vibrant East Village (east of Broadway), which until the 1950s was viewed as part of the Lower East Side.

Manhattan

Area of map detail

THE VILLAGES

1 Judson Memorial Church 2 Church of the Ascension 3 First Presbyterian Church 4 Merchant's House Museum 5 Grace Church 6 Stuyvesant–Fish House 7 St.-Mark's-in-the-Bowery 8 Ukrainian Museum

The West Village's reputation as a haven for free-thinkers, free-lovers, artists, poets, writers, rebels, and revolutionaries dates back to the turn of the 20th century; and that reputation applies now equally to the East Village. Even the street plan of the West Village is bohemian—the diagonal streets defy the grid plan imposed on the rest of the city starting at 14th Street. Here, streets follow divisions that once marked farms, and are lined with low-rise houses and green courtyards from an earlier era.

Today, in addition to poets and artists, you will find students, skateboarders, matrons pushing baby carriages, and old men playing chess at outdoor tables in Washington Square in the West Village or Tompkins Square, along with that unfortunate fixture of urban life, the drug dealer. Washington Square is well protected by the New York city police but the same is not yet true of Tompkins Square. There are beautiful, quiet, tree-lined streets in the Villages, but there are mean streets as well.

Nothing keeps away visitors and new residents of late, even Wall Street types, who are able to pay the ever soaring rents.

The West Village is unique, alluring, and always on the go, an attraction for New Yorkers from all over the city and tourists from all over the world. They are drawn by the Italian groceries, antique stores, and outdoor art shows, and they seek the past in coffee-houses, bars, and streets where the now famous once hung out. Bob Dylan sang his folk songs in the '60s in Washington Square. There are historic watering holes such as the White Horse Tavern at the corner of Hudson and West 11th Streets, an 1880s saloon popular with writers. Here the Welsh poet Dylan Thomas had his final drink. In the East Village, there is McSorley's Old Ale House on East Seventh Street, founded in 1854 and dedicated to "Good Ale, Raw Onions, and No Ladies" (until 1970 when women were admitted). At CBGB's on the Bowery, American punk was born.

EARLY VILLAGE

Long before settlement, Canarsee Indians used the marshy area of what would become Greenwich Village for hunting and fishing. When the Dutch arrived, they grew tobacco along Minetta Brook, and the area became the best tobacco plantation in the colony. In 1644 slaves who had been given partial freedom by the West India Company settled near Minetta Lane, which would later become part of the Underground Railroad. When the English took over, the section became Greenwich, meaning Green Village. As the city spread northward, the West Village attracted well-to-do New Yorkers fleeing yellow fever and cholera epidemics in the 1820s. Among the 19th-century residents was Henry James, who used his grandmother's house at 18 Washington Square North (now demolished) as the setting for his novel *Washington Square* (1881). The immigrants, intellectuals, writers, and struggling artists who gave Greenwich Village its reputation arrived at the end of the 19th century. ∎

Washington Square Park

At the foot of Fifth Avenue, the Washington Arch dominates Washington Square Park.

WASHINGTON SQUARE PARK WAS CLOSED TO TRAFFIC IN the 1960s, turning it into one of the city's great gathering places—for students, performers, dog walkers, tourists, and, to keep an eye on things, police. The focal point is the landmark 86-foot-tall Washington Arch, which was designed by Stanford White and dedicated in 1895, six years after the city enthusiastically observed the centennial of Washington's Presidential inauguration.

The city used the eight-acre parcel of land as a potter's field, public gallows, and parade ground, before redesigning it in 1826 as Washington Square Park. With it came fashionable town houses, including the 12 exquisite Greek Revival brick houses (1831–33) known as "the Row" on Washington Square North.

Although the Row and northern environs housed writers and artists—Edith Wharton, Willa Cather, John Dos Passos, and Mark

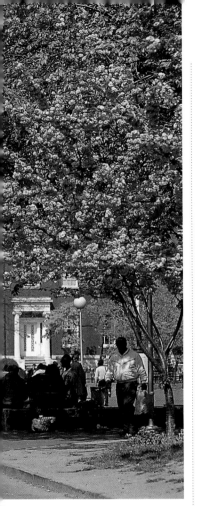

1841 Gothic Revival **Church of the Ascension** *(10th St. & 5th Ave., tel 212/254-8620)*. The stained glass and altar mural are by John La Farge. The 1846 **First Presbyterian Church** *(West 12th St., tel 212/675-6150)* has a tower that is based on one at Oxford's Magdalen College.

Across from the arch, however, in the direction of Bleecker Street, the atmosphere becomes more ethnic and earthy. **Judson Memorial Church** (1892) is to this day known for its political activism. This Romanesque basilica has stained-glass windows by John La Farge and a marble relief by Augustus Saint-Gaudens. The church's social/political mission was to bring together the square's aristocratic northern residents with the immigrants moving into the south.

Struggling writers and artists moved into the Village along with the immigrants. Mrs. Blanchard's boardinghouse at 61 Washington Square South became famous as the "House of Genius": From the 1890s it was home to writers Stephen Crane, Theodore Dreiser, and Frank Norris. Nearby, at 139 MacDougal Street, Provincetown Playhouse was founded in 1917, where the works of Eugene O'Neill were produced. The radical writer John Reed (1887–1920), resident at 42 Washington Square South between 1911 and 1912, celebrated the Village as a place where "nobody questions your morals, and nobody asks for the rent...."

Nowadays the situation has changed: No one's rent remains delinquent long. The Village is among the city's most sought-after addresses, home to such writers as Stanley Crouch and Grace Paley and actors Richard Gere and Kathleen Turner. ■

Judson Memorial Church

🅜 Map p. 76
✉ 55 Washington Square South
☎ 212/477-0351

Twain, among others—there was never anything bohemian about this neighborhood. The writer Djuna Barnes described the difference between the north and south sides of Washington Square in early 20th-century terms: "satin and motorcars on this side, squalor and pushcarts on that." Even today, the square separates two very different neighborhoods. Along the northern side, near the arch, the streets are quiet, tree-lined, and patrician. Two churches a short distance north of the arch on Fifth Avenue continue the sense of restraint. At West Tenth Street, Richard Upjohn designed the

A walk in Greenwich Village

This 90-minute walk in the West Village historic district wends its way through quiet
residential areas, charming nooks and enclaves, and busy thoroughfares.

Begin at Sixth Avenue and Ninth Street,
by the landmark **Jefferson Market
Courthouse Library** ❶. Its name derives
from a market named for President Thomas
Jefferson that opened on the site in 1833.
The present redbrick Gothic structure (1877)
was designed by Calvert Vaux, one of the
designers of Central Park, and Frederick
Withers. In the 1960s, crusading Villagers,
including poet e.e. cummings, saved the
structure from demolition.

Go left on West Tenth Street to tiny
Patchin Place ❷, a cul-de-sac of ten brick
houses from 1848, originally built to house
waiters from the nearby Hotel Brevoort. e.e.
cummings lived at No. 4 for 40 years until his
death in 1962 and was regularly visited by
luminaries including Ezra Pound and T.S.

Eliot; author Djuna Barnes lived at No. 5 until
her death at age 90 in 1982.

Turn left on Greenwich Avenue, right on
Christopher Street, and left again on **Gay
Street** ❸. This short curving street is a perfect introduction to the irregular street pattern
in the Village, which refused to adopt the grid
plan imposed on the city north of 14th Street.
Once an alley, Gay Street became famous as
the birthplace of *My Sister Eileen* (1938), a
book about life in zany Greenwich Village.
The author, Ruth McKenney, was a young
woman from Ohio who lived with her sister,
a struggling actress, here at 14 Gay Street.

Turn left on Waverly Place. Edgar Allan
Poe, master of the macabre, lived for a time
at No. 137. When he had a cold, he simply
walked down the street for treatment—to

**George Segal's sculptured gay
couples in Christopher Park**

🅰 Map inside front cover
► Sixth Avenue and
   Ninth Street
↔ 1.5 miles
🕐 1.5 hours
► Sixth Avenue or
   Bleecker Street

NOT TO BE MISSED
• Gay Street
• Sheridan Square

The picturesque streets of Greenwich Village are rewarding to wander.

follow his path, turn back, walking west on Waverly Place. The triangular building just ahead is the 1827 **Northern Dispensary** ❹, where the city provided Poe and others free medical care.

Turn left on Stonewall Place (part of Christopher Street), named after the **Stonewall Inn** ❺, where the gay liberation movement began on June 27, 1969. The present Stonewall bar occupies part of the space of the original inn *(53 Christopher St.)*, and plaques on the wall inside detail the events of 1969. Christopher Park, across from the bar, has a George Segal sculpture of gay couples.

Ahead is Seventh Avenue. This area is known as **Sheridan Square** ❻, and it is a pulse of Village life today, as in the past. Early in her career, Barbra Streisand appeared at the Duplex cabaret *(61 Christopher St. at 7th Ave., tel 212/255-5438)*. The Village Vanguard *(178 7th Ave., tel 212/255-4037)* has been preeminent among jazz clubs since 1935.

Go south on Seventh Avenue and turn right on Grove Street. Revolutionary-era writer Thomas Paine lived for a time at No. 59, where an 1839 building now houses Marie's Crisis *(Tel 212/243-9323)*, a sing-along bar.

Continue to Bedford Street and turn right to No. 102, Twin Peaks. In 1926 financier Otto Kahn remodeled the building after one in Nuremberg, as an inspirational home for artists. Continue to Christopher Street and turn left, then left on Hudson Street to No. 485, **St. Luke in the Fields** ❼ (restored 1981). Around the corner is a peaceful garden path with benches open to the public.

Turn left on Barrow and then right on Bedford Street (or meander onto Commerce Street to see the 1924 Cherry Lane Theater, one of the first off-Broadway theaters). Don't miss **Chumley's** *(86 Bedford St.)*, a signless 1873 building. This speakeasy from the 1920s is lined with old book jackets from its writer patrons. Note the "secret" back exit.

Return to Bedford Street, walking left (east). Actor John Barrymore lived at 75½ Bedford around 1915, and poet Edna St. Vincent Millay from 1923–24. Just 9.5 feet wide, this is the city's narrowest house.

Turn right on Morton Street, left on Hudson Street, and left onto St. Luke's Place, with its fine 1850s brownstones. New York's popular mayor, Jimmy Walker, lived at No. 6 from 1886 to 1934. Resident writers here included Theodore Dreiser (No. 16) and Marianne Moore (No. 14).

Cross Seventh Avenue to Leroy Street; Jimmy Walker was born at No. 100. This returns you to Bleecker Street, the Village's main street, where there are shops and restaurants from one end to another.

Benches await you at Bleecker Street and Sixth Avenue in **Father Demo Square** ❽, named for a priest of the 1926 **Church of Our Lady of Pompeii** *(Carmine & Bleecker Sts.)*, which has lovely murals.

If you have leftover energy, cross Sixth Avenue and continue down Bleecker Street to the heart of the legendary coffeehouse district, and pilgrimage on to the Bitter End at No. 147 *(Tel 212/673-7030)*, famous as a springboard for such comics and musicians as Woody Allen, Bob Dylan, and many more. ■

A banner year for the arts

In 1913, the Village—and its artists and intellectuals—came to the attention of the outside world. A building on West Eighth Street, once the Village's best shopping street, is a link with that 20th-century heyday. Then, 8 West Eighth Street housed the gallery and residence of Gertrude Vanderbilt Whitney, one of modern American art's most influential patrons. It was in salons such as hers, and another hosted by the wealthy and well-connected Mabel Dodge Luhan, that Village artists and intellectuals gathered. Out of these salons came plans for two extraordinary events: the 1913 Armory Show, critical in the recognition of American art; and the Paterson Strike Pageant, a theatrical extravaganza staged by the Villagers to support striking silk factory workers in Paterson, New Jersey.

THE 1913 ARMORY SHOW

Greenwich Village had been the center of artistic activity for decades and it was out of the tradition of artists gathering to share ideas that the Armory Show grew. In the 1840s, Herman Melville and Edgar Allan Poe were among those frequenting a salon at 116 Waverly Place. In 1858 a wealthy businessman commissioned Richard Morris Hunt to build an artists' studio building on West Tenth Street, which had 25 studios grouped around a large central exhibition space. Tenants of the Tenth Street Studio Building included architect Hunt himself, and painters John La Farge, Winslow Homer, Frederic Church, and Albert Bierstadt, whose collection of American Indian objects was an added public attraction.

By the early 20th century, artistic gatherings in the Village became more avant garde and radical. Whitney herself was an accomplished but conventional sculptor, but as a patron and collector, she was dedicated to modernism. The 1913 Armory Show that she helped sponsor was held at the 69th Regiment Armory at 25th Street and Lexington Avenue. Featuring more than 300 artists and drawing 70,000 people, this was the single most important art exhibition ever held in America. Disturbingly abstract pieces like Marcel Duchamp's "Nude Descending a Staircase" were ridiculed in the press—one critic called the show "a toss-up between madness and humbug"—but the exhibition had an immediate and lasting impact, altering America's assumptions about what art ought to be.

After the show, Whitney expanded her Eighth Street studio into exhibition space and an artists' club. In 1929 she offered to give her collection of modern American art to the Metropolitan Museum of Art. When her offer was refused, she established her own museum, the Whitney Museum of American Art, in four town houses at 8–14 West Eighth Street. This was the first museum in the world devoted to American art, and the origin of today's Whitney Museum (see pp. 164–65).

THE PATERSON STRIKE PAGEANT

Mabel Dodge Luhan's salon at 23 Fifth Avenue was another influential Village institution. Luhan was a hostess, not an artist or intellectual, who had mastered the art of bringing creative people together. Regulars included radicals Emma Goldman and John Reed, photographer Alfred Stieglitz, and birth-control advocate Margaret Sanger. It was at a Luhan soirée that Village intellectuals first learned of violence against workers striking at the silk factories in Paterson, New Jersey. The result of the meeting was an extraordinary pageant, staged on June 7, 1913, at Madison Square Garden: More than a thousand of the strikers reenacted scenes from the confrontation.

Luhan supported the Paterson Strike Pageant production financially; Reed wrote and directed it; and painter John Sloan, member of the so-called Ashcan school, did the scenery. Performed on a 200-foot-long stage, the pageant was attended by 15,000 people. Although it lost money, it encouraged radical and experimental theater in New York. Afterward, Reed and Luhan became lovers and she nursed him through a bout with diphtheria, but eventually he moved on. Her autobiography revealed that Village artistic life was not without heartache. She wrote: "That I have so many pages to write signifies, solely, that I was unlucky in love." ∎

Left: A dramatic poster advertising the Paterson Strike Pageant.
Below left: The re-enactment of the Paterson Strike.
Below right: A banner outside the Armory for the 1913 modern art show.

New York University

New York University
www.nyu.edu

- 🅰 Map p. 76
- ✉ Washington Square
- ☎ 212/998-1212
- 🚇 Subway: A, B, C, D, E, F, Q to W. 4th St.-Washington Sq.

Cryptically called "The Alamo," Tony Rosenthal's giant steel cube dominates a traffic island at Astor Place.

WASHINGTON SQUARE IS THE NERVE CENTER OF NEW York University (NYU); its library, law school, and administrative buildings line the park, and its students are visible all around. The rest of NYU, the largest private university in the country, is scattered throughout the city. Founded in 1831 as the University of the City of New York, the school was intended to provide a nonsectarian alternative to Columbia University.

Although its early buildings are gone, signs of their history are scattered about. In 1833 stonecutters rioted, protesting the use of prison labor in the construction of the university's first building. A memorial to the event is in Washington Square. In 1835 the Gothic Revival University Building (demolished in 1894) opened on Washington Square East. Among those who taught and worked in its tower were architect Richard Morris Hunt, artist Winslow Homer, poet Walt Whitman, and Samuel F. B. Morse —who demonstrated his new invention, the telegraph, there. Part of the tower is on display at Gould Plaza on West Fourth Street. The University Building itself appears in Morse's painting "An Allegorical Landscape Showing the University."

The university moved to the Bronx in the 1890s, but retained a presence in Washington Square. In 1911 its community witnessed a horrific event. On the site where the Brown Building now stands, 146 young women died in a fire at the Triangle Shirtwaist Company. The city's worst factory fire, it led to the creation of workplace safety laws.

In 1973, NYU sold the Bronx campus to the city and returned to Washington Square. Among its buildings there now are 1972 Bobst Library (Washington Sq. South); Tisch Hall (40 W. 4th St.); Andre and Bella Meyer Hall (4 Washington Place); and the exotic Hagop Kevorkian Center for Near Eastern Studies (50 Washington Sq. South). A number of 19th-century converted stables stand on **Washington Mews,** the charming alleyway north of Washington Square North. The **Grey Art Gallery** (100 Washington Sq. E., tel 212/998-6780) specializes in late 19th- and 20th-century art. ■

Astor Place

ASTOR PLACE IS AT THE CENTER OF A LIVELY STUDENT-filled neighborhood formed by the junction of exotic St. Mark's Place, businesslike Fourth Avenue, the derelict Bowery, and the architecturally distinguished Lafayette Street.

Historically, Astor Place is identified with the 1849 Astor Place riots that happened where an opera house stood on the plaza. When English actor William Macready was hired over Irish-American actor Edwin Forrest to play Hamlet, more than 10,000 Irish Americans gathered in protest. Police fired on the crowd, killing and wounding many. Today many know the area as the home of the Italianate redbrick building housing the highly respected Cooper Union for the Advancement of Science and Art, commonly called **Cooper Union.**

Founded in 1857–59 by Peter Cooper to provide a free higher education for worthy sons and daughters of the poor, Cooper Union is still tuition free. Every President since has spoken here. Cooper, who built the country's first steam locomotive, was a self-taught entrepreneur and reform-minded politician. His statue, by Augustus Saint-Gaudens, stands at the school's entrance.

Astor Library opened in 1854 as the city's first free library, with a bequest from John Jacob Astor. It is now the **Joseph Papp Public Theater,** named for the dynamic late producer who, in 1965, persuaded the city to convert the building into theaters. Excellent plays and films are regularly scheduled. Also worthy of note is the 1886 **De Vinne Press Building** *(393–399 Lafayette St.),* built in the Romanesque Revival style, and **Colonnade Row** at Nos. 428–434, four houses remaining from a row of nine 1833 marble-fronted Greek Revival residences. ■

Cooper Union
- ✉ 41 Cooper Sq.
- ☎ 212/353-4100
- 🚇 Subway: 6 to Astor Place

Joseph Papp Public Theater
- ✉ 425 Lafayette St.
- ☎ 212/260-2400
- 🚇 Subway: 6 to Astor Place

The Cooper Union Building lies just south of Astor Place. In the 19th century it was the first free college in the United States.

"Right makes might"

On the snowy evening of February 27, 1860, 1,500 people packed Cooper Union to hear Abraham Lincoln, soon to be a presidential candidate, speak about slavery. Arguing that the Constitution gave the federal government power to control slavery in the federal territories, he closed with these now-famous words: "Let us have faith that right makes might, and in that faith, let us, to the end, dare to do our duty as we understand it." ■

East Village

ONCE PART OF THE ETHNIC LOWER EAST SIDE, THE EAST Village has attracted artists, musicians, writers, and political activists since the 1960s. Large numbers of immigrants still live here as well. Explore the many bookstores, record stores, and specialty shops. Eateries—from two-table storefronts to Jewish delis, Polish coffee shops, an entire street of Indian restaurants (East Sixth Street), and atmospheric gourmet restaurants—reflect the area's zesty ethnic mix.

Merchant's House Museum
- Map p. 76
- 29 E. 4th St.
- 212/777-1089
- Closed a.m. & Tues.–Wed.
- $
- Subway: 6 to Astor Place

Ukrainian Museum
- Map p. 77
- 203 2nd Ave. between 12th & 13th Sts.
- 212/228-0110
- Closed a.m. & Mon.–Tues.
- $
- Subway: L to 3rd Ave.

Youth-oriented St. Mark's Place is the East Village's short but vital main drag.

At the East Village's heart is Tompkins Square Park, named for Daniel Tompkins (1774–1825), a governor of New York. Dutch governor Peter Stuyvesant is buried behind **St. Mark's-in-the-Bowery** (*E. 10th St. at 2nd Ave., tel 212/674-6377*) and some say his ghost walks the grounds, tapping his wooden leg. The church is a center of activism and the arts, especially poetry—the Beats frequently appeared here, and there are open readings weekly (*Danspace, tel 212/674-8194*).

Across from the church is a classic federal-style structure, the 1803 **Stuyvesant-Fish House** (*21 Stuyvesant St., not open to the public*). Architect James Renwick built the 1861 Italianate town houses here (Nos. 23–35) and at 114–28 East Tenth Street, comprising the Renwick Triangle. South of the church, Janis Joplin, the Doors, and others appeared at Bill Graham's now extinct psychedelic Fillmore East (*2nd Ave. at 6th St.*).

West of St. Mark's is an 1846 Renwick Gothic Revival masterpiece, the Episcopal **Grace Church** (*Broadway and E. 10th St., tel 212/254-2000*). The interior has exquisite stained glass and a mosaic floor. North of Grace Church is a must for bibliophiles, the **Strand Book Store** (*828 Broadway, tel 212/473-1452*), a large used bookstore.

East Village museums include the **Merchant's House Museum,** dating from 1832 and providing an authentic look into 19th-century life. The **Ukrainian Museum** has a fine collection of folk art, embroidered textiles, jewelry, and *pysanky,* decorative Easter eggs. ■

Midtown South has many faces: quiet enclaves such as Gramercy Park; libraries of unsurpassed riches; one of the city's busiest shopping districts; a building shaped like an iron; and two of New York's favorite skyscrapers.

Midtown South

**The unusual geometry
of the Flatiron Building**

Midtown South

THE DIFFERENCES BETWEEN MIDTOWN SOUTH AND THE CITY'S TRUE CENTER farther north are ones of pace, style, and age. Whereas Midtown North aggressively races through the day, its southern neighbor has pockets of tranquility along with areas of frenzied activity. Midtown South has quiet enclaves where the bustle of a modern city hardly penetrates. But it also has Herald Square, home to Macy's, and the garment district, where traffic and crowds are among the densest anywhere in the city.

Midtown South's buildings are older than the more famous skyscrapers uptown, but they are no less significant or beautiful. In its 19th-century heyday, Midtown South was the center of the city, boasting everything that its uptown neighbor has today: the best hotels, restaurants, theaters, opera houses, department stores, and the opulent residences of the rich and powerful.

The New York Public Library was erected in 1898–1922 on the site of an 1842 walled reservoir that was part of the 41-mile-long Croton Aqueduct. Madison Square Garden, the city's famous sports arena, is still a Midtown South fixture. The first "Garden" (1879) was located in a converted railroad depot on the east side of Madison Square Park, near 23rd Street.

Stanford White's elaborate replacement opened on the same site in 1892. A nude statue of the goddess Diana atop its tower was controversial in a city still in the throes of Victorian prudery. White himself was anything but a prude; his fast lifestyle caught up with him in 1906, when a jealous husband shot and killed him in the building's roof garden. When the Garden moved uptown in 1925, the building was demolished.

In the 19th century, Midtown South became the center of the city's clothing factories. From its beginnings on the Lower East Side, the garment industry moved first to the Madison Square area around 23rd Street, then to the West 30s, the now famous Garment District. Here even today a pedestrian's way might be blocked by racks of clothes moving through the streets. A 1984 bronze statue—Judith Weller's "The Garment Worker," a man at a sewing machine—honors the Jewish immigrants who helped build the industry. The Fashion Institute of Technology (7th Ave.

at 27th St., tel 212/217-7999), a training ground for the trade, hosts frequent fashion exhibits and operates a museum with over four million textile swatches in its collection.

The past two decades have seen renewal in the region. Stores, restaurants, nightclubs, and businesses such as advertising agencies, and publishing companies are reoccupying buildings abandoned by similar businesses almost a century before. The area around the Flatiron Building is now known as the Photography

District: Photographers converted lofts to studios and labs and art stores followed.

The neighborhoods above 14th Street continue to change, as rents skyrocket Uptown and Downtown and the demand for "affordable" housing grows. ■

MIDTOWN SOUTH

1 Jacob K. Javits Convention Center 2 General Theological Society 3 St. Peter's Episcopal Church 4 Church of the Holy Apostles 5 General Post Office 6 Madison Square Garden 7 Holy Communion Church 8 New Amsterdam Theater 9 Macy's 10 Flatiron Building 11 Worth Monument 12 Museum of Sex 13 T. Roosevelt Birthplace 14 Con Edison H.Q. 15 N.Y. State Supreme Court 16 N.Y. Life Insurance Co. 17 American Radiator Building 18 Church of the Incarnation 19 Daily News Building

Manhattan

Area of map detail

0   600 yards

0   600 meters

Chelsea

CHELSEA, ALONG THE WEST SIDE FROM 14TH STREET TO 30th Street, has blossomed into the city's most dynamic neighborhood. Now home to more than 190 art galleries plus trendy shops and restaurants, it retains its past aura in 19th-century row houses and well-preserved churches. The former Ladies Mile emporiums along Sixth Avenue bustle with new stores, while on Eighth Avenue high-tech companies occupy buildings long vacant.

St. Peter's Episcopal Church

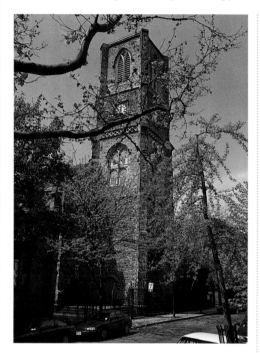

The innovative **Dia Center for the Arts** *(Tel 212/989-5566)* opened its 40,000-square-foot exhibition facility at 548 West 22nd Street *(bet. 10th and 11th Aves.)* in 1987, leading the way for droves of galleries to follow, many from SoHo. At Dia you can see modern art that is too big to be shown elsewhere. A recent seven-projector large-scale video installation by Bruce Nauman, for example, recorded the nocturnal activity of his cat and an infestation of mice in his studio.

Dia Center for the Arts
www.diacenter.org
- ✉ 548 W. 22nd St.
- ☎ 212/989-5566
- 🕐 Closed a.m. & Mon.–Tues.
- 💲 $
- 🚇 Subway: C, E to 8th Ave. & 23rd St. or 1, 9 to 7th Ave. & 23rd St.

Plan a day or a weekend to explore Chelsea's banquet of art venues, from those gritty and industrial, to one of the city's most beautiful locations for fine art photography, the John Stevenson Gallery *(338 W. 23rd St., bet. 8th & 9th Aves., tel 212/352-0070)*. Also featuring art is the new **Museum of Sex** *(233 5th Ave. at 27th St., tel 212/689-6337, adm. fee)*, the country's first major cultural institution devoted to human sexuality.

CHELSEA HISTORIC DISTRICT

Chelsea was originally Dutch—Jacob Somerindyck owned a farm here which English army captain Thomas Clarke bought in 1750 for his retirement and named Chelsea, after London's Chelsea Royal Hospital. His grandson, the versatile professor and writer Clement Clarke Moore, became Chelsea's first developer. Moore is best remembered for penning the children's classic, *A Visit from St. Nicholas*, popularly known as *The Night Before Christmas.*

Moore donated a square block of land on Ninth Avenue at Chelsea Square for the **General Theological Seminary,** the oldest Episcopal seminary in the country, where he taught biblical languages. The interior courtyard is ringed by buildings including the West Building (1836), the city's oldest example of Gothic Revival style. The modern St. Mark's Library

(1960) contains an impressive collection of Latin Bibles.

Across from the seminary, **Cushman Row** (*406–418 W. 20th St.*) comprises seven Greek Revival houses, some adorned with window wreaths and pineapples on the stair posts, both signs of hospitality. They were built in 1839–1840 for merchant and developer Don Alonso Cushman, who also built the four Italianate buildings (1858–1860) on the street's north side (Nos. 355–361). Nearby the **James N. Wells Row** of narrow Italianate houses (*400–412 W. 22nd St.*) is named after another prominent developer of this era. Wells's own 1835 home, a Greek Revival mansion with five bay windows, still stands next door at No. 414.

AN AREA OF CHURCHES

Clement Clarke Moore was also a founder of **St. Peter's Episcopal Church** (*346 W. 20th St. at 8th Ave.*), a trio of buildings erected in 1836–38. The rectory is the city's oldest Greek Revival building. Its 1790 iron fence came from St. Paul's Chapel on lower Broadway.

Richard M. Upjohn, son of Trinity Church's architect, designed the outstanding **Church of the Holy Communion** (*49 W. 20th St. at 6th Ave.*) in 1846. Together, the Upjohns designed the transepts for the **Church of the Holy Apostles** (*9th Ave. at 28th St.*) in 1858. The church itself, with its unusual spire of bronze and slate, was built in 1848 by Minard Lafever. John and William Jay Bolton, the first stained-glass makers in the U.S., created the windows. Before the Civil War, the church was an abolitionist center and a stop on the Underground Railroad.

CHELSEA HOTEL

Distinguished by its ornate iron balconies, the Chelsea Hotel (*222 W. 23rd St. between 7th and 8th Aves.*) was built in 1884 as a cooperative apartment, but soon became a hotel catering to the literati. Plaques on the facade honor distinguished guests, who have included Mark Twain, Dylan Thomas, and Tennessee Williams. There are comfortable seats in the lobby and art on display. ■

General Theological Seminary
www.gtu.edu
✉ 175 9th Ave.
☎ 212/243-5150
🕐 Closed a.m. & Sun.
🚇 Subway: 1, 9, C, or E to 23rd St.

Above: A venerable city landmark, the Chelsea Hotel has a history rich in legend, literature, and scandal.

Left: Brownstone town houses were built from an inexpensive form of sandstone in the mid-1800s.

Gramercy Park

GRAMERCY PARK IS THE CITY'S ONLY PRIVATE PARK—AND, for that reason alone, one of the city's most desirable addresses. The park is surrounded by a tasteful but formidable iron fence, and, unless you live in the immediate vicinity or know someone who does, you will not be able to go in. The rule restricting the use of the park to residents, who have keys to the locked gate, was relaxed only once—when troops were bivouacked there during the Draft Riots of 1863 (see p. 26). Today, it is often used for film shoots, such as Martin Scorcese's *Age of Innocence.*

The name was originally Dutch, Krom Moerasje, meaning "little crooked swamp," which the English, somehow, anglicized to Gramercy. In 1822, Samuel Ruggles purchased and drained the swamp, laid out the park, and sold lots. Early residents included lawyer and diarist George Templeton Strong, and James Harper, a publisher and New York City mayor (1844–45), whose home at 4 Gramercy Park West still has the traditional outdoor lampposts that marked it as the mayor's residence.

Erected in 1917, the statue of Edwin Booth faces the actor's former home.

Writers of Renown

One of the city's first cooperative apartment buildings, the 1883 Gramercy (*34 Gramercy Park E.*), has housed such prominent figures as playwright DuBose Heyward, and the late actors James Cagney, Mildred Dunnock, and Margaret "Wicked Witch of the West" Hamilton.

On the south side of the park, 144 East 20th Street was built in 1860 as a Quaker Meeting House and now serves as a synagogue. At the corner of Irving Place, the 1845 brick building at 19 Gramercy Park South was owned in the 1880s by financier Stuyvesant Fish; more recently the house was home to actor John Barrymore and, later, the colorful public relations genius Ben Sonnenberg.

Actor Edwin Booth (see sidebar below) gave his home at 16 Gramercy Park South to the **Players' Club;** Stanford White remodeled the 1845 brownstone in

The melancholy thespian

Inside locked Gramercy Park but visible through the fence, stands a bronze statue of Edwin Booth (1833–1893), the most famous American actor of his day. In April 1865, he received unwanted notoriety when his actor brother John Wilkes Booth, assassinated President Lincoln in Washington, D.C., and died trying to elude capture.

After the assassination, Edwin retired temporarily, then built his own theater to stage his own productions. In 1888 he founded the Players' Club for actors at 16 Gramercy Park South. Twenty-five years after his death, the club commissioned the statue of Booth, a small, lithe figure, as Hamlet, a role at which he excelled—perhaps because the prince's melancholy matched his own after his brother's murderous deed. ∎

EDWIN BOOTH
1833 1893

1888. Next door, Calvert Vaux built No. 15 in 1884 for Samuel Tilden, a former New York governor. Fearful of populist revolt, Tilden had an underground escape tunnel dug to 19th Street. The restored brownstone is now the **National Arts Club,** where literary events often take place.

The **Gramercy Park Historic District** extends several blocks in each direction beyond the park itself. Developer Ruggles named the six-block-long street between the park and 14th Street Irving Place, after his friend, writer Washington Irving. The gesture led to the misconception that Irving lived on the street; however, he did visit his nephew who lived at 45 Irving Place. In the early 20th century, the house was the home of the society interior decorator Elsie de Wolfe, who was famous for the mix of high society and bohemia at her salons and her open relationship with her lover, the literary agent Bessie Marbury. Another well-known Gramercy Park figure, William Sydney Porter (pen name: O. Henry) did much of his writing and drinking at Healy's (today called Pete's Tavern) at Irving and 18th Street, where—in the second booth from the right—he supposedly penned his most famous short story, *The Gift of the Magi*.

West of Gramercy Park, the **Theodore Roosevelt Birthplace N.H.S.** is a replica—right down to the slate shingles on the mansard roof—of the 1845 building, which was demolished in 1916. Roosevelt was born here in 1858 and lived in the house until 1872; he later recalled the "gloomy respectability" of the library. Operated now by the National Park Service and open to the public, the birthplace was rebuilt in 1923 by Theodate Pope Riddle, the country's first woman architect. ■

Gramercy Park in winter

National Arts Club
www.nationalartsclub.org
- ✉ 15 Gramercy Park S.
- ☎ 212/475-3424
- 🚇 Subway: 6 to 23rd St.

Theodore Roosevelt Birthplace N.H.S.
- 🅰 Map p. 89
- ✉ 28 E. 20th St.
- ☎ 212/260-1616
- 🕐 Closed Sat.–Sun.
- 💲 $
- 🚇 Subway: 6, N, or R to 23rd St.

Walk down Ladies' Mile

In the relatively short distance covered by this walking tour—which spans two pleasant parks, Madison Square on the north and Union Square on the south—you will see a neighborhood in the process of reestablishing its original image on a walk that will take about an hour, depending on stops.

In the 1870s, so many of the city's fashionable retailers were located along this stretch that it became known as Ladies' Mile. The stores moved northward, but many neglected buildings survived and today they are being renovated and reinhabited. Businesses have returned, bringing with them bars and restaurants. The Ladies' Mile Historic District also includes Fashion Row on Sixth Avenue, a cluster of late 19th-century structures centered between 18th and 19th Streets.

Start at the north of **Madison Square Park** ❶ near East 26th Street. When Madison Square opened in 1847, it was already home to the city's first organized baseball team, the Knickerbockers. The park contains excellent sculpture, notably the 1881 "Admiral Farragut Monument" by Augustus Saint-Gaudens, with a base by Stanford White.

Three eminent skyscrapers abut the park. Cass Gilbert designed the block-long neo-Gothic **New York Life Insurance Company Building** ❷ (51 Madison Ave. between E. 26th and E. 27th Sts.) in 1928. Another massive building is at the north corner of East 25th Street and Madison Avenue, the 1900 beaux arts **Appellate Division** of the **Supreme Court**. The interior is sumptuously decorated with stained glass and murals, the exterior by statuary, including "Justice" by Daniel Chester French. Napoleon LeBrun's tower for the huge art deco **Metropolitan Life Insurance Company Building** ❸ (1 Madison Ave. between E. 23rd and E. 24th Sts.) was built in 1932. Walk south to Fifth Avenue and East 23rd Street to see architect Daniel Burnham's 20-story **Flatiron Building** ❹ (1902); it was called Burnham's Folly by those who feared high winds would blow it over. The Flatiron was the city's tallest building until it was dwarfed by the Metropolitan Life Tower (Madison Ave. at 24th St.).

Head downtown (south) on Broadway to **901 Broadway** (at E. 20th St.), an Empire-style cast-iron building that was, until 1914,

the Lord & Taylor Store. One block south, there are three more impressive 19th-century survivors. The Queen Anne-style 1884 building at 889–891 Broadway was once a retail outlet of the Gorham Manufacturing Company, the American silver manufacturer. The **Arnold Constable Dry Goods Store** (881–887 Broadway at E. 19th St.) is an 1869 building; its cast-iron extension up to Fifth Avenue has an impressive mansard roof. On the southeast corner of East 19th Street, **884 Broadway** once housed W. & J. Sloane, purveyors of rugs, curtains, and fabric. Note the striking cast-iron storefront and carved columns.

Continue south about three blocks to **Union Square** ❺, successfully renovated in 1986, ridding the area of drug dealers and making it once again a popular park and shopping area. To the north, at 33 East 17th Street, the **Century Building** (1881), faced with red brick and whitestone, housed Century magazine, an illustrated publication devoted to the reunification of the country after the Civil War. It is now a Barnes and Noble megabookstore. Number 31 Union Square West at East 16th Street, is the original 1903 Bank of Metropolis building, designed by Bruce Price, an innovative architect of skyscrapers; the **Coffee Shop** (29 Union Sq. W.) is a trendy restaurant. On the square's east side (Park Avenue South), the ill-proportioned but imposing Greek temple was built in 1907 as the Union Square Savings Bank.

When Union Square opened as a park in 1831, it was at ground level; it was later raised to accommodate the subway tracks beneath it. From the Civil War until recent times, the park was a stump for political orators. Today Union Square holds a year-round **Green Market** (Mon., Wed., & Sat.), where farmers

For nearly a century the elegant and unmistakable Flatiron Building has attracted attention.

sell a range of fresh produce, including home-made cheeses, ciders, baked goods, and flow-ers. The park's impressive statuary includes heroic statues of Abraham Lincoln, the Marquis de Lafayette, and George Washington.

If you are hungry, there are good places to eat along Park Avenue South, which begins at the east side of Union Square. Or you can stroll farther down Broadway toward New York University. If you're in a shopping mood, sample the discount merchants all along 14th Street heading west. ■

- Map inside front cover
- ▶ Madison Square Park
- ⬌ 0.5 mile
- ⏱ I hour
- ▶ Union Square

NOT TO BE MISSED
- Flatiron Building
- Metropolitan Life Insurance Company Building

Empire State Building

Empire State Building

www.esbnyc.com

 Map p. 89

350 5th Ave.

212/736-3100

$$

Subway: B, D, F, Q, N, R to 34th St.

THE TALLEST IN THE WORLD FOR MORE THAN 40 YEARS, the Empire State Building will always be the quintessential skyscraper. From most places in Manhattan you will see it. As a destination, it draws many visitors night and day. A high-speed elevator whisks you to the 86th-floor outdoor observation deck, and to a higher observatory on the 102nd floor. The view from the top, uptown and down, is matchless and essential to understanding Manhattan's lay of the land. Building attractions include the Guinness Exhibition of World Records, and Skyride, a motion-flight simulated tour of the city in a theater that moves.

Visible night and day, the Empire State is no longer a chic address, but still one of the world's great buildings.

Work on the new building proceeded at unprecedented pace, with an average of 4½ stories added every week; in one 10-day spurt, the project's 3,500 workers completed 14 stories. The Empire State Building opened on May 1, 1931, ahead of schedule and 5 million dollars under its 50-million-dollar budget. It was a hit with tourists from the start, but during the Depression about half of the two-million-plus square feet of floor space was unrented, hence its nickname, the Empty State Building. In 1945 a U.S. Air Force B-25 crashed into the 78th and 79th floors, without harming the building's structural integrity.

The 102-story building is 1,250 feet tall. Its 6,400 windows are designed to project beyond the limestone surface, thereby avoiding the mottled look that marred other skyscrapers. The five-story base covers two acres along Fifth Avenue between 33rd and 34th Streets. Its shaft rises to the 86th story. The metal-and-glass tower on top, 16 stories tall, was intended as a mooring mast for dirigibles but was only used twice. Some said the mast detracted from the essential beauty of the building, but that was before a giant ape used it as a perch in the classic 1933 film *King Kong*. Today the top is illuminated in different colors to celebrate holidays and special occasions. During the spring and fall migrations, the tower lights are turned off so as not to confuse large flocks of birds.

The Empire State Building lost its title as the world's tallest building in the 1970s. But that has not diminished its grace, its popularity, or its place in the consciousness. As a critic once said in its praise, "That it is the world's tallest building is purely incidental." ∎

Herald Square

Inside the steel-
and-glass Javits
Convention
Center, designed
by I. M. Pei

IN 1904, WHEN SONGWRITER GEORGE M. COHAN WROTE
"remember me to Herald Square," it was the merchandising center of
the city. Most of the stores have moved or disappeared, but the area—
where Broadway and Sixth Avenue cross at 34th Street—has retained
a grimy vitality.

Macy's opened here in 1902; still
the world's largest department
store, it has endeared itself to millions with its annual Thanksgiving
Day Parade extravaganza.

The square is named for the
New York Herald, headquartered
here in a Renaissance-style building
from 1894 to 1921. All that remains
of the building is the ornamental
clock. On the hour, two bronze
bell ringers, nicknamed Stuff and
Guff, appear and strike the bell
with mallets.

To the west, **Madison Square
Garden** (familiarly, the "Garden")
stands on the site of the former
Pennsylvania Station. Today's **Penn
Station,** serving long-distance
Amtrak trains and commuter trains
to Long Island and New Jersey, is
housed underground. The Garden
itself, home to the New York Knicks
and New York Rangers, is a major
arena for sports, concerts, trade
shows, and performing arts events.

At 2 Penn Plaza, the entrance to
the present Penn terminal, are two
Adolph A. Weinman sculptures
from the 1910 Penn Station: a ten-
foot-high statue of a railroad president, and two large granite eagles
from the cornice. The present Penn
Station is soon to be installed in
grander quarters. Senator Daniel
Patrick Moynihan spearheaded an
effort in the 1990s to move the
terminal into the monumental
General Post Office, located on
the west side of Eighth Avenue
between 31st and 33rd Streets.
McKim, Mead & White designed
the building in 1913 to visually
blend with the old Penn Station's
grander entrance across the avenue.

Farther west, on 11th Avenue
between 34th and 39th Streets, is
the **Jacob K. Javits Convention
Center,** a huge, modernistic, all-
glass pavilion designed by I.M. Pei
and named for New York's longtime
Republican senator. ■

Macy's
- Map p. 89
- ✉ 151 W. 34th St.
- ☎ 212/695-4400
- 🚇 Subway: N, R, B, D,
  F, Q to 34th St.

**Madison
Square Garden**
- Map p. 89
- ✉ 2 Pennsylvania
  Plaza
- ☎ 212/465-6741 for
  information and
  daily tours
- 💲 $$–$$$$
- 🚇 Subway: A, C, E, 1,
  2, 3, 9 to 34th St.

**Jacob K. Javits
Convention Center**
- Map p. 88
- ✉ 655 W. 34th St.
- ☎ 212/216-2000
- 🚇 Subway: A, C, E to
  34th St.

Pierpont Morgan Library & Murray Hill

NAMED FOR QUAKERS ROBERT AND MARY MURRAY, WHO owned an estate here in colonial times, the Murray Hill neighborhood extends, north to south, from 40th to 34th Street and east to west, from Third to Madison Avenues. Although it intrudes on Manhattan's busy Midtown, its tree-lined side streets are reminiscent of a more tranquil era when some of the city's richest and most socially prominent people lived here. Among them was financier John Pierpont Morgan (1837–1913), one of the world's richest men in a time when there were few restraints on making money.

PIERPONT MORGAN LIBRARY

Morgan was also a leading collector of the Gilded Age. His library, quipped its first director, "contains everything but the original tablets of the Ten Commandments." Contemporaries were divided on Morgan's connoisseurship, but the Pierpont Morgan Library today is recognized as one of the world's great collections. Visit it with the same reverence you would take to a great museum and wander amid the artistic and literary treasures on view in this marble palace. There is also a delightful café and gift shop.

Morgan began collecting books and manuscripts, such as the *Mainz Psalter* of 1465, and expanded to sculpture, Renaissance painting, old master drawings, and music manuscripts. When his collection grew too large for his mansion, Morgan commissioned Charles McKim to design the one-story, neoclassic building on East 36th Street.

The library was built, in classical fashion, from marble blocks put together without mortar. Adolph A. Weinman created the sculptured panels on the exterior representing the arts and other disciplines; Edward Clark Potter's lions at the entrance are forerunners of those he made for the New York Public Library. The interior consisted of a Rotunda at the entrance, the book-lined East Room, the North Room (an office), and Morgan's study, called the West Room. A biographer described Morgan during the panic of 1907, sitting here calmly "in a red plush armchair by the fire with a Madonna and Child by Pinturicchio looking down over his shoulder ...."

The collection

Morgan's son opened the library to the public in 1924. Four years later, Morgan's home at the corner of 36th Street and Madison Avenue was torn down and replaced by an annex, which became the entrance to the library. Hans Memling's "Portrait of a Man with a Pink" (circa 1475), perhaps the most famous painting in the collection, is displayed on the red damask walls of the West Room. One of three Gutenberg Bibles Morgan acquired is on display in the East Room. This room, with its spectacular domed ceiling and stone fireplace, is lined with three tiers of bookcases.

The collection continues to expand through acquisitions: in 1992, a signed copy of Lincoln's Emancipation Proclamation and other American historical documents; in 1998, the Carter Burden Collection of American literature, with more than 80,000 volumes dating from 1870, valued at eight to ten million dollars. In 1988, the library purchased Morgan House, the 45-room home of Morgan's son (*37th St. and Madison Ave.*), which was renovated as the education center and bookstore. A garden court connects the library and Morgan House.

AROUND MURRAY HILL

A tip of the hat to the wealthy Mr. Morgan is the luxurious hotel, **Morgans** (see p. 243), well worth seeing. Nearby, **De Lamar Mansion** (No. 233), now the Polish Consulate, was built in 1905 for a Dutch-born business-man. At Nos. 205 and 209 (at 35th Street), the 1864 **Church of the Incarnation and the Rectory** (1906) contains stained-glass windows by William Morris, Louis Comfort Tiffany, and John La Farge and sculpture by Daniel Chester French and Augustus Saint-Gaudens.

A block east on Park Avenue, No. 57 was designed by Philadelphia architect Horace Trumbauer, with sculptured friezes, for socialite Adelaide L.T. Douglas. The 1911 building now houses the Guatemala Consulate General and related offices. Number 23, the former Advertising Club, now apartments, is another McKim, Mead & White structure designed as a millionaire's mansion. Between Lexington and Third Avenues, Murray Hill's eastern border, lies **Sniffen Court** (*150–158 E. 36th St.*), the city's smallest historic district. This intriguing mews of ten brick carriage houses dates from the 1850s. ∎

Pierpont Morgan Library
www.morganlibrary.org
◪ Map p. 89
✉ 29 E. 36th St. at Madison Ave.
☎ 212/685-0008
🚇 Subway: 6 to 33rd St.

Church of the Incarnation
http://churchoftheincarnation.org
◪ Map p. 89
✉ 209 Madison Ave.
☎ 212/689-6350
🕐 Open Sun.–Wed. & Fri. 11:30 a.m.– 2 p.m.
🚇 Subway: 6 to 33rd St.

New York Public Library

New York Public Library Central Research Branch
www.nypl.org
- Map p. 89
- 5th Ave & 42nd St.
- 212/869-8089 for announcements of exhibits & events
- Closed Sun.
- Subway: B, D, F, Q to 42nd St.; 7 to 5th Ave.

The oak tables of the library's Main Reading Room shine after a recent renovation.

GUARDED BY EDWARD CLARK POTTER'S SCULPTURED PAIR of all-knowing lions, "Patience" and "Fortitude," the New York Public Library is one of the world's great cultural institutions. Founded in 1895, it grew out of the consolidation of two private libraries, those of millionaire John Jacob Astor and the reclusive real estate heir James Lenox.

The New York Public Library opened in 1911 on the site of the old Croton Reservoir. The broad steps and terraces leading up to its grand exterior entrance, framed by Corinthian columns, have become a favorite gathering place for New Yorkers. The library is widely considered the greatest example of beaux-arts design in the country. What's more, it works. In an enlightened move, librarians themselves assisted the architects Carrère & Hastings in designing a building that was not only beautiful, but also functional. The behind-the-scenes system for moving its more than nine million books is still state of the art. The library's collection includes some 21 million other items, among them priceless manuscripts, recordings, periodicals, historical maps, prints, photographs, and family histories. Regular, changing exhibitions are drawn from these.

Rooms throughout display elegant design and clever use of natural light. The Main Reading Room, lined by windows adjoining interior courtyards, is two blocks long, with chandeliers and a magnificent wood-paneled ceiling. The skylit Bartos Forum and the Periodicals Rooms with murals by Richard Haas are also superb, and the gift shop/bookstore has many unusual items.

Stretching behind the library to Sixth Avenue, **Bryant Park** is named for poet and editor William Cullen Bryant (1794–1878); beautifully restored in the 1990s, there are public benches and a fine indoor-outdoor restaurant, Bryant Park Grill *(25 W. 40th St., tel 212/840-6500)*. To the south, the 1924 **American Radiator Building** *(40 W. 40th St.)*, faced with black brick and gold terra-cotta, was Raymond Hood's first New York skyscraper. ∎

The library holds one of the most precious documents of Americana in existence, Christopher Columbus's 1493 letter describing how "in thirty-three days I passed from the Canary Islands to the Indies ...." ∎

From the East River to the Hudson, from Times Square to Rockefeller Center, this is the city's must-see area. Almost everything is nearby—restaurants, music, theater, art, enduring architecture, and much that is ephemeral.

Midtown North

**Architectural detail
at Rockefeller Center**

Midtown North

THE ENTRANCE COURT TO ROCKEFELLER CENTER'S INTERNATIONAL building features a massive statue of Atlas supporting on his broad shoulders an open sphere representing the world. The four-story statue is impossible to miss. To many, it is a symbol of Midtown North, that slice of Manhattan running river to river between 42nd and 59th Streets. This nerve center for business, culture, and entertainment has abundant office buildings and theaters, a most venerable concert hall, landmark structures such as the Chrysler Building, as well as museums, art galleries, synagogues, churches, hotels, and restaurants. Grand Central Terminal has long welcomed visitors from all over the country; and the United Nations Plaza hosts the entire world.

Manhattan

Area of map detail

You can even live here, and New Yorkers pay a great deal of money to do so. Beekman Place and Sutton Place, on and near the East River, are among the city's most expensive addresses. Supermarkets are in short supply but sustenance can be found at such a variety of restaurants, cigar bars, delicatessens, and upscale stores— Bloomingdale's among them—that no one with money need ever go hungry. Another exclusive area is Central Park South along 59th Street, Midtown's northern edge. Rents are more affordable to the west along the Hudson, where the changing working-class neighborhood Hell's Kitchen is becoming known as Clinton.

No places better illustrate the diversity found in Midtown North than two focal points: frenetic Times Square in the 40s (where Broadway and Seventh Avenue cross) and staid Rockefeller Center in the 50s (between Fifth and Sixth Avenues). In Times Square you will be assaulted by traffic, noise, pedestrians, and the constant presence, night or day, of its gigantic animated signs. Rockefeller Center, though bustling, is quite different, the atmosphere proper and restrained. Its buildings and well-kept open spaces radiate a conviction that all is well with the world.

Midtown North was created as the wealthy elite led the city northward. Fifth Avenue was chosen as the site for St. Patrick's Cathedral in 1848 by a bishop who wanted to put his

Roman Catholic congregation on an equal footing with the Protestant establishment. In 1926 an area nearby was selected by the Metropolitan Opera for its new home. When the plan floundered one of its key investors, John D. Rockefeller, Jr., instead built one of the world's great urban centers. Park Avenue developed into prime residential property—and later a business district—after 1903, when New York Central decided to put the railroad tracks serving Grand Central below ground.

Midtown's southern boundary, 42nd Street, was designated a major crosstown street in the city's 1811 grid plan. Still, the *New York Times*'s decision in 1904 to move to its western part was considered daring. Then called Longacre Square, it was a red-light district with stables and shops

> ## MIDTOWN NORTH
>
> 1 Former McGraw Hill Building 2 Lyceum
> 3 International Center of Photography
> 4 Columbus Circle 5 Carnegie Hall
> 6 Algonquin Hotel 7 Chanin Building
> 8 American Folk Art Museum 9 Grand
> Army Plaza 10 Trump Tower 11 Sony
> Building 12 Citicorp Center 13 Waldorf-
> Astoria 14 News Building

catering to the carriage trade. *Times* publisher Alfred Ochs persuaded the city to run the subway there, ensuring development. The newspaper's building became Times Tower, the area Times Square. A decade later, the *Times* moved to their present home on West 43rd Street and Times Tower became One Times Square: The name was there to stay.

As the theater district developed in the area in the early 1900s, Times Square also became home to the "Great White Way." Once and forever the area became a defining part of Midtown North and one of the most popular of all city destinations. ■

Grand Central Terminal & along 42nd Street

STAND ON THE BALCONY ON GRAND CENTRAL TERMINAL'S Vanderbilt Avenue side and enjoy the view of the Main Concourse; witness the ebb and flow of New York, timed to the rhythm of the daily rush hours. Grand Central Terminal is the gateway to the city, used by 150,000 commuters a day, and thousands of pedestrians.

Grand Central Terminal

- Map p. 103
- 42nd St. & Park Ave.
- 212/532-4900, 212/490-6650 (Oyster Bar)
- Subway: 4, 5, 6, 7, S to Grand Central

The terminal opened in 1913. Warren Whitney designed the beaux-arts facade facing south on 42nd Street. Atop the entrance is a clock topped by the figure of Mercury whom sculptor Jules-Felix Coutan described as "the god of speed, of traffic, and of the transmission of intelligence." The firm of Reed & Stem, architects, made the station work by devising a rail system that brings trains in on two levels.

As part of a 196-million-dollar, nine-year restoration, the East Waiting Room was completed in 1992, followed by an impressive overhaul of the Main Concourse. This immense space—measuring 120 feet by 175 feet with arched windows soaring 75 feet on either end—has a floor of Tennessee marble and 125-foot-high vaulted ceilings, which are painted to resemble the constellations. Between the two levels is the **Oyster Bar,** famous for its oyster stew and its ceiling of Guastavino tiles, which was restored after a fire in 1966.

"The Jolly Green Giant." Across the street is the **Holy Cross Church** *(Tel 212/246-4732),* an 1870 Byzantine-style building and the parish church of Father Francis P. Duffy, chaplain of the Fighting 69th in World War I. Duffy Square (see p. 108) is named for him.

Past the renovated theaters (see pp. 114–15) is the former

The elegant lobby of the St. Regis Hotel has a beautifully painted ceiling.

ALONG 42ND STREET

The following are a few sights to help orient you as you visit 42nd Street.

The former **McGraw-Hill Building** *(330 W. 42nd St.)* is a 1930 avant-garde skyscraper by architect Raymond Hood. You can visit its art deco lobby, which is green like the exterior terra-cotta tiles, hence the building's nickname,

Knickerbocker Hotel *(1466 Broadway at 42nd St.).* Built in 1906 by John Jacob Astor, the hotel's Maxfield Parrish mural now hangs in the King Cole Bar in the St. Regis Hotel. In 1924 George Gershwin's "Rhapsody in Blue" premiered at a concert hall across from New York Public Library. Next door, the contoured **W. R. Grace Building** *(43 W. 42nd St.)* is a rarity in a city where horizontal and vertical lines are the architectural norm. Cross Fifth Avenue and walk about three blocks to the **Whitney at Philip Morris,** a satellite of the Whitney Museum of American Art (see pp. 164–65). The enclosed sculpture garden makes a relaxing stop. Pass Grand Central Terminal, then continue to the **Chanin Building,** at No. 122. This 56-story, 1929 skyscraper was the first in the area; the interior bronze art deco grillwork is by Rene Chambellan, whose sculptures also grace Radio City Music Hall. Across Lexington is the **Chrysler Building** (see p. 106), and across Third Avenue, the art deco **Daily News Building** *(220 E. 42nd St.),* home until 1995 of the city's first tabloid, and another 1930 Raymond Hood classic. The building is the fictional Daily Planet in the *Superman* movies. Cross to the **Ford Foundation Building** at No. 320, a 1967 glass box enclosing a public plaza and atrium. Reachable by steps near First Avenue is Tudor City, a Tudor-Gothic self-contained community. ∎

Whitney Museum of American Art at Philip Morris

www.whitney.org

✉ 120 Park Ave. at 42nd St.

☎ 917/663-2453

🕐 Closed Sat.–Sun.

🚇 Subway: 4, 5, 6, 7, S to Grand Central

Grand Central, a landmark building with a practical purpose

Chrysler Building

THE ART DECO CHRYSLER BUILDING IS THE FAVORITE skyscraper for many New Yorkers and visitors alike. A historic landmark since 1971, it was built for automobile magnate Walter P. Chrysler, who wanted a corporate headquarters that reflected the glory of America's automotive industry.

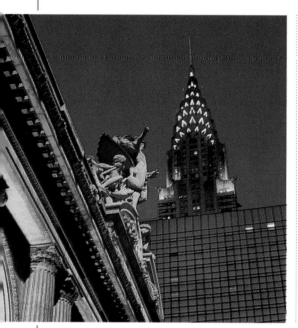

To this end, architect William Van Alen adorned the facade with symbols such as wheels and radiator caps, adding stainless steel gargoyles that resemble Chrysler hood ornaments. The stainless steel pinnacle, called the vertex, is an art deco version of a radiator grill. The lavish granite and marble lobby, with its Edward Trumbull ceiling mural, was once a Chrysler showroom.

From the start, the building was a favorite with artists. Georgia O'Keeffe rendered it as a painting, and a famous photograph by Margaret Bourke-White shows her perched on a gargoyle high above the city. ∎

Chrysler Building

Ⓜ Map p. 103

✉ Lexington Ave. at 42nd St.

☎ 212/682-3070

🚇 Subway: 4, 5, 6, 7, S to Grand Central

A block away from Grand Central Terminal, the Chrysler Building's famous spire dominates the night sky.

Ever higher

In the late 1920s an architect had only to announce a new skyscraper and he made the front page. In this charged atmosphere, the competition between the Chrysler Building's architect, William Van Alen, and his rival, H. Craig Severance, whose Bank of Manhattan building at 40 Wall Street was going up at the same time, was much in the news. Van Alen started at 56 floors, then, to top Severance, went to 65. Severance countered by adding a tower and, looking like a sure winner, finished at 71 stories. Van Alen, however, had secretly assembled a 185-foot steel spire within the Chrysler Building's fire shaft. At his signal, he recalled, "the spire gradually emerged like a butterfly from its cocoon ...." The Chrysler Building won, with a height of 1,048 feet. Opened in 1930, it was also briefly the world's tallest building, surpassing the Eiffel Tower. But Van Alen's triumph was short lived; a few months later the Empire State Building opened. However, the Chrysler Building remains a jazz age masterpiece, and its spire, lit since 1978, a distinctive skyline presence night and day. ∎

United Nations Plaza

IN 1946 THE YEAR-OLD UNITED NATIONS ORGANIZATION decided to locate its headquarters in the United States. Although other cities were in the running, it was a John D. Rockefeller gift of 8.5 million dollars, for the purchase of an 18-acre plot on the East River, that made New York the chosen site.

The entrance is lined with flags of the 191 member nations. At the heart of the complex is the 39-story **Secretariat Building,** designed by France's Le Corbusier. Stretching north is the **General Assembly,** with its concave roof and central dome. The **Conference Building,** where the Security Council meets, extends east, over F.D.R. Drive. Guided tours leave from the General Assembly lobby, and there is a gift center and postal counter selling unique stamps.

Artwork donated by member nations is throughout. On the grounds, Barbara Hepworth's bronze monolith rises from a fountain at the entrance; see also Yugoslavian Antun Augustincic's statue "Peace," and the Japanese Peace Bell. Inside the Secretariat Building's Dag Hammarskjöld Memorial Chapel you can see Marc Chagall's stained-glass windows.

Construction on the plaza began in 1947, in what was then an area of tenements, slaughterhouses, and breweries. The library is a 1963 addition. Other buildings surrounding the plaza include the office-hotel complex and UNICEF Building. Steps at 43rd Street lead to **Ralph Bunche Park,** dedicated to the African-American U.N. delegate and Nobel Peace laureate. Upon its Isaiah Wall are engraved the words, "They shall beat their swords into plowshares ....": fitting for this area, a symbol of world peace and freedom. ■

United Nations Plaza
www.un.org/tours/
⚠ Map p. 103
✉ 1st Ave. & 46th St.
☎ 212/963-8687
💲 $$ (tours)
🚇 Subway: 4, 5, 6, 7, S to Grand Central

The General Assembly of the U.N. can accommodate representatives of the more than 185 member nations.

Times Square

STAND AT FATHER DUFFY SQUARE BETWEEN 46TH AND 47TH Streets, to the north of Times Square. Traffic and pedestrians sweep by as Broadway and Seventh Avenue intersect: This is the Crossroads of the World. Night or day, gigantic neon signs blaze their messages. Here are theaters, Restaurant Row on 46th Street, and buildings that are destinations unto themselves. Such splendor is the gateway to the city's newest extravaganza, new 42nd Street. This legendary strip between Eighth Avenue and Broadway will add attractions into the 21st century.

Times Square Visitors Center
- ✉ 1560 Broadway at 46th St.
- ☎ 212/869-1890
- 🚇 Subway: 1, 2 3, 7, 9 N, R, S to 42nd St.- Times Square

TKTS
- ✉ Broadway at W. 47th St.
- ☎ 212/221-0013
- 🚇 Subway: 42nd St.- Times Square

Times Square today is a very different place from the tawdry tenderloin it had become by 1989. Buildings have sprouted, including one on **Duffy Square** designed especially for electric billboards. The new building at Four Times Square, housing the Condé Nast offices of *Vogue, Vanity Fair,* and the *New Yorker,* has been nicknamed the Citadel of Chic. Just a few years ago, the thought of a *Vogue* editor in Times Square would have been inconceivable.

A decade ago, 42nd Street between Seventh and Eighth Avenues, known as The Deuce, was somewhat dangerous, a place of hustlers, deteriorating second-run X-rated movie theaters, peep shows, and sex shops. Times Square had become a blot on the city's image and a place to steer clear of. Today it is clean, policed, and visitor-friendly. Commuters, tourists, and school groups on class trips to New York are much in evidence, as are sightseeing New Yorkers, proud to see this neighborhood reclaimed.

Before leaving Duffy Square, give your regards to the statues of actor-producer George M. Cohan, and Father Francis P. Duffy, Chaplain of the 69 Regiment during World War 1 and pastor of Holy Cross Parish, at their statues, then get your bearings. With the TKTS discount ticket booth behind you (where you can purchase same-

Opposite: The crossing of Broadway and Seventh Avenue forms the two triangles at the heart of Times Square.

day discounted tickets), the Times Square Information Center is left (east) of Duffy Square. Located in the landmark **Embassy Theater,** the first U.S. theater to show newsreels, it offers many tourist services and tickets. The tower straight ahead (south) of Duffy Square is One Times Square, where the glittering ball on New Year's Eve drops. Remember that between 45th and 42nd Streets, both Broadway and Seventh Avenue have Broadway addresses. East at 43rd and Broadway, the seven-stories-high **Market Site Tower** dominates the corner, illuminating the area 24 hours a day. It houses a state-of-the-art digital broadcast studio transmitting 175 live market updates from major networks: CNN, CNBC, BBC, and more. You may forget the occupants, but not the high-tech electronic display wrapping the cylindrical building with up-to-the-minute NASDAQ information. To immerse yourself in a family interactive amusement center, walk south to **Broadway City** (241 W. 42nd St., between 7th and 8th Ave.).

LANDMARK BUILDINGS
You can also seek out landmarks. The theaters (see pp. 114–115) are architectural gems. The 1931 **Brill Building** (1619 Broadway at 49th St.) was known as Tin Pan Alley when it was the center of America's popular music industry. For an old-

At the stroke of midnight

It was the opening of the Times Tower on New Year's Eve 1904 that first brought the crowds into Times Square. Marked by fireworks, the celebration was reported in the newspaper: "The instant the first flash on the Times Tower showed, a great shout went up, and an ear-splitting blast was sounded from the horns of the myriad merrymakers on the streets below."

Thus the *Times* unwittingly gave birth to a tradition that continued after it moved out of the building in 1913. Today, half a million people pack Times Square on New Year's Eve, to watch a lighted ball begin its countdown fall one minute before midnight. Millions more watch the spectacle on television. ■

fashioned, well-stocked music store, visit **Colony Records** *(1619 Broadway, tel 212/265-2050)*. There at street level the **Paramount Building** *(1505 Broadway)*, a 1926 landmark with setbacks, towers, and clocks, once housed the Paramount Theater. An opulent movie palace of the day, it is also remembered for a 1944 concert when bobby soxers, as teenage girls were then called, went into a frenzy over Frank Sinatra.

Experience "hotel as theater" at the **Paramount Hotel** *(235 W. 46th St., tel 212/764-5500)*. A light tableau animates the sweeping lobby staircase; the Whiskey Bar is trendy; and the Mezzanine Restaurant offers Latin-inspired cuisine. Downstairs is where Billy Rose had his famed Diamond Horseshoe. It is much in tune with Rose's rule for the shows he staged there in the 1940s: "No subtlety allowed." Less ostentatious is **Sardi's** *(234 W. 44th St., tel 212/221-8440)*, a theatrical restaurant and landmark. Opened in 1921, it is famous for the caricatures of celebrities on its walls and for the low-priced "actor's menu" it offers to members of Actors' Equity.

There have been casualties of changing tastes and times. Nathan's, specializing in the hot dog made famous at Coney Island, is gone. The Latin Quarter, with its chorus line, closed long ago. The original Lindy's (Mindy's in Damon Runyon's short stories) of cheesecake fame also shut its doors. Also gone are Hubert's Museum, a long-lived Times Square institution featuring freaks; Dr. Heckler's Flea Circus; revelations on sex from "The French Academy of Medicine, Paris"; and transvestite bars and streetwalkers. Some might argue that renewal has washed away Times Square's distinctive character, but even naysayers have begun to welcome a renaissance long overdue, a boon to tourism and the city economy, and a catalyst to revitalization elsewhere. An earlier renewal plan fortunately found no funding—it would have turned the area into a staid office district. Instead, in new Times Square the pulse of New York beats at its most vital. ■

43rd & 44th Streets

For a break from high-pressured Times Square, sample West 43rd and 44th Streets (between Fifth and Sixth Avenues), streets of almost oppressive dignity—whose buildings hold some wonderful interiors.

Start with the 1902 **Algonquin Hotel** (see p. 245), famed home of the literary Round Table. This 1920s group included Dorothy Parker, Robert Benchley, and other writers and artists whose clever conversation set the standard for jazz age sophistication. The venerable Oak Room, Blue Bar, and Rose Room—no longer rose—are open for dining and periodic cabaret shows. The lobby, delightful for tea, remains genteel: Ring a bell for the waiter. Celebrity spotting is better across the street at the 1898 **Royalton Hotel** (see p. 246), renovated in 1988 by Philippe Starck. Nearby, a plaque identifies the building that housed The *New Yorker*, whose offices (25 W. 43rd St.) also opened onto here. Visit for free the **Mossman Collection of Locks** in the building housing the General Society Library. The 400-lock collection holds fascinating antique to contemporary locks.

Exclusive associations occupy other turn-of-the-20th-century buildings. The limestone-clad 1895 **Bar Association of the City of New York Building** runs through the block and has two addresses (42 W. 44th St., 37 W. 43rd St.). More fanciful is the 1899 **New York Yacht Club** (37 W. 44th St., tel 212/382-1000), home of the America's Cup from 1857 to 1983. Its beaux-arts window bays have a nautical air. Architects McKim, Mead & White designed the 1894 brick-faced **Harvard Club** (27 W. 44th St.) as well as the 1891 Italianate-style building for the **Century Association** (7 W. 43rd St.), a men's dining club. ■

Mossman Collection of Locks

✉ 20 W. 44th St.

☎ 212/840-1840 (call beforehand)

🕐 Closed Sat.–Sun.

🚇 Subway: 1, 2 3, 7, B, D, N, Q, R, S to 42nd St.-Times Square

The imposing entrance of the Royalton Hotel, renovated by fashionable designer Philippe Starck

The Great White Way

Good news! The Great White Way is alight as never before—electric signs blazing, blinking, and crowding each other as they vie like noisy children for our attention.

O.J. Gude, whose company did many of the early Times Square signs, coined the term "The Great White Way" around the turn of the century. This referred to Broadway's appearance when lit up by signs, which at the time used only white light bulbs. Gude believed that electric signage was art. He was also the first to understand its effectiveness: "Everybody must read them, and absorb them, and absorb the advertiser's lesson willingly or unwillingly." In another era, poet Ezra Pound saw them as "our poetry, for we have pulled the stars down to our will."

Gude and Pound were right: This kind of advertising surpasses mere communication. Here in Times Square developed a distinctly urban popular art form, one that wedded beauty, communication, architecture, and technology. Times Square's premier signmaker today is Artkraft Strauss. Look at any major sign and you can see their "signature," the name Artkraft along the bottom. To view the Great White Way, start at Times Square's southern perimeter, by the subway entrance on 42nd Street and Seventh Avenue, and look north to Broadway's main stem. Across from you, the gigantic Oreo Cookies sign wraps the corner (note the Artkraft signature); to your left the marquees of the newly restored theaters fan out toward the multiplex cinemas. Cross 42nd Street and look back at the British Airways supersonic Concorde (actually a half-scale model) atop Hansen's Times Square Brewery. Proceed uptown, choosing your favorite signs. At Duffy Square, the stacked signs soar skyward. By electronic magic, the cap lifts off the 42-foot-tall Coke bottle and its contents disappear through a straw.

The first electric sign was an 1898 advertisement for Coney Island, erected at 38th Street and Broadway. The 1904 move of the *New York Times* created Times Square, where electric signage would come into full flower. In 1910 the *Times* introduced its popular news ribbon for the Jim Jeffries-Jack Johnson fight in Nevada. This blow-by-blow account ran along the outside of Times Tower, the words rendered by 15,000 bulbs flashing 72,000 times a second. The technique is used today, in digital ribbons known as zippers.

A 1916 change in zoning regulations removed size restrictions, and in 1917, Wrigley Spearmint Gum erected what it claimed was the world's largest electric sign. Eighty feet tall and two hundred feet long, the ad featured animated spear-thrusting elves. In the 1920s, neon lighting brought color to the Great White Way, whose name was not to change. Everyone with memories of Times Square recalls specific signs. Many cite the Pepsi-Cola extravaganza of the 1950s, an immense waterfall flanked by huge Pepsi bottles. Someone calculated that it would have taken 7,812

New technology, including digital imaging, has made the advertising signs of Times Square brighter than ever.

gallons of Pepsi to fill the bottles. Artkraft Strauss did the Pepsi sign and such other landmarks as the Camel man who blew gigantic smoke rings, one every 20 seconds. The source of the smoke: Con Edison steam.

The fifties have been called the heyday of the Great White Way, but with redevelopment under way—and many signs of even grander scale in the works—that title may be lost, or two heydays acknowledged, for there are differences. Today, colors are brighter, more intrusive. Many of the signs advertise foreign imports. Although today's signs are spectacular, the contrast between past and present creates a certain nostalgia for the old days. On assignment to photograph Times Square, Jack Pierson deliberately made his pictures blurry: "I still like to believe that the signs say 'Franks One Nickel' not 'Casio' or 'TDK'— so, if they're out of focus, I've got my New York Dream." ■

Broadway theaters

Broadway theater information
☎ 212/302-4111 or 888/Broadway

IF YOU HAVE HEARD THAT THE BROADWAY THEATER IS dead, don't believe it. In one recent year, 11,890,000 people paid $666,000,000 for theater tickets, and had a choice of more productions—close to 40—than at any other time in recent memory. Since 1880, "Broadway" has been a term for large-scale theater that opens in New York City and often travels elsewhere; but since 1929, when movies took over many theaters, most plays have opened not on Broadway, but nearby, on the narrow streets off Times Square.

1903 beaux-arts masterpiece. Note the graceful marquee, ornate columns, and theatrical masks across the entablature on the grandiose facade. Two blocks away, Marlon Brando debuted in *A Streetcar Named Desire* in 1947 at the **Barrymore** *(243 W. 47th St., tel 212/239-6200)*.

Although the architecture of many theaters is a show in itself, the wonder is what happens on stage. The boards echo with great performances, from the early Barrymores to Christopher Plummer playing Barrymore in 1997 to unknowns creating a success in the musical smash, *Rent*. The best way to savor Broadway is to buy a ticket and go. You might find yourself in a Moorish palace inside the **Martin Beck Theater** *(302 W. 45th St.)* or amid plasterwork seemingly from the Renaissance at the Shubert or gazing at a French garden dance above the proscenium arch of the **Cort** *(138 W. 48th St.).* The exterior, by the way, was based on Marie-Antoinette's Petit Trianon at Versailles. You can also tour some theaters, such as the sumptuously renovated **New Amsterdam,** which one reviewer called "walking into a dream."

One of Broadway's most enduring hits has found a home in one of the area's most traditional theaters, the Majestic.

New Amsterdam
✉ 214 W. 42nd St.
☎ 212/282-2900 or 800/755-4000 (Ticketmaster) for show tickets
🚇 Subway: N, R, S, 1, 2, 3, 7, 9, to Times Sq.

You can still step back into the past wandering these streets. Begin with the **Belasco Theater** *(111 W. 44th St.)* and walk west to the theaters along "Rodgers & Hammerstein Row," from the **Shubert** *(225 W. 44th St.)* to the **Broadhurst,** the **Majestic,** the **Helen Hayes,** and the **St. James.** Farther along is the **Actors Studio** *(432 W. 44th St., tel 212/757-0870, closed Sat.–Sun.),* founded by Elia Kazan in 1947. Here director Lee Strasberg taught his students, including Marlon Brando, Marilyn Monroe, and Al Pacino.

Starring on the next block is the **Lyceum** *(149–57 W. 45th St.),* a

PRESERVATION
A 1980s decision to give most of Times Square's legitimate theaters the status of historic landmarks was an important step in saving

them. Unfortunately, five venerable theaters, the Bijou, the Astor, and the original Helen Hayes among them, had already been destroyed. Preservationists turned their attention to the nine 42nd Street theaters west of Times Square, decayed almost to the point of ruin or converted to "grind houses," showing pornographic movies and "adult" fare. Disney's 1995 commitment of eight million dollars to restore the New Amsterdam changed the area's fate. Now the nonprofit Times Square Business Improvement District guides the plan that is rescuing the theaters and revitalizing the area.

The stunning renovation of the New Amsterdam set the standard to follow. The original theater was the height of opulence, with promenades and a roof garden. From 1913 to 1927, the Zeigfeld Follies were produced here. Today the theater has been returned to use in all its art nouveau splendor; it opened with *The Lion King*, theater the whole family can enjoy.

So stand in line at TKTS (see p. 108) at Father Duffy Square, mingle with the crowds to get your discount seats (cash only), feel the excitement build until you are in your seat. As the lights go down, let Broadway theater sweep you off your feet. ∎

The beautifully renovated New Amsterdam theater has featured *The Lion King* since 1997.

Skyscrapers walking tour

This zigzag tour passes buildings pivotal in the city's architectural history. It begins with the baroque-towered Helmsley Building straddling Park Avenue, crosses Park Avenue a number of times, and ends with the art deco Fuller Building on Madison Avenue.

Built in 1929 as the New York Central Building—to house the railroad company—the **Helmsley Building** ❶ *(230 Park Ave. between E. 45th and E. 46th Sts.)* is stunning inside, and its white-towered outline impressive. Unfortunately, in 1963 the Pan Am Building (now Met Life) went up, blocking any clear view of the building. Continue north three blocks to 301 Park Avenue, the famed art deco **Waldorf-Astoria Hotel.** Its twin 625-foot Towers are residences for the rich and famous. The hotel is a favorite of royalty and presidents

alike, and far grander than the original Waldorf. Visit its luxurious art deco marble-columned lobby, filled with bronze and rich mahogany. A highlight is "The Wheel of Life"(1931), a 148,000-piece tile mosaic depicting the drama of human existence, by the French artist Louis Rigal.

Turn left (west) on East 50th Street, crossing Park Avenue, and go right at Madison Avenue to the **Villard Houses** *(Nos. 451-455),* with the **Helmsley Palace Hotel** rising behind. Built for railroad tycoon Henry Villard, beginning in 1883, the Villard Houses are six brownstones joined to look like a single Renaissance palace. The complex was saved from demolition in the 1980s by incorporating the east wing into the Helmsley Palace Hotel lobby. The north wing now houses the Municipal Art Society and the Urban Center Galleries. You can stop for tea beneath the gilded ceiling in the

Helmsley Palace Gold Room.

Take a right at 51st Street and right at Park Avenue for **St. Bartholomew's Church** ❷. This 1919 Byzantine-style Episcopal church exemplifies the city's movement north; the congregation was formerly located on Madison Avenue and East 44th Street. The Stanford White porch, with carvings by Phillip Martiny and Daniel Chester French, came from the earlier church. Go left (east) on East 50th Street to Lexington Avenue and turn left. The art deco **General Electric Building** ❸ *(570 Lexington Ave.),* built in 1931 as the RCA Victor Building, was sheathed in brick and terra-cotta to complement St. Bartholemew's next door.

Go left at East 51st Street and right to 370 Park Avenue, the **Racquet and Tennis Club** (1916–19). This members-only male bastion by McKim, Mead & White is a copy of an Italian Renaissance palazzo. Across the street rises the 1958 bronze-glass-and-steel **Seagram Building** ❹ *(375 Park Ave.).* It is the city's only building by the great German-born American architect Mies van der Rohe. The design of the slab set back on a plaza became widely imitated. A block north at 390 Park Avenue, the landmark 1952 **Lever House** was the city's first glass slab office building. Turn right at East 54th Street to **Citicorp Center** ❺ (1978), an aluminum-clad cantilevered tower. Its chisel-shaped top is a modern reference point on the skyline. Inside are stores and St. Peter's Lutheran Church. On the corner of 55th Street and Lexington Avenue is the city's oldest continuously used synagogue, the onion-domed **Central Synagogue** ❻ *(123 E. 55th St., tel 212/838-5122, ext. 219).* Dating from 1872, it has been rebuilt since a 1998 fire.

Go left on East 55th Street two blocks and right to Philip Johnson's 1984 **Sony Building** ❼ *(550 Madison Ave.),* the first postmodern skyscraper. Inside visit the **Sony Wonder Technology Lab** *(Tel 212/833-*

8100, closed Mon.), a free multimedia exhibit where you can even design a music video. A personalized voice chip lets you use the interactive games. Farther along, the green granite 1983 **IBM Building** ❽ (590 Madison Ave.) has an atrium for rest and refreshment amid soothing bamboo trees. The final stop is the art deco **Fuller Building** ❾ (41 E. 57th St. at Madison Ave.), built in 1929 for the construction company. Note the Elie Nadelman sculpture, "Construction Workers," above the entrance. There are galleries inside. ∎

Opposite: The art deco Waldorf-Astoria
Right: The Sony Building

Rockefeller Center

ROCKEFELLER CENTER—WITH ITS WALKWAYS, SUNKEN plaza, gardens, outdoor sculpture, and architecturally related art deco buildings—has been copied but never surpassed. Bounded by Fifth and Sixth Avenues and 48th and 51st Streets, this 19-building city within a city is arguably the most successful urban development ever.

**Radio City
Music Hall**
www.radiocity.com
🅰 Map p. 103
✉ 1260 6th Ave.
☎ 212/247-4777
💲 $$
🚇 Subway: B, D, F, Q
to 47th–50th Sts.-
Rockefeller Center

Note: Tours of Radio City
leave daily from its
lobby.

As a visitor, a good place to start is **Radio City Music Hall,** where the high-kicking, 36-member dance team, the Rockettes, still performs at Christmas and Easter shows and where top singers perform throughout the year. Here you stand at the edge of the original 14 buildings that comprised the center when it opened in 1940; five buildings west of Sixth Avenue were added after 1945. For a detailed guide to the complex, go to the **General Electric (GE) Building** at 30 Rockefeller Plaza. Headquarters for NBC is here, and outside *(between W. 49th and W. 50th Sts.),* the morning *Today Show* with Katie Couric and Matt Lauer films live. Watch it through the glass-enclosed set and maybe you will see yourself on TV. In the center of the complex is a flag-lined sunken plaza. Here you can skate outdoors in winter, or in summer dine at American Festival Café, which takes over the rink. Past the rink is the sloping Promenade, where the lighting of an immense Christmas tree is the focus every holiday season. Sit by the floral displays and sculpture in the Channel Gardens and then wander onto Fifth Avenue, but be sure and turn back for another look.

The elegant **Rainbow Room** (see p. 248) atop 30 Rockefeller Plaza, long a favorite spot for its revolving floor, cocktails, and spectacular views, changed its policy in December 1998, and is now open for private parties and on a limited basis to the public. It is worth checking hours to see if there is a chance of visiting this landmark 65 floors up. In good or bad weather you can explore the many shops and eateries in the complex's underground concourse.

Although Mitsubishi now owns the controlling interest in Rockefeller Center, it was John D. Rockefeller who developed it. The site was originally intended as a home for the Metropolitan Opera but when the stock market crashed the Met reneged. In late 1929 Rockefeller announced a plan for a commercial complex to house the new radio and television industry. When the Radio Corporation of America (RCA) moved into the building, the entire complex became known as Radio City, a name that soon gave way to Rockefeller Center. The name of the adjacent Radio City Music Hall stuck. It remains, with 6,200 seats, the country's largest theater, and it is a link with a time when RCA, RKO, and NBC were primary tenants. Rockefeller Center now houses publishing and communications organizations.

Not part of the complex but nearby are two historic streets. "Swing Street," 52nd Street between Fifth and Sixth Avenues, was the world center of jazz in the 1930s. All that remains of that era is the brownstone housing the swank restaurant, **21 Club** *(21 W. 52nd St., tel 212/582-7200).* Still vital as a district is "Diamond Row," along 47th Street; the diamond cutters who formed it were European Jews fleeing Nazism. ∎

Opposite: The lighting of the immense Rockefeller Center tree is a highlight of the New York holiday season.

St. Patrick's Cathedral

ST. PATRICK'S IS HUGE—AT 332 FEET LONG AND 174 FEET wide, it is among the world's largest cathedrals. Offering quiet refuge in busy Midtown, it is in constant use for weddings and other events, while its entrance steps are the ideal platform from which to watch the parade of pedestrians.

St. Patrick's Cathedral

- Map p. 103
- 5th Ave. & 50th St.
- 212/753-2261
- Subway: B, D, F, Q to 47th–50th Sts.- Rockefeller Center; 6 to 51st St.

Lee Lawrie's "Atlas" in silhouette with St. Patrick's Cathedral in the background

Its architecture is timeless; James Renwick, Jr., modeled it on the Gothic cathedral in Köln, Germany, borrowing elements from others in Europe. The spires were finished in 1888; at 330 feet tall, they towered above the city until the 1930s, when skyscrapers appeared. Renwick's original east front was replaced in 1906 by the Lady Chapel, designed by Charles Matthews. The three sets of bronze doors on Fifth Avenue are a 1949 addition. Elizabeth Ann Seton, the first American-born saint, is among the saints of New York depicted on the central doors; inside is a shrine to her, with a bronze statue.

Go inside—visitors are expected to respectfully wander to view the interior. The central nave can seat 2,500 people. It is 108 feet high and 48 feet wide. Be sure to visit the Lady Chapel Cathedral honoring the Blessed Virgin, where there is a marble Pietà (1906, by William O. Partridge). Unlike most Gothic cathedrals, there are no flying buttresses, but above the altar is a 57-foot bronze baldachin. Note, too, the entryway, especially magnificent when light streams in through the 26-foot-wide Rose Window above the Great Organ over the Great Bronze Doors.

Archbishop John Hughes announced plans for the church in 1858. His successor, Archbishop John McCloskey, opened the church on May 25th, 1879. The 1.9-million-dollar cathedral is dedicated to the patron saint of Ireland. ■

Fifth Avenue today

MIDTOWN FIFTH AVENUE BEARS SMALL RESEMBLANCE today to its residential past as millionaires' row. Still, there are signs of that history among all that is new. Architecturally, the stretch covered here features Grand Army Plaza, St. Patrick's Cathedral, Rockefeller Center, and other historic buildings.

The aristocrat of toy stores, **F.A.O. Schwartz** *(767 5th Ave.)* is the place to pick an Eloise book or toy: The six-year-old fictional character of Kay Thompson's series lived nearby at the Plaza Hotel. **Tiffany & Co.** *(727 5th Ave.)* originated on lower Broadway, but the glitter of gems remains the same, and there are a few affordable purchases, so look inside.

Experience the Donald Trump aesthetic of glamour, glitz, and sparkling brass—plus shopping and a waterfall—at the bronze-colored **Trump Tower** *(725 5th Ave., tel 212/832-2000)*; you ride crisscrossed escalators up the mirror-lined atrium to the retail floors. On opposite corners at 55th Street are two fine hotels, the **Peninsula New York,** a 1905 beaux-arts landmark, and the 1904 **St. Regis,** built by John Jacob Astor. Visit its King Cole Bar and Lounge to see the Maxfield Parrish mural of the merry old soul. For city views, try the Pen Top Bar and Terrace atop the Peninsula.

In 1917 **Cartier** *(653 5th Ave.)* converted two turn-of-the-20th-century mansions into its jewelry emporium, while the design company **Versace** occupies a house built in 1902–05 by George W. Vanderbilt *(647 5th Ave.)*. **Saks Fifth Avenue** *(611 5th Ave.)* has occupied this landmark Renaissance-style building since it was built in 1922. The 1927 **Fred F. French Building** *(551 5th Ave.)*, with its multicolored faience, is a classic example of setback architecture, and its exotic lobby is a treat. ∎

Above: Cartier—gift wrapped for Christmas
Below: Alternative transport outside Tiffany's

Museum of Modern Art

Museum of Modern Art
www.moma.org
- Map p. 103 & 205
- **Queens site:** 33rd St. at Queens Blvd., Long Island City, Queens
- 212/708-9400
- $$$
- Subway: Local 7 to 33rd St., Queens
- **Manhattan site:** 11 W. 53rd St. between 5th & 6th Aves.
- Subway: E, F to 5th Ave.

Note: Complimentary shuttle buses leave hourly on weekends from the Manhattan main location although the museum there is closed. Call 212/708-9750.

THE MUSEUM OF MODERN ART (MOMA) IS AN EXCITING place to explore, attracting more than 1.6 million visitors annually with its outstanding collection of 20th-century art and blockbuster shows. Bursting at the seams with ever growing audiences and a burgeoning collection needing more space, MoMA closed in 2002 for major construction. Until 2005 MoMA's main operations have shifted to MoMA Queens, a temporary location in a redesigned Swingline Staple factory. Here the shows continue that have earned the museum worldwide fame.

MoMA has it all, from Cézanne to Chuck Close, from the earliest daguerreotypes to interactive video displays. Exhibits at MoMA Queens are in part drawn from this large repository of art.

From its beginnings in 1929, the museum's guiding principle was to move beyond the narrow definition of art, which included painting, sculpture, and drawing, to embrace all the visual fields. MoMA was a pioneer in the fields of architecture and graphic, industrial, and textile designs. It collected and exhibited photographs long before other major museums, and was early to

collect and preserve significant films. Since then its holdings have steadily increased, and its physical structure has steadily grown. The MoMA Design Store across from the main museum on 53rd Street, specializing in objects chosen for their felicity of design, remains open, and directions to MoMA Queens are available there.

THE COLLECTION
MoMA'S permanent collection includes more than 100,000 paintings, sculptures, drawings, prints, photographs, design objects, and architectural drawings and

models. There are, in addition, some 14,000 films, 4 million film stills, and 120,000 books, periodicals, and artists' books.

MUSEUM HIGHLIGHTS

The urban/suburban location of MoMA Queens is an exhilarating contrast to bustling Manhattan. And getting there is a great social outing. In fact, William Wegman, famous for his dog photographs, published a lighthearted book on the subject, *How Do You Get to MoMA QNS?* In it Chip, one of Wegman's weimaraners, journeys from Manhattan to Queens with ease. You can, too.

A ride on the local 7 subway to Queens offers a unique experience. As the train pulls into the 33rd Street Station, the name MoMA QNS, spelled out in shifting white letters painted onto boxes on the museum roof, becomes visible, only to disappear as the train moves on. Patterned lighting elements lead you on the short walk to the block-long blue stucco building. Inside, gallery space is flexible, with move-able walls. High ceilings and the open architecture make the space seem larger than its 160,000 square feet. A mezzanine overlooking the lobby houses a small café and store.

During its stay in Queens, the museum will always feature one exhibit called "To Be Looked At," which rotates 75 works from its permanent collection. Various special exhibitions are scheduled as well, including "Max Beckmann"; "Ansel Adams at 100"; and "Kiki Smith: Prints, Books & Things."

Lectures and talks take place onsite and at satellite locations. These include MoMA's affiliate just walking distance away, **P.S.1 Contemporary Art Center** (see p. 224); and, in Manhattan, both the **Gramercy Theatre** *(127 E. 23rd St. at Lexington Ave., tel 212/777-4900)* and the **Arts Consortium Auditorium** *(1 E. 53rd St., bet. 5th and Madison Aves., tel 212/708-9400)*, with the latter offering a brown-bag lunch series and family-oriented artist talks and programs. Once MoMA reopens in Manhattan, the Queens location will

There's no mistaking the location of MoMA QNS.

become a permanent home for storage of MoMA's collection as well as a place for study and research.

PAINTING & SCULPTURE

Containing some 3,200 works from the late 19th century to the present, MoMA's modern painting and sculpture collection is the world's largest and most inclusive. A portion will always be displayed in the MoMA QNS' "To Be Looked At," with pieces being changed on a rotating basis. Perhaps you will be fortunate to see its earliest work, Paul Cézanne's Postimpressionist painting "The Bather" from the 1880s. Some of the most recent works, from the 1960s and later, feature such artists as Andy Warhol, James Rosenquist, and Susan

Rothenberg. The museum has large holdings by Claude Monet and Pablo Picasso, among others, and exceptional groups of work by Henri Matisse, Joan Miró, Piet Mondrian, Frida Kahlo, Jasper Johns, Roy Lichtenstein, and Jackson Pollock.

PHOTOGRAPHY

The photography department was established in 1940 by Beaumont Newhall, who was succeeded in 1947 by Edward Steichen. The "Family of Man" exhibit that Steichen curated at MoMA in 1955 raised awareness of photography as an art form. The collection holds more than 25,000 photographs and works by such artists as Alfred Stieglitz, Man Ray, Imogen Cunningham, and Cindy Sherman.

DRAWINGS, PRINTS, & ILLUSTRATED BOOKS

This collection includes more than 6,000 drawings in all mediums and almost 40,000 prints and illustrated books. Among highlights are drawings by Jean Dubuffet, Robert Rauschenburg, and others; and prints by Toulouse-Lautrec.

ARCHITECTURE & DESIGN

The architecture collection documents buildings and contains more than 60 models and 1,000 drawings plus the large **Ludwig Mies van der Rohe Archive.** The design collection has more than 3,000 objects, ranging from appliances, furniture, and classic cars to textiles and silicon chips;

the 4,000-piece graphic design collection includes typography and posters.

HISTORY

The idea for the museum was conceived in the winter of 1928–29 when Abby Rockefeller, the wife of John D. Rockefeller, Jr., and Lillie P. Bliss met in Cairo, Egypt. They decided that America must have a museum devoted to modern art and sculpture, works other museums refused to exhibit. Mary Quinn Sullivan became the third partner in the enterprise.

The "ladies," as they were called, enlisted the aid of A. Conger Goodyear, a museum trustee and collector who had shocked the art world by spending $5,000 for a

Picasso and Matisse feature largely at MOMA QNS.

The American Folk Art Museum's glimmering new facade

Picasso, and art historian, Paul J. Sachs. Soon the museum opened in a small gallery on the 12th floor of the Heckcher Building (*750 5th Ave. at 57th St.*) with a brilliant 27-year-old art scholar, Alfred H. Barr, Jr., as its director. Barr shaped the museum during its formative years and insisted on expanding the museum's horizons to include all the visual arts.

In 1932 the museum moved into a town house, at its current location on West 53rd Street. The same year, director Barr, in collaboration with

Philip Johnson and Henry-Russell Hitchcock, held the museum's first exhibit on architecture. This groundbreaking event introduced the controversial international style—of Walter Gropius, Mies van der Rohe, Le Corbusier, and J.J.P. Oud of Holland—to the American public, and converted the museum's trustees to the international style.

In 1936, MoMA commissioned architect Edward Durell Stone and Philip Goodwin, a museum trustee, to design a new building for its West 53rd Street site. The new museum, which opened in 1939, was fronted by a sheath of glass and marble and was one of the country's first examples of international style. The museum doubled in size in 1984, when Cesar Pelli designed an addition, a garden hall, and two wings in a condominium tower.

The latest phase of growth is the most extensive to date. Acclaimed architect Yoshio Taniguchi created an elegant design for the new building, scheduled to open in conjunction with MoMA's 75th anniversary year. The space for its exhibitions and programs more than doubles in the 630,000 square feet of new and redesigned space. The enlarged Abby Aldrich Rockefeller Sculpture Garden will be framed by a new gallery building housing the main exhibition galleries, and a stand-alone Education/Research Center. ■

American Folk Art Museum: Midtown

American Folk Art Museum: Midtown

This new $22-million, 30,000 square-foot, eight-story building, on Museum Row along 53rd Street, quadrupled gallery space for the American Museum of Folk Art (a branch museum remains at its original location in the Upper West Side; see p. 179). Designed by the New York architectural firm of Tod Williams Billie Tsien and Associates, its modernist structure is clad in textured bronze alloy panels that catch and reflect sunlight. Dramatic cut-throughs on each floor allow light to filter inside. Within, wood floors add warmth and three interior staircases lead to the galleries, filled with fascinating folk art, traditional and contemporary, national and international. ■

International Center of Photography

THIS UNIQUE INSTITUTION IS THE LARGEST PHOTOGRAPHY museum-school in the world and the only museum in New York solely dedicated to photography. Formerly housed in a mansion on Fifth Avenue's Museum Mile, it completed in 2001 its relocation to an exciting new Midtown campus where Gwathmey Siegel & Associates Architects redesigned an ICP satellite museum and enlarged it to 17,000 square feet. Here changing exhibitions are installed, many drawn from the museum's 60,000 original prints spanning the history of photography. Across the street is the new state-of-the-art school facility, designed by the architectural firm Gensler.

International Center of Photography
www.icp.org
🅰 Map p. 103
✉ 1133 Avenue of the Americas (at 43rd St.)
☎ 212/857-0002 or 800/688-8171
🕐 Closed Mon.
💲 $$
🚇 Subway: B, D, F, Q to 42nd St.-5th Ave.

The redesigned ICP's opening exhibit promised visitors the unexpected.

The museum entry opens onto a large airy space. On the right is the museum shop filled with everything from hard-to-find books to Holga plastic cameras. Ahead the spacious gallery area begins, continuing downstairs. An elevator or a wide stairwell reaches the second floor, where there are more galleries plus a café. At least three shows are usually on display on the two floors.

Concurrent exhibits recently included "Weegee's Trick Photography"; "Bruce Davidson's Civil Rights Photographs"; and "William Henry Fox Talbot and the Birth of Photography." Retrospectives have showcased Imogen Cunningham, Man Ray, Annie Leibowitz, David Hockney, and more. Group and theme shows have ranged from "Rise of the Picture Press: 1918–1939" to "Life in the Post-Genome Era."

Cornell Capa, the former *Life* magazine photographer who founded the ICP in 1974, did so to present and preserve all aspects of photography—from photojournalism to the avant garde, from master photographers to emerging talent. He also wanted to preserve the work of founders of the Magnum cooperative

photo agency. These included his brother, Robert Capa (who was killed in Indonesia), Henri Cartier-Bresson, Chim (David Seymour), and others.

ICP also sponsors monthly lectures and symposia and more than 500 courses a year, taught by leading photographers. ∎

More Midtown sites

Midtown North is awash in museums, and some corporations hold significant art and host exhibitions. Two corporate standouts are at 51st Street: **PaineWebber** (*1285 6th Ave., tel 212/713-2885, closed Sat.–Sun.*), which has changing exhibits, and the **AXA Gallery** (*787 7th Ave., tel 212/554-4818, closed Mon.*). See the murals in AXA's atrium, including Roy Lichtenstein's huge "Mural with Blue Brushstroke."

INTREPID SEA-AIR-SPACE MUSEUM

This unique museum is moored at a Hudson River dock. The *Intrepid* is a decommissioned aircraft carrier that fought in World War II and the Korean and Vietnam Wars. Saved from the scrap heap in 1978, it opened as a museum of naval aviation history in 1982.
✉ Pier 86, One Intrepid Sq., W. 46th St. and 12th Ave. 💲 $$$ ☎ 212/245-0072
🚇 Subway: A, C, E to 42nd St.

JAPAN SOCIETY GALLERY

In addition to its own small collection of 20th-century woodblock prints by Shiko Munamata, the gallery exhibits art from other institutions. Founded in 1907, the society opened the gallery here in 1971. Its small lobby garden, with a pool and bamboo trees, provides a peaceful retreat.
✉ 333 E. 47th St. ☎ 212/832-1155
🕐 Closed Mon. 💲 $$ 🚇 Subway: E, F to Lexington Ave., B or 6 to 51st St.

MUSEUM OF ARTS & DESIGN

Here the line between craft and art is blurred; the museum seeks to raise crafts to the level of art. Displayed, in clay, metal, fiber, glass, and wood, are works that often fill no needs except aesthetic ones. There are also exhibits on such traditional crafts as quilts.
✉ 40 W. 53rd St. ☎ 212/956-3535 💲 $$
🚇 Subway: B, D, F, Q to 47th-53rd Sts.-Rockefeller Center

MUSEUM OF TELEVISION & RADIO

More than 70 years of broadcasting—and 60,000 individual programs—are preserved in this innovative museum, founded by CBS chairman William Paley in 1975. In 1991, it moved to its present quarters, designed by John Burgee and Philip Johnson. There are two theaters, two screening/listening rooms, exhibits, artwork, and artifacts. Computers allow you easy access to your favorite TV or radio episode, whether it be the 1937 live radio broadcast of the Hindenburg crash or an early Sid Caesar television show.
✉ 25 W. 52nd St. ☎ 212/621-6600
🕐 Closed Mon. 💲 $$ 🚇 Subway: E, F to 5th Ave. or Rockefeller Center

ROSE MUSEUM AT CARNEGIE HALL

Even if there wasn't this small museum on the second floor, a visit to Carnegie Hall would be in order. Andrew Carnegie built the famed concert hall in 1891, and Tchaikovsky conducting his own works was among the first to appear. Since then every major figure in classical music—and many in jazz, pop, and rock—have performed here. When Lincoln Center opened in 1962, Carnegie Hall was scheduled for demolition. Saved by the efforts of violinist Isaac Stern, the building was renovated in 1986 and a museum added in 1991. Here you can see changing exhibits of photographs, Carnegie Hall mementoes (such as Toscanini's baton), and musical manuscripts.
✉ 154 W. 57th St., at 7th Ave. ☎ 212/903-9629 🚇 Subway: N, R to 57th St.

TURTLE BAY HISTORIC DISTRICT

After visiting the UN, stroll around the brownstones once home to several illustrious writers and artists. E. B. White's *The Second Tree from the Corner* immortalizes a tree in the quarter's **Turtle Bay Gardens,** a large communal garden built in Italianate style in the 1920s. Other past and present luminaries of this lovely neighborhood include Katharine Hepburn, Dorothy Thompson, and Stephen Sondheim.
✉ 226-246 E. 49th St. bet. 2nd & 3rd Aves.
☎ Turtle Bay Association: 212/751-5465 ■

A curving wooden staircase, itself a feat of craftsmanship, leads to second-floor exhibits at the Museum of Arts & Design.

Central Park South

TWO VERY DIFFERENT PUBLIC SPACES ARE ONLY THREE blocks apart on Central Park South: European-style Grand Army Plaza, near Fifth Avenue, and hectic Columbus Circle, near Eighth. On streets in between, Midtown shoppers set a rapid pace.

Carnegie Hall

- Map p. 103
- 154 W. 57th St.
- 212/247-7800
- $ for tours, offered Mon.–Fri.
- Subway: N, R to 57th St.

Beyond a carpet of tulips stands the grande dame of New York hotels, the Plaza, a French château of immense proportions.

Gracing the plaza is the revered **Plaza Hotel,** designed in 1907 by Henry Hardenbergh as a high-rise French château. Drinks in the lobby Palm Court or dinner in the Oak Room offer the ambience of old New York. To the north stands Augustus Saint-Gaudens's last major work (1892–1902), a gilded monument to Civil War general William Tecumseh Sherman. For a family treat, cross over to the ultimate toy store experience, F.A.O. Schwartz (see p. 260), site of the piano-playing scene in the film *Big.*

Central Park South, lined with elegant hotels, echoes the clip-clop of horse-drawn carriages. Enjoy the scene from the sidewalk café of the **St. Moritz** *(50 Central Park S.).* Nearby, see the elaborate terracotta decorations on the **Alwyn Court Apartments** *(180 W. 58th St.)* and famed **Carnegie Hall.** Performers from Fats Waller to Luciano Pavarotti have graced its stages since 1891. Patrons paid one to two dollars on opening night to hear composer Pyotr Tchaikovsky conduct his "Marche Solennelle." Along 57th Street art galleries nestle among toney stores, theme restaurants, and cafés.

Be especially alert as you approach **Columbus Circle,** named for the statue atop the 77-foot obelisk in the center. Fast-moving traffic and people pouring forth from the subways are all around.

A group headed by Related Companies is transforming the New York Coliseum site west of the circle into a major arts/entertainment complex. Plans for the Columbus Center, as it is called, include twin towers (inspired by the twin-towered apartments of the Upper West Side) on a five-story base that will follow the contours of the circle. The group has signed Time Warner and its television studios as a major tenant. The complex's focal point will be a jazz theater entered through a grand glass rotunda.

Architect David Childs designed nearby Worldwide Plaza in Hell's Kitchen/Clinton and the neomodernist Mercantile Exchange in Battery Park City. ■

The Upper East Side is the most exclusive part of town, bar none. The elegant avenues and tranquil side streets are the haunts of the very rich. On Fifth Avenue, great fortunes, great architecture, and great art find one another.

Upper East Side

The dome of the Guggenheim Museum

Upper East Side

THE THREE MAGIC WORDS, UPPER EAST SIDE, CONJURE UP AN IMAGE OF wealth and upper-class privilege that accurately reflects part but not all, of this large section of Manhattan between Central Park and the East River. Certainly only the wealthy can afford to live on Fifth or Park Avenues. These magnificent thoroughfares are noted for such rarified sights as uniformed doormen hailing cabs for apartment house residents, exquisitely dressed matrons walking exquisitely groomed dogs, small children and their nannies on outings to Central Park. Such sights alone are enough to make a visit to the Upper East Side worthwhile.

Once there, you can savor life as the upper crust lives it. A visit to the Metropolitan Museum of Art, for example, can be enhanced by taking tea at Fifth Avenue's Stanhope Hotel—or on Madison Avenue, at the Carlyle or the Westbury Hotels. Many of Fifth Avenue's museums are housed in millionaires' mansions; inside you can absorb the ambience of wealth as well as the art treasures on view. Or go to the galleries, most on or near Madison Avenue, where the rich indulge their mostly conservative tastes. Two of the most prestigious, the Hirschl & Adler Galleries and the Knoedler Gallery, established in 1836, are housed in landmark residences on East 70th Street that were built for wealthy New Yorkers early in the 20th century.

But the Upper East Side is not all upper-class extravagance and ostentation. The avenues farther east—Lexington, Third, Second, and beyond—are today home to the middle class as well as the young and upwardly mobile, people to whom the term "yuppie" was first applied. Here the restaurants and bars are lively and trendy; even the literati enjoy mingling and being seen at Elaine's restaurant *(1703 2nd Ave., between 88th and 89th Sts., tel 212/534-8103).*

In an earlier incarnation, this part of the Upper East Side was the teeming home to immigrants. In 1878–79, elevated train lines (Els) were built along Second and Third Avenues, blocking out sunlight and bombarding the nearby tenements with noise. The first immigrants came from Germany, Ireland, and Bohemia. German Yorkville, its heart at 86th Street between Lexington and Second Avenues, was a thriving center of German culture that dwindled away after the tracks of the Third Avenue El were torn down in 1956. Today the

Heidelberg *(1648 2nd Ave. between 85th and 86th Sts., tel 212/628-2332)* is one of the few German restaurants surviving in an area where German cuisine was commonplace.

SPANISH HARLEM

The Upper East Side, at least from 96th Street north, is also a center of Latin American culture. These lively, overcrowded, and impoverished streets have almost nothing in common with the elegant avenues and side streets farther south. Called El Barrio or Spanish Harlem, the neighborhood was largely Italian until Puerto Ricans and other Latin Americans began settling there in great numbers after World War II. Museum Row's northernmost museum, El Museo del Barrio (see p. 159) embodies the culture of teeming Spanish Harlem. Its dynamic collection proves that there is more to the Upper East Side than wealth and its abundant trappings.

HISTORIC DISTRICTS

The historic buildings of the Upper East Side—mostly residences of one sort or another—are preserved in several historic districts. Among the hundreds of important buildings are early apartment houses, such as 998 Fifth Avenue (1912), which became, in form and function, the ideal to which other apartment houses aspired. On a much smaller scale is the Henderson Place Historic District, on a cul-de-sac off 86th Street, between East End and York Avenues, consisting of 24 relatively modest Queen Anne row houses built in 1881. ■

EAST DRIVE

GRAND ARMY PLAZA

5th Avenue

①

Manhattan

Area of map detail

0   600 yards
0   600 meters

El Museo
del Barrio

Museum of the
City of New York

EAST DRIVE

CENTRAL PARK

FIFTH AVENUE

FIFTH AVENUE

103rd
Street

102ND STREET

106TH STREET

Jewish
Museum

Cooper-Hewitt
National Design
Museum

National Academy
of Design and
School of Fine Arts

The
Guggenheim

96th
Street

96TH STREET

CARNEGIE
HILL

92ND STREET

PARK AVENUE

LEXINGTON

THIRD

SECOND

FIRST

Metropolitan
Museum of Art

86th
Street

86TH STREET

⑤

④

⑦

YORKVILLE

79TH STREET

CARL
SCHURZ
PARK

⑧

Whitney Museum
of American Art

77th
Street

UPPER
EAST SIDE

PARK AVENUE

AVENUE

AVENUE

72ND STREET

The
Frick
Collection

68th Street-
Hunter College

JOHN
JAY
PARK

FRANKLIN D. ROOSEVELT DRIVE

East River

CENTRAL

FIFTH

PARK AVENUE

MADISON

LEXINGTON

THIRD

SECOND

FIRST

YORK

LENOX
HILL

③

63RD STREET

Lexington
Avenue

Lexington
Avenue

59th Street

②

⑥

QUEENSBORO BRIDGE

UPPER EAST SIDE

① New York Academy of Sciences
② Bloomingdale's ③ Seventh
Regiment Armory ④ New York
Society Library ⑤ Neue Galerie
New York ⑥ Abigail Adams Smith
Museum ⑦ Church of the Holy
Trinity ⑧ Gracie Mansion

Frick Collection

Frick Collection

www.frick.org

- Map p. 133
- 1 E. 70th St.
- 212/288-0700
- Closed Mon. & a.m. Sun.; also open Fri. evenings
- $$
- Subway: 6 to 68th St.

Note: Children under ten are not admitted, and those under 16 must be accompanied by an adult.

The Frick's largest room, the skylit **West Gallery**, combines old masters and the ambience of a classic New York mansion.

A VISIT TO THE FRICK COLLECTION IS A TRIP BACK TO THE Gilded Age, when millionaires competed to build mansions along elegant Fifth Avenue and fill them with art treasures. Housed in the former residence of industrialist Henry Clay Frick (1849–1919), the collection has welcomed visitors from around the world since its celebrated opening as a museum and library in 1935.

In contrast to the monumental character of some of the city's museums, the Frick is just the right size for a serene immersion in the arts in a refined setting. Furnishings and artworks are arranged as though the Fricks were still in residence, without regard to chronology or period. A free acoustical guide (in 6 languages) and a brochure with a floor plan guide you through the collection's 19 rooms. A small shop is outside the Reception Hall, and across from it the entrance to a downstairs gallery for changing exhibits.

The main collection is on the first floor. The **Boucher Room** just off the East Vestibule is unforgettable—cloying to some—

adorned with a series of decorative panels entitled "The Arts and Sciences," depicting cherublike children engaged in various adult activities. Created by François Boucher (1750–52) for Madame de Pompadour, the artworks once graced **Mrs. Frick's bedroom** upstairs, reached by the grand staircase off the vestibule. Portraiture by Hogarth and Reynolds and others line the walls of the **Dining Room,** which also holds the fine "Mall in St. James Park" (1783), social landscape by Thomas Gainsborough.

The highlight of the **Fragonard Room** is the light-hearted 18th-century series of paintings, "The Progress of Love," by Jean-Honoré Fragonard. The austere **Living Hall** is dominated by masterworks including "Portrait of a Man in a Red Cap" by Titian (circa 1488–1576), "St. Jerome" by El Greco (1541–1614), and "Portrait of Sir Thomas More" (1527) by Hans Holbein the Younger. The Living Hall's furniture is by French cabinetmaker André-Charles Boulle. Beyond is the wood-paneled **Library,** where one of Gilbert Stuart's many portraits of George Washington is a lone American classic amid European masterpieces.

Be sure not to miss the offerings in the Halls. A portrait by Ingres, "Comtesse d'Haussonville" (1845) in the **North Hall** is among the most popular works in the collection. Dutch artist Johannes Vermeer's "Officer and Laughing Girl" (circa 1655–1660) hangs in the **South Hall.** Adjacent to the Halls is the Garden Court; save this for last.

Visitors take a breath as they enter the **West Gallery;** it is long, high, and skylit, very unlike what has preceded. A gallery of this sort characterized 19th-century upper-class homes. Here is a formidable grouping not to be missed: Rembrandt's self-portrait, "Portrait of a Young Artist" (1658) plus important works by Vermeer, Van Dyck, Hals, Velázquez, and more. The **Enamel Room** at one end is intimate, replete with French Limoges enamels, including the exquisite "The Seven Sorrows of the Virgin" (1500–1550). Frick acquired most of these from the estate of J. P. Morgan. The **Oval Room,** formerly Frick's office, has large portraits by Van Dyck and Gainsborough and a life-size Houdon sculpture of Diana. In the **East Gallery,** a pair of Whistlers handsomely frame the doorway, and Claude Lorrin's "The Sermon on the Mount" (1656) is on the far wall.

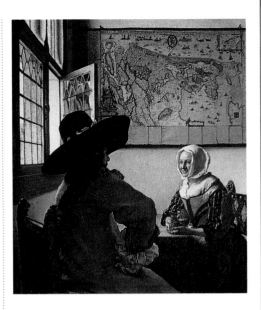

Johannes Vermeer's "Officer and Laughing Girl" (circa 1655–1660)

Proceed to the enclosed **Garden Court,** with a pool, greenery, benches, portrait busts, and a charming bronze angel by Jean Barbet, with the year 1475 engraved on its left wing. In this soothing place you may reflect upon all you have seen and decide what to revisit.

FRICK FAMILY LEGACY

Frick, a self-made man, was criticized at an early age as being "a little too enthusiastic about pictures." Starting in coal mines, he was a millionaire by age 30. By 40 he was president of Carnegie Steel. He moved to New York in 1900, partly to protect his collection from the polluted Pittsburgh air. Philanthropically inclined, he built his mansion with the idea of eventually turning it into a museum open to the public. In 1920, Frick's daughter opened the **Frick Art Reference Library** (*10 E. 71st St.*), with 750,000 photographs and 174,000 books and catalogs. Today the Library is a research center and a photoarchive. ∎

Metropolitan Museum of Art

THE METROPOLITAN MUSEUM OF ART IS THE LARGEST museum in the Western Hemisphere. Its collection, some two million items, is not only broad—the entire world, from antiquity to the present—but deep with holdings so large in a number of areas that some collections might be considered museums unto themselves. The best way to approach this vast repository is to understand the museum's arrangement and select a limited number of areas to see during your visit. Those who do not, usually come away feeling overwhelmed.

The museum itself is a very large structure. Study it from the Fifth Avenue side before you go in. Large hanging banners announce important temporary exhibits. You might decide to choose one of these, but if you plan to stay longer, orient yourself to the building and identify basic locations for some of the most popular collections. Think of the museum as a rectangle with a central stairway in the middle that divides right and left. Then divide each side into front and back. Look at the twin columns flanking the entrance. On the front right side of those columns is the Egyptian Collection (and the Temple of Dendur), and on the back side, the American Wing (which continues in the same position onto the second floor). To the front left side of the columns you will find Greek and Roman art and then a self-service cafeteria and restaurant. On the back left side is the Lila Atcheson Wallace Wing with 20th-century art. In between are the arts of Africa, Oceania, and the Americas.

Once you enter and pay your admission, if you walk up the grand staircase immediately in front of you, you will be on the second floor in what many consider to be the heart of this museum, its superior collection of European painting, sculpture, and decorative arts.

There you will find masterpieces by Botticelli, Brueghel, Rembrandt, Vermeer, Degas, Rodin, plus the Petrie Sculpture Court, a delightful and contemplative place to relax. Although things will feel more complicated once you enter the museum, if you can keep in mind the rough locations of these six areas (Egyptian; American; Greek and Roman; eating; Africa, Oceania, and the Americas; and 20th century) on the first floor, and, at the top of the stairs on the second floor, European paintings, you can be assured of finding them, and once you are in them, finding your way back out. As you walk up the exterior steps, notice how they level off repeatedly, allowing one to pause. So, too, it is best to stop off periodically when sampling the collections. If you keep track of where you are, you will avoid the anxiety of getting lost.

PLANNING WHAT TO SEE

When you enter, pick up a floor plan and take time to look it over and write your choices on it and then plan where to start. If you do not want to go on your own, there are guides and recorded tours to take you through almost every part of the museum. A relaxing way to enjoy the ambience, architecture, and sheer beauty of the interior is to visit after 5 p.m. on Friday and

Metropolitan Museum of Art
www.metmuseum.org
Map p. 133
5th Ave. at 82nd St.
212/535-7710
Closed Mon.
Donation ($$) includes admission to The Cloisters (see pp. 196–197)
Subway: 4, 5, 6 to 86th St.

Note: Some wings are closed certain days due to funding problems. Visitors should call ahead if they are interested in a particular wing.

Opposite: The Great Hall of the Met, where visitors can orient themselves before plunging into the seemingly endless collections

19th-century European paintings & sculpture

Drawings, prints, & photographs

European paintings

The American Wing

SECOND FLOOR

Japanese, Asian, Southeast Asian, & Chinese art

Islamic art

FIRST FLOOR

Robert Lehman Collection

Egyptian art

20th-century art

Arms & armor

The Costume Institute

Greek & Roman art

Arts of Africa, Oceania, & the Americas

20th-century art

Medieval art & European paintings & sculpture

Musical instruments

Greek, Roman, Egyptian, & Ancient Near Eastern art

Asian, Oriental, & Islamic art

Africa, Oceania, & the Americas

Arms, armor, & costume

American art & architecture

Drawings, prints, & photographs

Saturday. Then you can take tea or have drinks on the balcony, while in the Great Hall a string quartet performs classical music, often playing on ancient instruments from the Metropolitan's own collections. Many people are drawn by blockbluster shows. Some of these—the 1978 "Treasures of Tutankhamun," for example, or the Mona Lisa's frantic visit to the Metropolitan in 1963—are major events in the cultural life of the city. But just as important to the world of art are some of the works unveiled for the first time, such as a 1998 exhibit of photographs done by the painter Edgar Degas later in life.

Some visitors return again and again to the same galleries. Certain adults are drawn back to the galleries they knew as children, particularly the Egyptian tombs and medieval arms and armor. There is, in fact, something here for everybody.

There are even reasons other than art to visit the Met. In addition to lectures, concerts, and films, there is a reference facility and print study rooms. The **Uris Center** on the ground floor has its own library and classrooms, and publishes educational books and films. The museum also offers an array of shopping options. The first-floor museum store is stocked to overflowing with separate boutique shops and features not just books and reproductions covering the whole history of world art, but fine jewelry, scarves, children's toys and games, recordings, three-dimensional reproductions, and more. It is a unique source of gifts for all occasions, with a mail-order catalog as well (plus ancillary city shops, including one across from the main branch of the Public Library on 42nd Street). Food options include the rooftop café and the first-floor cafeteria and

restaurant. But there is no truer New York pastime than buying food from a vendor outside and sitting on the steps, often never even venturing a foot inside.

HISTORY

In 1866 John Jay, a diplomat, lawyer, and grandson of America's first chief justice, told a group of American businessmen visiting Paris that the time had come "for the American people to lay the foundation for a national institution and gallery of art." His words so stirred them that, on their return, they put poet and newspaper editor William Cullen Bryant at the head of a committee charged with founding the Metropolitan Museum of Art. Bryant enlisted the help of other leading New Yorkers, mostly members of the Union League Club; but it was Bryant himself, wrote critic Russell Lynes, "more than any other New Yorker who nursed the concept of a museum of art from a hope into a solid stone-and-mortar reality."

In 1870 the museum opened in temporary quarters. The next year it acquired a collection of 174 European paintings and hired Calvert Vaux and Jacob Wrey

Visitors stand back in a painting gallery.

Mould to design its first building. This small, redbrick high Gothic building had a steel-and-glass roof and was situated in Central Park at 82nd Street and Fifth Avenue, the very spot that Vaux and his partner Frederick Law Olmsted, in their "Greensward plan" for Central Park, had set aside for a museum. The front entrance of the museum originally faced Central Park.

As the Metropolitan grew, the Vaux-Mould building was literally swallowed up by new wings and additions. Portions of the original building are now visible from the Lehman Wing and the European Sculpture Court. The signature Fifth Avenue facade, with its neo-classic features, and Great Hall were added in 1902, designed by Richard Morris Hunt and executed by his son. McKim, Mead & White added the north and south wings in 1911 and 1913. Roche, Dinkeloo & Associates have been in charge of recent additions, among them the Lehman Wing in 1975, the Skaler Wing added in 1979 for the Far East collection, and the Rockefeller Wing added in 1982 to house the arts of Africa, Oceania, and the Americas. The museum's new American Wing (1980) was built around the old, and provides generous new space for the Americana collection, by then the largest in the country. The Lila Atcheson Wallace Wing for 20th-century art was added in 1987. Renovations and changes are constantly under way.

BUILDING THE COLLECTION

In 1883 the museum purchased a large collection of architectural casts. At the time, the museum assumed, wrongly, that important European masterpieces would never become available for purchase, so "casts and reproductions" were considered important parts of the collection. For years, according to a 1917 guide, "models, on a scale of one-twentieth of the original, of the Parthenon, the Pantheon, Notre-Dame, and the Hypostyle Hall of Karnac" greeted visitors in the Great Hall.

In 1887 an extraordinary loan of 37 European paintings from railroad financier Henry Gurdon

Marquand instantly made the museum one of the best in the country. The works included Vermeer's "Young Woman with a Water Jug," still considered one of the finest works in the collection, as well as paintings by Van Dyck, Rembrandt, Franz Hals, Petrus Christus, Turner, and Gainsborough. In 1913 a bequest from the department store owner, Benjamin Altman, which included almost 500 Chinese porcelains and a number of Rembrandts, came with several strings attached, one being that the paintings hang "in a single line, not one above the other," as was then the custom.

After financier J.P. Morgan died in 1913, his son gave about 40 percent of his huge collection to the museum. Other important acquisitions included, in 1929, the collection of French Impressionists assembled by Louisine Havemeyer. It took the museum decades to develop an interest in American art. In 1930 it rejected Gertrude Vanderbilt Whitney's offer of 500 modern American paintings so quickly that her representative did not have a chance to add that the offer included a new wing to house them. Since that time, the museum has welcomed many important donations and gifts.

OVERVIEW, GROUND FLOOR

Many might overlook **The Costume Institute** because of its location, but if your interest is fashion, this is an essential stop. Noted for its imaginative exhibits, the institute began independently as the Museum of Costume Art, which became part of the Metropolitan in 1946. The 60,000 items (15th century to the present) include high fashion and native garb from around the world. A recent show called "Rock Style" featured costumes of rock musicians including Elvis Presley, the Beatles, and Madonna. There is a museum shop near the Costume Institute.

OVERVIEW, FIRST FLOOR

The founders of the Metropolitan believed that American painting, decorative arts, and furniture had no place in a serious museum. The

The popular Garden Court of the American Wing offers views of American art and of Central Park beyond.

attitude began to change after the museum's first exhibit of American furniture and silver in 1909 proved immensely popular. American arts and crafts became a separate department in 1922 and the **American Wing** opened in 1924. In 1980, it was renovated and expanded: It now occupies galleries on three floors, and is a world unto itself where one can easily spend an entire day. The collection here is indeed varied with everything from an unsurpassed assemblage of American paintings, to a rare Honus Wagner baseball card, to a room from the Frank Lloyd Wright Prairie House in Minnesota. Period rooms are organized chronologically, beginning with the earliest colonial ones on the third floor.

Highlights include the wing's focal point, the glass-covered **Garden Court** on the first floor, which features fountains, Central Park views, an 1824 bank facade from Wall Street, and stained glass by Louis Comfort Tiffany. In the courtyard, flooded with natural light, the work of well-known sculptors, including Gutzon Borgum (of Mount Rushmore fame) is displayed on a rotating basis. There are many significant American paintings, including those of the Hudson River school, Winslow Homer, Childe Hassam, and Mary Cassatt. Try to see the largest painting in the Metropolitan, John Vanderlyn's "Panorama of the Palace and Gardens of Versailles" (1818–19), displayed in its own oval gallery. On the second floor in the new wing there are portraits of George Washington by Charles Willson Peale and Gilbert Stuart. Emanuel Leutze's popular "Washington Crossing the Delaware" (1851) is also here.

Located on the first floor to the right of the staircase and past

European and Decorative Arts, the **Arms and Armor** collection is one of the first sought out by all enamored of Camelot. Especially popular here is the Equestrian Court, whose armored knights on horseback evoke the world of King Arthur and the Knights of the Round Table. The Japanese armor is highlighted by fierce face masks worn in battle. American arms include a Kentucky rifle and a Colt revolver.

Located on a first-floor wing donated by Nelson Rockefeller, in memory of his son, Michael, who died on an expedition in New Guinea, is the **Arts of Africa, Oceania, and the Americas.** The collection incorporates

In the museum's unrivaled collection of paintings, George Washington by Gilbert Stuart (1755–1828)

Rockefeller's former Museum of Primitive Art that used to be in midtown Manhattan. Don't miss the sculptures of the Buli Master, one of the first African artists recognized as an individual.

Any tour of the museum would devote considerable attention to the extensive Egyptian Collection, even if it did not have its counterpart next door: the exquisite three-room **Temple of Dendur** (circa 23–10 B.C.). Since 1978, the temple has rested in isolated splendor in its own high-ceilinged gallery in the **Sackler Wing.** Originally the Roman emperor Augustus had the temple built as a tribute to the Nile god, Osiris. The Gateway leading to the temple is adorned with reliefs showing Augustus honoring local gods. What is most fascinating is how the temple came to rest in New York City. When it was threatened with destruction because of the Aswan High Dam, it was given to the United States, transported block by block, and then reassembled.

The **Egyptian Collection,** in adjacent galleries, spans more than three and a half millennia, from circa 3000 B.C. to A.D. 641. It is organized chronologically. The tomb of Perneb (circa 2440 B.C.), a reconstruction of the *mastaba,* or tomb, in which an official of the Old Kingdom was buried, is impressive, with vivid reliefs of servants preparing and carrying food.

A room dedicated to modern art and sculpture

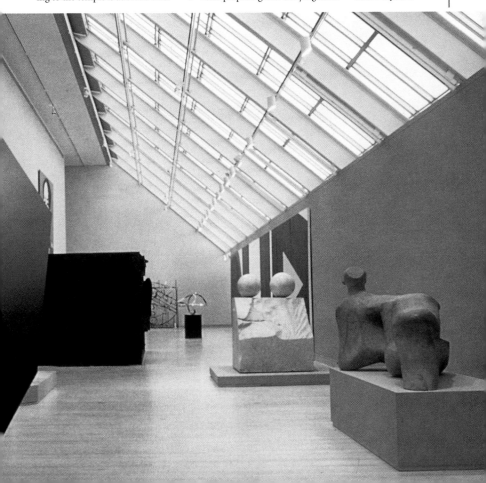

Also of note are the statues from the funerary temple of Queen Hatshepsut (circa 1502–1482 B.C.), including one in which she wears masculine garb. Finally, see the remarkably detailed models of daily life in Dynasty XI (circa 2009–1998 B.C.).

The Arms and Armor collection has been a favorite ever since the museum acquired its first pieces in the early 20th century.

Near the stairs you will find the department of **European Sculpture and Decorative arts,** which surrounds the department of medieval art. Its galleries include works from the Renaissance to the early 20th century. Be sure to visit the **European Sculpture Court.** Noteworthy is Auguste Rodin's "The Burghers of Calais" (1885–1895), depicting citizens who saved Calais from English reprisals. The **Jack and Belle Linsky Galleries,** a collection of furniture, bronzes, exquisitely detailed objects, and paintings includes Fra Bartolomeo's "Portrait of a Man" (after 1497).

This department also encompasses the **Robert Lehman Collection,** which came to the museum with the stipulation that the art be displayed in rooms re-created from the donor's home. Thus it is that one of the country's most outstanding private art collections came to reside in a modern glass pyramid-shaped pavilion, the **Robert Lehman Wing,** in the back corner of the first floor of the museum. Among the seven re-created rooms, the **Grand Gallery** includes works by Corot, Monet, van Gogh, but the collection covers old masters to the 20th century. Among the highlights are Gauguin's "Tahitian Woman Bathing" (1891); and El Greco's "St. Jerome as a Cardinal" (circa 1600–1610). The 15th-century Italian masterpieces in the exquisite Red Velvet Room include Giovanni de Paolo's "Expulsion from Paradise" (circa 1445), and Botticelli's "Annunciation" (circa 1490).

By the turn of the 20th century, the Metropolitan had acquired considerable **Greek and Roman art,** including Cypriot statues and artifacts donated by Louis Palma di Cesnola, director of the museum from 1879 to 1904, and the Roman and Etruscan glass from Henry Gurdon Marquand. Don't miss the Boscoreale frescoes, from a villa buried under volcanic ash by the eruption of Vesuvius in A.D. 79; the Kouros (700 B.C.), the earliest Greek marble statue in the museum; and the Euphronios vase (circa 515 B.C.), depicting detailed scenes from the Trojan War.

Originally based on the collection made by J.P. Morgan, the **Medieval art** galleries, on the first floor behind the staircase, span 12 centuries, from 300 to 1500. Included are early Christian art, the Romanesque Chapel, medieval tapestries, paintings, and sculpture, plus the **Medieval Treasury,** containing items of gold and other precious metals. Of particular importance are the Antioch Chalice, a sixth-century liturgical cup; the 15th-century "Annunciation" tapestry from Arras, France; and the glazed terra-cotta altarpiece by Andrea Della Robbia depicting the Assumption. Those interested in this period will want to visit the Metropolitan's museum devoted to medieval art in a medieval setting, The Cloisters (see pp. 196–97).

Housed in the first-floor **Lila Acheson Wallace Wing** (1987), named for a founder of the *Reader's Digest* magazine, the **20th-century art** department is strong in an area the museum once spurned—modern American paintings. The wing housing it is worth a visit for its own sake: There are glass curtain walls and an attractive roof garden. This department began with Alfred Stieglitz's collection of modern painting, sculpture, and drawings that his widow, Georgia O'Keeffe, gave to the museum in 1949. Important to the development of art in New York is "Nasturtiums" (1912), one of the first works by Henri Matisse to be shown in this country—it debuted at the famous 1913 Armory Show (see pp. 82–83). Also be sure to see the work of the New York innovators known as The Eight and the abstract expressionists.

OVERVIEW, SECOND FLOOR

On this floor you'll find the remaining exhibits from the **American Wing.**

Spanning 6000 B.C. to the 7th century A.D., the **Ancient and Near Eastern art** galleries include Assyrian art, Mesopotamian art, pre-Islamic antiquities from Iran and Achaemenid, Parthian, and Sasanian art. Be sure to see the gypsum statue of a bearded Sumerian worshiper (circa 2750–2600 B.C.) or, if in residence, the statue of Ur-Ningirse, whose body belongs to the Louvre, but the head to the Metropolitan; the entire statue alternates between Paris and New York.

A highlight of the newly renovated **Chinese art** galleries at the top of the stairs is Dong Yuan's "The Riverbank," a monumental 10th-century hanging scroll landscape. Also, visit the **Astor Court Garden** on the third floor, a 16th century-style garden for medita-

tion. It was constructed for the museum in 1979 by Chinese craftspeople using ancient techniques and tools.

The **drawing, painting, and photograph** collections hold some extraordinary works, including drawings by Michelangelo and Matisse, prints by Rembrandt, and photographs collected by Alfred Stieglitz. Visit the **Howard Gilman Gallery,** inaugurated in 1997. Three changing exhibits yearly display photographs from the private 5,000-piece collection of the late Howard Gilman.

The 30 galleries devoted to **European paintings** form an especially rich part of the museum, spanning five centuries. Two of the galleries are devoted to Italian Renaissance painting (Mantegna, Botticelli, Della Robbia) and Dutch painting (Rembrandt, Hals, Vermeer, Ruisdael). These works came from the Benjamin Altman

Seated on the hard marble floor, a student sketches a statue by the 17th-century Italian, Gianlorenzo Bernini.

Collection, bequeathed to the museum in 1913 by the department store millionaire. The masterpieces in this gift made the Metropolitan one of the world's leading museums. The galleries are arranged by school: 18th-century Venetian painting (Tiepolo); 15th-century Italian painting (Filippo Lippi, Ghirlandaio, Signorelli, Perugino); 17th-century Dutch portraits (Rembrandt, Hals); English portraits (Reynolds, Gainsborough, Lawrence); and so forth. A highlight here is Rembrandt's "Aristotle with a Bust of Homer" (1653), purchased by the museum in 1961 for a record sum at the time of 2.3 million dollars.

Extensive **Far Eastern art** galleries wind through the second floor and encompass three major areas: Chinese art, Japanese art, and the art of South and Southeast Asia—the last areas comprising 18 galleries, with works from India, Tibet, Nepal, Thailand, Indonesia, Cambodia, Burma, and Vietnam. See the collection of Chinese ceramics, which dates back to

China's historical beginnings, the Shang dynasty (17th–11th centuries B.C.); the collection of large Chinese Buddhist sculptures; a 5th-century Standing Buddha from northern India; and the **Khmer Courtyard,** featuring the Angkor period (9th–13th centuries) of Cambodia, Vietnam, and Thailand.

The **Greek and Roman art** galleries continue onto the second floor. They include a fine collection of Greek vases.

One of the jewels of the museum is the **Islamic art** collection. It starts with the reign of the four caliphs in A.D. 632, extends into the 19th century, and stretches geographically from Spain east to Southeast Asia. One gallery is devoted to the museum-sponsored excavations of Nishapur in Iran, once a great Islamic center, and a re-created early 18th-century reception room from a wealthy Ottoman home in Damascus. Highlights include art from the Mughal period in India (1526–1858)—carpets, miniature painting, jewelry, and jade carving.

The sweeping display of **Japanese art** in familiar settings is spread out over ten galleries. Chronological and thematic displays include some exquisitely detailed tapestries and ceremonial costumes and a re-creation of a *shoin*, or study.

If you have children, or if you love music, turn right at the top of the stairs to the collection of rare and fascinating **musical instruments**. Dating from prehistory to the present, instruments are from Europe, and the Americas, Asia, and Africa. Among the distinguished objects here is the oldest (1720) surviving piano by Bartolomeo Cristofori, inventor of the instrument, Andres Segovia's guitars, and Native American pipes. Visitors can hear the sounds of instruments on audio. Mrs. Mary Crosby Brown's donation, in 1889, of 270 instruments from around the world is at the heart of the collection. As many other donors, she continued to collect and donate to the museum; by 1906 there were 3,500 instruments.

The **19th-century Euro-pean painting and sculpture** collection is one of the greatest of its kind in the world and one of the museum's most popular. The collection is displayed in galleries that reflect the spirit of the period. Two galleries are named for the collection's great benefactors, Louisine and H.O. Havemeyer. Mrs. Havemeyer's interest in European Impressionist and Postimpressionist paintings began with her friendship with the American painter, Mary Cassatt. The museum's holdings include many works by such well-known artists as Courbet, Corot, Degas, Manet, Monet, Cézanne, Seurat, van Gogh, and Rodin. There are also sections or galleries devoted to Neoclassicism, Romanticism, the Barbizon school, French still lifes, pastels, and salon painting. The paintings are displayed in a loose chronological order, starting with neoclassicists David and Ingres and ending with such turn-of-the-20th-century work as Pissarro's "Garden of the Tuileries" (1899) and Rousseau's "The Repast of the Lion" (1907). ■

The Temple of Dendur, a gift from Egypt to the U.S., stands alone as it did on the Nile, in its own gallery.

The Guggenheim

WHEN YOU VISIT THE SOLOMON R. GUGGENHEIM Museum, keep in mind that it is the only building in New York by Frank Lloyd Wright, possibly America's greatest architect ever. To architects the museum is circular form in a rectilinear space. To the rest of us, it is a round building amid square ones. However you put it, it is a presence; today, four decades after Frank Lloyd Wright's concrete spiral opened on Fifth Avenue, it is impossible to visit, talk, or think about the museum without considering the building. Before the structure was renovated in the early 1990s, it was emptied of its paintings, but visitors came anyway—just to see Wright's building.

Solomon R. Guggenheim Museum
www.guggenheim.org
- Map p. 133
- 1071 5th Ave.
- 212/423-3500
- Closed Thurs.
- $$
- Subway: 4, 5, 6 to 86th St.

The Guggenheim, as it is called, grew out of the private collection of the millionaire Solomon R. Guggenheim. He began collecting old masters but expanded into modern art under the influence of Hilla Rebay von Ehrenwiesen, a European artist and baroness, opening the Museum of Non-Objective Painting in 1939. In 1943 it was Rebay who selected and hired Wright as the architect for a new museum. In a letter that must have appealed to his considerable ego, she wrote: "I need a fighter, a lover of space, an originator, a tester and a wise man … I want a temple of spirit, a monument!" Non-objective painting, as Rebay defined it, "represents no object or subject known to us on earth. It is simply a beautiful organization arranged in rhythmic order of colors and forms to be enjoyed for beauty's sake."

Wright responded that he was "eager to build to objectify the non-objective point of view." That was 1943. Over the next 16 years Wright submitted six sets of plans and 749 drawings. Wright informed his clients that he was striving for "one extended expansive well-proportioned floor space from bottom to top … gloriously lit from above." Guggenheim died in 1949 but left two million dollars to build the museum. In 1956 construction began. The museum opened to the public in October 1959. Wright had died six months before, on April 9.

TODAY'S COLLECTION

The present collection covers the history of modern art, including European art of the first half of the 20th century as well as late 19th-century and postwar European and American art. Ongoing curatorial efforts include recent acquisitions in film, photography, multimedia, and high-technology art. In the 1980s, the Guggenheim began its growth into a bicontinental entity. In addition to its Fifth Avenue site in New York, it now occupies locations in Venice, Berlin, and Bilbao. All of this expansion has made the Guggenheim an institution uniquely equipped to present the evolution of 20th-century art in the global arena.

THE ROTUNDA & THE RAMP

Immediately upon entering from Fifth Avenue you confront the daring design. To the left is the museum store and to the right, the admission desk, but ahead is the Great Rotunda, spiraling upward 92 feet to the domed skylight. The Rotunda at street level is often filled with an exhibit entitled "1900: Art at the Crossroads," featuring 250 works by more than 170 artists from 24 countries. In 1998 a cluster of gleaming machines greeted

Above and below: The Guggenheim's spiral ramp, reaching some 90 feet above the main floor, offers easy access to the collection.

visitors when "The Art of the Motorcycle" camped in the space.

You do not need to walk all the way to the top (the cantilevered ramp that circles the interior through five levels is a quarter of a mile long); instead, thankfully proceed to the elevators straight ahead.

A visitor ponders a minimalist painting at an exhibit of Russian avant-garde art.

Wright expected visitors to start at the top and work their way down. Though many find the experience unnerving, the 1992 renovation and addition of the ten-story **Gwathmey Siegel Tower** adjacent to the original building has provided the viewer relief during the descent. You may now leave the gradually pitched ramp at each level and walk into a gallery in the tower (where floors do not slope), and then return to the ramp. The alternation of sloping and level gallery experiences reduces the disconcerting effect of a single circular descent.

EXPLORING THE COLLECTION

Exhibits frequently change and not all of the permanent collection is on display at any given time. However, you can always find some examples of works by key artists. The museum's collection includes more than 200 works by Kandinsky. It also has

works by Brancusi, Calder, Delaunay, Klee, Miró, Nevelson, and Piet Mondrian, naming but a few. Favorites include Chagall's "Paris Through the Window" (1913), Léger's "Great Parade" (1954), Modigliani's "Nude" (1917), and Picasso's "Woman Ironing" (1904).

The **Thannhauser tower galleries** (named for Justin K. Thannhauser, a dealer and collector who donated 75 Impressionist and Postimpressionist works) display both the permanent collection and contemporary changing exhibits. Levels 2, 5, and 7 contain larger works, while level 4 is low-ceilinged and holds drawings and smaller paintings, plus the **Robert Mapplethorpe Gallery** for photography. There are also four video viewing rooms integrated in the exhibition galleries, and a fifth-floor sculpture terrace.

Ramp exhibits change frequently, often containing a blockbuster, such as the 1998 Rauschenburg show that flowed over into tower galleries. On ramp 3 are the **Guggenheim Family Galleries.** In 1963, Solomon's niece, Peggy Guggenheim, a gallery owner, collector, and, briefly, wife of Max Ernst, gave the museum works representing surrealism, cubism, and abstract expressionism.

Many of the special exhibits draw large crowds and often forge new artistic or curatorial ground. Jenny Holzer's "Untitled" (1989) from her "Truisms" series consisted of a strip of electronic display signboard mounted along the inside of the ramp. Messages such as "When Something Terrible Happens People Wake Up" appeared on the display, casting a neon glow over the spiral interior. Recent exhibits have featured Jeff Koons's large paintings of modern "food, fashion, and fun" and Rachel Whiteread's sculptures transformed from ordinary objects and architectural spaces. ■

National Academy of Design

LIKE THE FRICK, THIS MUSEUM GIVES THE VISITOR A TASTE of what it was like to be wealthy early in the 20th century. Since 1940 the academy has been housed in this beaux-arts town house, built in 1914 for the railroad heir Archer Huntington and donated by him to the academy in 1940. Archer's wife, Anna, was an academy member. So were Winslow Homer, Augustus Saint-Gaudens, and Frank Lloyd Wright. Recent members include painters Isabel Bishop, Jim Dine, Robert Rauschenberg, and Chuck Close, sculptor Louise Bourgeois, and architects I. M. Pei, Philip Johnson, and Maya Lin.

National Academy of Design and School of Fine Arts
www.nationalacademy.org
- Map p. 133
- 1083 5th Ave. between 89th & 90th Sts.
- 212/369-4880
- Closed Mon.–Tues.
- $$
- Subway: 4, 5, 6 to 86th St.

The National Academy of Design was formed by Asher Durand, Samuel F. B. Morse, and others in 1825 in protest against the domination of the American Academy of Fine Arts by businessmen. With the purpose of increasing recognition of the role of art in America, the new organization helped to make New York the art capital of the nation and left a rich legacy of art treasures that continues to grow. Uniquely governed by member artists, its full name (National Academy of Design and School of Fine Arts) reflects the academy's scope and breadth—the institution encompasses a museum, school of fine arts, and honorary association of artists. Elected by their peers, members are established architects, painters, sculptors, and printmakers. All members are required to donate representative work.

The result is one of the country's largest public collections of 19th- and 20th-century American art. It comprises more than 5,000 works in almost every artistic style, and it is constantly enriched by member gifts. New acquisitions hang in the lobby, an intimate space with a gift shop where original works are for sale. Prominent in the entrance foyer is a bronze sculpture of Diana by Anna Hyatt Huntington.

Galleries on the second and fourth floors offer changing exhibits; the third floor is closed to the public. One popular show mounted from the permanent collection in 2002, for example, was "Transformations: American Paintings from Frederic E. Church to Wayne Thiebaud." For a look at the latest from the national art scene, time your visit to coincide with the month-long Annual Exhibition in late spring, held every year since 1826. ∎

The National Academy of Design and School of Fine Arts' Fifth Avenue home

Cooper-Hewitt National Design Museum

Cooper-Hewitt National Design Museum, Smithsonian Institution

www.ndm.si.edu

🅰 Map pp. 132–33
✉ 2 E. 91st St.
☎ 212/849-8400
🕐 Closed Mon. & a.m. Sun.
💲 $$
🚇 Subway: 4, 5, 6 to 96th St.

Extensive grounds surround the mansion housing the Cooper-Hewitt.

THIS IS THE ONLY DESIGN MUSEUM IN THE UNITED STATES. Its fascinating collection of some quarter of a million objects from all over the world constitutes a history of design, from the sixth century B.C. to the present. And a visit to its home, the former Andrew Carnegie mansion, provides a glimpse of history. It was built between 1899 and 1903 when only squatters lived in this section of Manhattan. Part of the appeal of the 64-room mansion today is its expansive garden and lawn, a reminder that there was much vacant land along Fifth Avenue when Carnegie built his house.

Founded in 1897 as the Cooper Union Museum for the Arts of Decoration, the Cooper-Hewitt has occupied its present quarters only since 1976. Though the museum was undertaken as a resource for decorators, architects, and other professionals, its appeal today is wide-ranging, and its eclectic collection remarkable. Thematic exhibits on urban architecture and graphic design change constantly, weaving material from the collection's four main areas: applied arts and industrial design; drawings and prints; textiles; and wall coverings. There is a small exhibition area on the ground floor and primary galleries on the street-level first floor and second floor. The library and archives on the third floor are open by appointment. An appointment is also needed to visit the Design Resource Center. This deluxe study facility opened in 1998 as part of a four-year, 20-million-dollar renovation.

The house itself is extraordinary, so plan to spend time looking at the interior as well as the collection. On entering the first-floor **Great Hall,** note the wood paneling throughout. Carnegie's use of Scottish oak reflects his love of his homeland. Always interested in new technology and design, Carnegie had his home equipped with the first domestic electric elevator and state-of-the-art air-conditioning and heating systems. On the west side of the hall is a gallery that was formerly his study. The low doorway is a clue to Carnegie's height, for he was only about five foot two.

Other first-floor rooms now identified only as galleries include the **Music Room,** with a bagpipe motif in the ceiling; the Garden Vestibule, with leaded Tiffany windows; the formal **Dining Room,** where guests included such luminaries of the day as Booker T. Washington, Mark Twain, and Madame Curie; and the **Breakfast Room,** overlooking the garden and leading to the skylit conservatory. A popular 1999 exhibit occupying the first floor was "The Architecture of Reassurance: Designing the Disney Theme Parks."

The museum is at its most enjoyable when it pays serious attention to everyday objects— buttons, watches, razors, wallpaper, cameras, computers—almost anything imaginable. One exhibit was devoted to the lowly doghouse—as rendered by leading architects—and another entirely devoted to kitchen utensils. "Design for Life," staged on the museum's centennial in 1997, illustrated the range of the collections. The 300 offerings included 1930s wallpaper, a 1936 cocktail shaker shaped like a penguin, a scale model of the Marmon 16—a sedan designed in 1930 to compete with the Cadillac—and a Tiffany goblet made for Andrew Carnegie in 1907.

INTERIOR DECORATION STARTED HERE

Sarah and Eleanor Hewitt, founders of the museum were, like other wealthy young women of the time, well traveled. They were impressed by the Musée des Arts Decoratifs in Paris and the Victoria and Albert Museum in London and set out to emulate them in their museum in New York.

New York is the undisputed center of American interior design. It owes that status to the Hewitt sisters and others working to develop the field at the turn of the century. The Hewitts believed that by educating the wealthy and the decorators who worked for them, taste would filter down to the masses. Author Edith Wharton echoed the Hewitt philosophy in her influential *The Decoration of Houses:* "When the rich man demands good architecture his neighbors will get it too…every carefully studied detail, exacted by those who can afford to indulge their taste, will in time find its way to the carpenter-built cottage" (1897).

In 1905, Elsie de Wolfe, the country's first professional interior decorator, began catering to the wealthy. That same year, Frank Alvah Parsons introduced interior decoration courses at his art school—today the Parsons School of Design. In 1913 Wanamaker's opened the first interior decorating department in a store. Three years later architect Augustus Sherrill Winton founded the New York School of Interior Decoration (today Design), now a thriving institution at 155 East 56th Street. By the 1970s, interior design was the preferred term. ■

Jewish Museum

HOUSED IN A FRENCH GOTHIC CHÂTEAU-STYLE MANSION, this esteemed institution is an important repository of Jewish culture and art. Through exhibits ranging from contemporary art to rare ethnographic material, and programs designed to engage all ages, Jews and non-Jews alike, it illuminates the remarkable scope and diversity of Jewish culture. The museum's collection holds some 27,000 items, from coins and medals to ceremonial objects, paintings, and archaeological treasures, capturing four thousand years of history.

Jewish Museum
www.thejewishmuseum.org
- Map p. 133
- 1109 5th Ave. at 92nd St.
- 212/423-3200
- Closed Sat.–Sun.
- $$
- Subway: 4, 5, 6 to 96th St.

Right: Near the north end of Museum Row, the Jewish Museum is housed in the former mansion of financier Felix Warburg. Below: An 1803 Jewish Omer calendar from Italy depicts Hercules destroying the Philistine temple.

The first and second floors are devoted to special temporary exhibits, which may be historical or contemporary in nature, and which often attract very large crowds. Recent special exhibitions have included "Paris in New York: French Jewish Artists in Private Collections," featuring painters and sculptors who were influenced by key avant-garde figures such as Henri Matisse and Pablo Picasso.

First-time visitors will not want to miss the permanent exhibition "Culture and Continuity: The Jewish Journey," which begins on the fourth floor and continues throughout the third. Vibrantly installed in 17 galleries, highlights on the fourth floor are a re-creation of an ancient synagogue; a gallery devoted to the Sabbath with an audio installation; and a silver menorah collection.

On the third floor, among the more spectacular artifacts, are the 18th-century Bavarian ark and the Urbino Ark (circa 1500).

On this floor, you can also view selected television and radio programs from the museum's archives or visit the delightful interactive **Children's Gallery.**

Founded in 1904, the Jewish

Museum is operated by the Jewish Theological Seminary. For 40 years the museum's collection was housed in the seminary's library. An important addition was the 1947 purchase of the **Benjamin and Rose Mintze Collection,** 500 items from Poland—kiddush cups, Torah crowns and mantles, and Hanukkah lamps. The museum opened at its present location in 1947. Originally designed by architect C.H.P. Gilbert, the mansion had been built in 1908 for Felix M. Warburg, a Polish-born banker, philanthropist, and leader of the Jewish-American community. ■

Left: A painting by Russian-born Max Weber (1881–1961)

Museum of the City of New York

Museum of the City of New York
www.mcny.org

⚠ Map p. 133

✉ 1220 5th Ave. at 103rd St.

☎ 212/534-1672

🕐 Closed Mon.

💲 Donation

🚇 Subway: 6 to 103rd St.

IN 1923 NEW YORK CITY DECIDED THAT, LIKE PARIS AND London and other great cities, it must have a museum to document its history. The result of this decision is the Museum of the City of New York, a treasure-house of some 1.5 million objects from Dutch colonial times to the present. This is a place for many tastes and audiences, from those who simply want to sample the broad range of the city's history, to those with specialized interests, be it firefighting, toys, furniture, silver, theater, prints, or paintings.

Here you can find such seemingly unrelated displays as the charred timbers from a 17th-century merchantman that burned off Manhattan; furniture of New York cabinetmaker Duncan Phyfe; and Gypsy Rose Lee's "chaste G-string with her name embroidered in blue silk by her own hand." There is an outstanding collection of Currier &

A stunning collection of theatrical costumes and memorabilia tells the story of the Broadway show.

Ives prints and a photo archive that includes the **Jacob Riis Collection.** If you're lucky, perhaps you'll catch some of the museum's treasures not often displayed, including vintage Barbie dolls, a lock of George Washington's hair, and Bill "Bojangles" Robinson's shoes. The museum continues to search for larger premises so that more of the collection can be shown.

The museum left its original home in Gracie Mansion, today's Mayoral Mansion, and opened at its present neo-Georgian building in January 1932. Exhibits here spread out over five floors, changing frequently. On the entry-level first floor are a gift shop and three galleries devoted to major changing exhibitions. Shows here are the most publicized and attract large crowds. Examples of recent shows include "Last Day of Penn Station," photographs by Aaron Rose, "Raíces: The Roots of Latin Music in New York City," and "The Lubavitch of Brooklyn, An Intimate Portrait: Photography by Steve Hoffman."

An elevator down to the ground floor brings you to the **Fire Gallery.** This unusual themed exhibition is filled with prints, paintings, artifacts, and other memorabilia related to fires, plus antique fire engines. One is the "Big Six," the 1851 fire engine belonging to the volunteer fire company that gave William Marcy "Boss" Tweed his start in city politics. A snarling tiger, the symbol of Tammany Hall, is painted on the front panel.

Also on the ground floor is the **City Partners Gallery,** where city-based organizations partner with MCNY to tell their stories. A recent exhibition was "The Mount Sinai Hospital, 1852–2002: Extraordinary People, Extraordinary Medicines."

UPPER FLOORS

On the second floor you may wish to see "The Big Apple," a 22-minute short on New York City that is shown often. Also on this floor is an ongoing installation of cityscapes from the collection called "Painting the Town." Beyond are the **Period Alcoves,** six rooms re-creating the unique interiors of New York houses from the late 17th to the early 20th century. The Flagler Drawing Room, from a 1906 Park Avenue home, was originally inspired by the Sala Della Zodiaco in the Ducal Palace at Mantua, while an 18th-century colonial parlor has Chinese handpainted wallpaper. At the other end of the hall, dioramas, artifacts, paintings, and models are devoted to New York's maritime history.

The third floor holds **New York Toy Stories,** always a popular exhibit. A highlight is its collection of dollhouses and doll furniture from 1769 to the present. Especially captivating is the dollhouse created by Carrie Stettheimer in the 1920s. Its interior includes an art gallery with miniatures of paintings by Marcel Duchamp and other artists of the first New York Avant Garde. "Broadway! A History of the American Theater" is also on the third floor, plus a gallery for changing exhibits that held "Richard Rodgers' Broadway" in 2002. The fourth floor is closed to the public.

On the fifth floor visit the **Rockefeller Rooms,** an opulent 1880s master bedroom and dressing room from the West 54th Street home of John D. Rockefeller, Sr. With such details as woodwork with floral inlays, red damask chairs and chaises, and even a "Turkish corner" in the bedroom, the rooms are no more extravagant than you might expect in the quarters of one of the city's most prominent businessmen. ■

The sumptuous late 19th-century bedroom of John D. Rockefeller, Sr., has been reassembled in the Museum of the City of New York.

Neue Galerie New York

**Neue Galerie
New York**
www.neuegalerie.org
🅰 Map p. 133
✉ 1048 5th Ave.
(enter on 86th St.)
☎ 212/628-6200
🕐 Closed Tues.–Thurs.
💲 $$
🚇 Subway: 4, 5, 6 to
86th St. at
Lexington Ave.; or
B, C to 86th St. at
Central Park West

Note: Children under
12 not admitted;
those 13-15 must
be accompanied by
an adult.

**The museum's
lovely Louis XIII-
style beaux-arts
facade**

FOR A MUSEUM WITH A EUROPEAN FLAVOR, VISIT THIS newcomer to Fifth Avenue's Museum Mile. Housed in a splendid 1914 beaux-arts limestone mansion once owned by a Vanderbilt, the Neue Galerie New York is devoted to early 20th-century German and Austrian art and design. Its works represent the pinnacle of the modernist German Expressionism and Bauhaus movements in Vienna and Berlin between 1900 and 1938, after which the Nazis banned experimental art.

The transformation of one of Fifth Avenue's most opulent landmark residences into a museum began with the dream of two collectors. Ronald Lauder, philanthropist and businessman son of cosmetics magnate Estee Lauder, and art dealer Serge Sabarsky envisioned a museum that would exhibit the best examples of the German and Austrian art they loved. Sabarsky purchased the building for the Neue Galerie in 1994. After Sabarsky's death in 1996, Lauder bought the building and made their dream a reality. Neue Galerie means "new gallery" in German and comes from the modernist wave of European galleries, especially Vienna's Neue Galerie, founded in 1923.

The collection is made up of more than 800 works from the Sabarsky Foundation, 500 from the Lauder family, and 100 purchased by the museum. Included are more than 100 paintings and graphic works by the artists Gustav Klimt and Egon Schiele, the largest holding of works by these artists outside Vienna.

VISITING THE GALLERY
On the first floor are a bookstore; a design center selling many items exclusive to the museum; and the Viennese-style Café Sabarsky, with authentic Austrian meals and superb pastries and coffee. Expect a line, but it is well worth the wait.

On the second floor, you'll find galleries containing paintings and drawings from turn-of-the-20th-century Vienna. Signature works include Klimt's "Dancer" in oil (1916–18) and numerous Schiele self-portraits. Oskar Kokoschka, Max Beckmann, and Emil Nolde are also represented.

The third-floor galleries feature German movements and artists, from Vasily Kandinsky and Paul Klee to Laszlo Moholy-Nagy and Ludwig Mies van der Rohe.

Decorative arts from the Wiener Werkstätte and Bauhaus design movements, including sleek furniture, decorative jewelry, ceiling fixtures, and flatware, are also on display.

Lectures, music, films, and cabaret performances are offered; ask the museum for a schedule. ∎

El Museo del Barrio

EL MUSEO DEL BARRIO, AT THE NORTH END OF MUSEUM Row, is dedicated to the art and culture of Latin America, especially Puerto Rico, the homeland of so many residents of nearby East, or Spanish, Harlem. Del Barrio preserves and documents both traditional folk arts and the contemporary urban art of the barrio, the city's Spanish-speaking enclave.

Founded in 1969, the museum grew out of the turmoil of the 1960s, when local Puerto Rican artists began protesting their lack of representation in downtown museums. The permanent collection contains more than 8,000 objects from all over Latin America and the Caribbean: pre-Columbian ceramics and vessels from the Taino culture of Puerto Rico and the Dominican Republic; Mexican masks; santos, or carved saints; paintings, sculptures, works on paper; and photographs by artists of Latin American descent.

The spacious white-walled museum occupies the ground floor in the Heckscher Building. This city-owned structure houses other organizations and a theater where del Barrio presents films and videos. After entering the building, turn left to access the museum through its gift shop. Works are exhibited in a number of spaces, beginning with the **Contemporanea Gallery** for

recent works. An important aim of the gallery is to disseminate art of the barrio, and work by the artists of El Taller, an artist-run collective, may be seen here.

The **Borinquen Gallery** is named for the Taino Indian word for Puerto Rico. It holds the highlight of the permanent collection of sculptural works, "Santos de Palo," an assemblage of 240 carved and painted saints. Made by artisans from Puerto Rico, Spain, Mexico, Guatemala, and the Philippines, usually for home devotions, most date from the 19th and early 20th centuries.

Major exhibitions are in the **East Gallery** and **Alegria Gallery.** Examples from the past include "The Art of Jack Delano," the first show to gather the complete range of photographs, films, posters, and book illustrations Delano created in Puerto Rico over the past 50 years, and "Gods, Spirits, and Legends," 20th-century art from El Salvador. ■

El Museo del Barrio
www.elmuseo.org
- Map p. 133
- 1230 5th Ave. at 104th St.
- 212/831-7272
- Closed Mon.–Tues.
- Donation
- Subway: 6 to 103rd St.

Above & below: Wooden santos, highlights of the museum's permanent collection

More stops along Upper Fifth Avenue

FRENCH EMBASSY, OFFICE OF CULTURAL SERVICES

Housed in a 1904 bow-front mansion, one of Stanford White's "most successful Italian High Renaissance-inspired designs," this organization mounts small exhibits in the second-floor parlor of the former home of Harry Payne Whitney and his wife, Gertrude Vanderbilt Whitney, founder of the Whitney Museum.
✉ 972 5th Ave. at 79th St. ☎ 212/439-1400 🕐 Closed weekends 🚇 Subway: 6 to 77th St.

GOETHE HOUSE

Founded in 1957, Goethe House is run by the Goethe Institut in Munich for the purpose of promoting German language study and cultural exchange and offers changing exhibits on German culture. Its 1907 beaux-arts town house was extensively renovated in 1991. An exhibit, "Interrelations and Migrations: Contemporary Sculpture from Germany," marked its reopening following the renovation.
✉ 1014 5th Ave., between 82nd and 83rd Sts. ☎ 212/439-8700 🕐 Closed Sun. 🚇 Subway: 4, 5, 6 to 86th St.

NEW YORK ACADEMY OF SCIENCES

Formed in 1817, the academy is housed in a Renaissance-style mansion (1919–1920) built for William Ziegler, Jr., president of a baking powder company. The academy mounts shows on subjects combining art and science, for instance, Berenice Abbott's photographs on "The Beauty of Physics."
✉ 2 E. 63rd St. ☎ 212/838-0230 🕐 Closed Sun. 🚇 Subway: 4, 5, 6, N, R to 59th St.

UKRAINIAN INSTITUTE OF AMERICA

Housed in a building that once belonged to a direct descendant of Peter Stuyvesant, the institute has a permanent collection that includes contemporary painting and sculpture, religious items, textiles, costumes, and *pysanky*, decorated Easter eggs. A Ukrainian immigrant, inventor William Kzus, founded the institute in 1955 and donated the building.
✉ 2 E. 79th St. ☎ 212/288-8660 🕐 Closed Mon. 💲 Donation suggested 🚇 Subway: 6 to 77th St. ■

Pysanky **from the collection of the Ukrainian Institute of America**

In & around the
Upper East Side

THE UPPER EAST SIDE HAS SUCH AN ABUNDANCE OF landmark buildings that you can wander its streets and avenues at will and spot eye-pleasing architecture, much of it from a more gracious past.

You can find elegant designer clothing and shoppers at stores along Madison Avenue in the 60s, or wander floor to floor at **Bloomingdale's** *(1000 3rd Ave., tel 212/705-2000),* which reigns over an entire city block. But for sightseeing, some places close to the East River deserve special notice, such as the tiny sunken parks overlooking the river at 57th Street and Sutton Place. Here, in one of New York's most exclusive neighborhoods, you may sit on benches and enjoy the river view.

A bird's-eye view of the city can be had by taking the aerial tram at 59th Street and Second Avenue to Roosevelt Island and back *(212/832-4555. $).* Also on the East River, **The Rockefeller University** *(1230 York Ave.)* is a world-renowned research institute for medicine and the physical sciences. Founded by John D. Rockefeller in 1901, the university moved here in 1906.

MOUNT VERNON HOTEL MUSEUM & GARDEN

This quiet site may seem out of place, but from 1826 to 1833, as an elegant country day retreat, it welcomed the city's burgeoning upper middle class. The museum illuminates early 19th-century hotel life. Originally the land was part of a 23-acre plot purchased in 1795 by Col. Stephen Smith and his wife, Abigail Adams (daughter of President John Adams), who christened the site Mount Vernon, after President

Washington's home. Finances forced them to sell before they could build, but the name remained. An enterprising merchant opened the first Mount Vernon Hotel on the site in 1808. Fire destroyed the building in 1826, but another hotel followed when the next owner converted the surviving stone carriage house into a much finer day resort. It was sold after 1833 for a private residence.

In the 1930s the Colonial Dames of America rescued the building. Its reinterpretation was completed in 2000 and its furnished rooms reflect its heyday. Men caroused in the Tavern Room or retreated to the more sedate Gentleman's Parlor. Women enjoyed singing and needlework in the richly decorated Ladies' Double Parlors. This is a rare architectural time capsule, replete with artifacts and a sense of times past. ∎

Mount Vernon Hotel Museum & Garden
www.mountvernonmuseum.org
- Map p. 133
- 421 E. 61st St. between 1st & York Aves.
- 212/838-6878
- Closed Mon. & Aug.
- $
- Subway: 4, 5, 6 to 59th St.

The Mount Vernon Hotel Museum, built of Manhattan schist, offers a rare glimpse into life in a 19th-century day resort.

The Cosmopolitan Club is an elite meetingplace for professional New York women.

Silk stocking district

10021. Just another zip code to most of us, but not to demographers who know it as the wealthiest postal zone in the United States: from East 61st to East 80th Street between Fifth Avenue and the East River. At its heart is the Upper East Side's wealthy silk stocking district. This is where the institutions of wealth, power, and social standing are located—the city's fanciest clubs, the best private schools, and architecturally distinguished churches and synagogues. The buildings that house them are often not open to the public, but many are landmarks well worth a look.

At the hub (but south of the geographic center) of the silk stocking district is the fortresslike 1880 Seventh Regiment Armory *(643 Park Ave. between E. 66th and E. 67th Sts.).* When socially prominent New Yorkers formed the unit in 1847, it was known as the Silk Stocking Regiment. The men designed their own uniforms and raised the money for the armory, which has distinguished interior rooms by Louis Comfort Tiffany and other designers. The drill room, 100 feet high and

measuring 200 by 300 feet, is the largest unobstructed interior space in the city. Instead of soldiering, bluebloods today go to the armory to play tennis. Though home to the National Guard, it is also home to the city's best antiques shows and a restaurant, the Seventh Regiment Mess.

From the armory it's only a few steps to the haunts of the elite, not all of whom, by any means, are men. Literally in the armory's shadow, the Cosmopolitan Club *(122 E. 66th St., closed to the public)* is a refuge for professional women. Its counterpart for society women, the Colony Club *(564 Park Ave. at E. 62nd St., closed to the public),* founded in 1903, is located in a 1916 building designed by Delano & Aldrich. The Lotos Club *(5 E. 66th St., closed to the public),* the city's oldest literary society, is in a 1900 house. It was designed by Richard Howland Hunt for William Schiefflin, a well-born (great-great-grandson of John Jay) and effective political reformer.

The Union Club *(101 E. 69th St., closed to the public),* founded in 1836, is only two blocks away in 1933 quarters designed by

Delano & Aldrich. The nearby Metropolitan Club *(1 E. 60th St., closed to the public)* was founded by Union Club members disgruntled when their friends and relatives were turned down for membership. The Metropolitan is housed in an 1893 building designed by McKim, Mead & White, who also did, in 1906, the Harmonie Club *(4 E. 60th St., closed to the public)*, founded by German Jews in 1852.

The spiritual needs of the silk stocking district are met by a variety of churches and synagogues. Within view of the armory, the neo-Gothic Central Presbyterian Church *(Park Ave. and E. 64th St.)*, built between 1920 and 1922, was originally the Baptist church where John D. Rockefeller worshiped. Socially prominent Episcopalians can still expect to be christened, confirmed, married, and eulogized at St. James Episcopal Church *(865 Madison Ave. at E. 71st St.)*. This neo-Gothic church (1884) was rebuilt in 1924 by architect Ralph Adams Cram.

Roman Catholics and Jews, once excluded from the seat of power, are today well represented in the silk stocking district. The 1929 Temple Emanu-El *(5th Ave. and E. 65th St.)*, a combination of western and Byzantine architectural styles, was the first reformed congregation in the city. It is one of the largest synagogues in the world, seating 2,500—more than St. Patrick's Cathedral.

Well-scrubbed schoolchildren accompanied by nannies or governesses, go to such prestigious and academically rigorous area institutions as Dalton, Chapin, and Brearley; there is also John Kennedy, Jr.'s alma mater, St. David's *(12–16 E. 89th St.)*, in a row of neo-Georgian town houses designed in 1919 by Delano & Aldrich.

It all seems so idyllic—genteel neighborhoods, beautiful people, elegant architecture—like a picture-perfect small town in the middle of a tumultuous city. But, before giving in to envy, consider the palatial 1931 limestone mansion at 56 East 93rd Street, home to impresario Billy Rose from 1955 until his death in 1966. Now it is a drug-and-alcohol rehabilitation center catering to the troubled among the privileged—proof that all is not bliss in paradise. ■

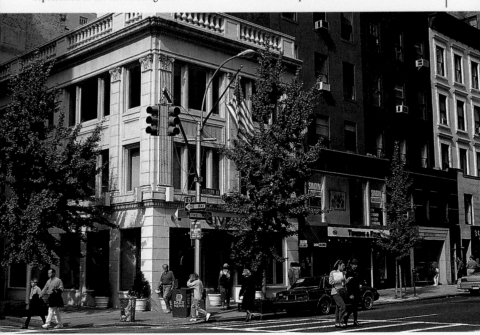

The elegant Upper East Side

Whitney Museum of American Art

THE WHITNEY MUSEUM IS UNUSUAL IN SEVERAL RESPECTS.
It is one of the few museums anywhere founded by an artist, in this
case, Gertrude Vanderbilt Whitney. A member of two of New York's
most prominent and wealthy families, she was also a sculptor with a
taste for the avant-garde. The Whitney is still one of the few museums
dedicated to American art of the 20th century, and one that energet-
ically seeks out independent artists in fields other places overlook,
such as film and video. Its invitational spring Biennial, first held in
1932, continues to stir up controversy with its exhibition of emerging
American artists and trends.

**Whitney Museum
of American Art**
www.whitney.org
🅰 Map p. 133
✉ 945 Madison Ave.
   at 75th St.
☎ 212/570-3676
🕐 Closed Mon.
💲 $$
🚇 Subway: 6 to 77th St.

The Whitney's present modern
home was designed by the Bauhaus
architect Marcel Breuer in 1966. The
massive three-story granite building
is cantilevered out like the steps of
an inverted pyramid, with an
entrance ramp above a "moat." That
area holds a popular brunch spot,
Sarabeth's *(Tel 212/570-3670)*,
accessed through the museum. On
the first floor is a bookstore and gift
shop and, past the turnstile, a small
gallery. Here and in galleries on the
next three floors, more recent hold-
ings rotate, interspersed with tem-
porary exhibits. Some are thematic,
such as one on the Beats, while oth-
ers feature contemporary artists,
such as William Wegman, and
African-American artist Bob
Thompson (1937–1966). One whole
gallery is devoted to photography, a
relatively new area for the Whitney.
Here the works of Diane Arbus,
Weegee, and Robert Mapplethorpe
are among those on display. The
**Whitney Museum at Phillip
Morris** *(120 Park Ave., tel 917/663-
2453)* also displays holdings from
the collection.

PERMANENT COLLECTION

A renovation and expansion pro-
ject, completed in 1998, created
new Permanent Collection galleries

on the museum's fifth floor and
mezzanine levels. The **Leonard
& Evelyn Lauder Galleries**
are devoted exclusively to the
Whiteney's collection of 20th-
century American art. They feature
a significant selection of works
from 1900 to 1950, including such
greats as Edward Hopper, Marsden

The building for
the **Whitney
Museum** is itself
an example of
20th-century art.
The severe
rectangular block
of granite-clad
reinforced
concrete was
designed by
Marcel Breuer
in 1966.

Hartley, Georgia O'Keeffe, Stuart Davis, Arshile Gorky, and Alexander Calder. Favorites include Calder's playful sculpture "Circus" (1926–1931); O'Keeffe's "Flower Abstraction" (1926); and Hopper's "Early Sunday Morning" (1930).

In 2000 the museum dedicated its second-floor **Mildred and Herbert Lee Galleries** to an ongoing exhibition of collection's key postwar and contemporary works. Willem De Kooning, Andy Warhol, Jasper Johns, Philip Guston, Alex Katz, Joseph Stella, Jackson Pollock, Louise Nevelson, and Kiki Smith are just some of the names you'll recognize here. Keep an eye out for Warhol's "Green Coca-Cola Bottles" (1962); Johns's "Three Flags" (1958); and Nevelson's "Black Majesty" (1955).

The Permanent Collection holds approximately 13,000 paintings, sculptures, prints, drawings, and photographs representing more than 2,000 artists.

A CONTINUING FORCE FOR CHANGE

The Whitney Museum was founded at a time when America did not take its own art seriously and regarded its artists, in John Sloan's words, "like cockroaches in kitchens—not wanted, not encouraged …" The Whitney Museum is largely responsible for changing that attitude—and the debates sparked annually by its Biennial are a sign that it is still an agent for change. The Whitney describes itself as "the Whitney Museum, the Advocate for 20th-century American Art." The new permanent collection galleries will allow the Whitney to continue to excel in the often fierce field of museum acquisitions and exhibitions. ∎

Edward Hopper's "Early Sunday Morning," a cornerstone of the Whitney collection

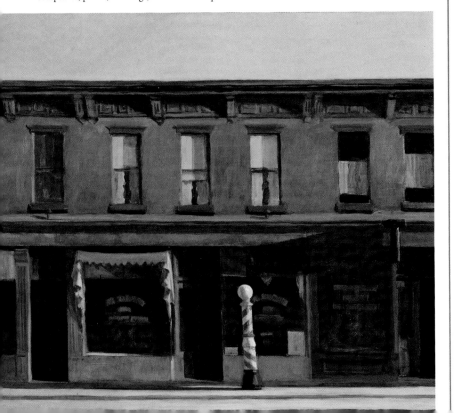

More places to visit

ASIA SOCIETY

This repository of Asian art and culture is housed in a 1981 red granite building designed by Edward Larrabee Barnes. Its permanent collection of Asian art and crafts is based on one compiled by John D. Rockefeller, III, who founded the society in 1956 to promote American understanding of Asian art and culture.
✉ 725 Park Ave. at 70th St. ☎ 212/517-2742 ⏱ Closed Sun. 💲 $ 🚇 Subway: 6 to 68th St.

GRACIE MANSION, THE MAYORAL HOME

This well-preserved federal house was built in 1799 by shipping merchant Archibald Gracie on the site of a Revolutionary fort. In 1924, the house, by then city-owned, became the first home of the Museum of the City of New York, which occupied it until 1932. In 1942 it became the mayor's official residence. Guided tours, on Wednesdays only, require reservations and include the mayor's study featuring Childe Hassam lithographs of New York street scenes and a permanent exhibit on the history of the house. Gracie

Once a country estate, Gracie Mansion today functions as the mayor's official residence and an uptown branch of City Hall.

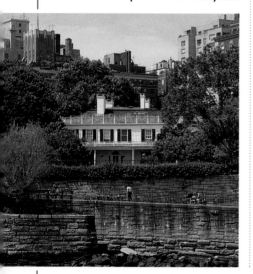

Mansion is located in **Carl Schurz Park,** an uncrowded, ten-acre, riverside tract with wonderful views of the East River and Roosevelt Island.
✉ 88th St. and E. End Ave. ☎ 212/570-4751 ⏱ Open Wed. only; reservations required (allow 2 weeks for processing) 💲 Donation 🚇 Subway: 4, 5, 6 to 86th St.

NEW YORK SOCIETY LIBRARY

The city's oldest library, housed in a landmark town house (1916–17). It is open to the public, although only members can borrow books.
✉ 53 E. 79th St. ☎ 212/288-6900 🚇 Subway: 6 to 77th St.

SOCIETY OF ILLUSTRATORS: MUSEUM OF AMERICAN ILLUSTRATION

This unusual museum exhibits commercial illustration, an art form not usually displayed. Housed in an 1875 carriage house, the society, founded in 1901 to promote the art of commercial illustration, had as early members such notables as Charles Dana Gibson, William Glackens, Norman Rockwell, and Frederic Remington. The museum's collection consists of some 1,500 original works from 1838 to the present. There is an extensive bookstore.
✉ 128 E. 63rd St. between Park & Lexington Aves. ☎ 212/838-2560 ⏱ Closed Sun.–Mon. 💲 Donation suggested 🚇 Subway: N, R to 60th St.

EPISCOPAL CHURCH OF THE HOLY TRINITY, YORKVILLE

This complex of French Renaissance-style structures was built in 1896–99 to serve the immigrant population of Yorkville. This once mainly German-Hungarian neighborhood runs from East 77th to 96th Streets between the East River and Lexington Avenue. For a bit of the ethnic East Side, there is a stretch along Second Avenue in the mid-80s with traditional German shops and delicatessens.
✉ 316–322 E. 88th St. ☎ 212/289-4100 🚇 Subway: 4, 5, 6 to 86th St. ∎

Central Park is aptly named. It is 800 or so acres of greenery located smack-dab in the middle of Manhattan. Nearly everyone in the city uses it at one time or another, be it for exercise or a rare commune with nature.

Central Park

At bat in Central Park

Central Park

ONE LITTLE-KNOWN FACT ABOUT CENTRAL PARK: ITS
gates—at least its 18 original ones—have names, although only
three are inscribed: the Inventors', Mariners', and Engineers'
Gates. Unbeknownst, you may be entering through the
Artists' Gate (Central Park South and Sixth Avenue) or, at
the opposite, northern end, the Warriors' Gate, or at
some other titled entrance. There are, however, no gates
named for the some 20 million people a year who use
the park: joggers, skateboarders, birdwatchers,
cyclists, softball players, sunbathers, chess players,
lovers, Rollerbladers, model boat sailors, kite
fliers, tourists, sketch artists, and more.

Manhattan

Area of map detail

0   600 yards
0   600 meters

110th Street-
Cathedral
Parkway

FREDERICK
DOUGLASS
CIRCLE

THE GREAT
HILL

103rd
Street

The Pool

WEST DRIVE

The
Loch

NORTH
MEADOW

96th
Street

97TH ST. TRANSVERSE

CENTRAL

Jacqueline
Kennedy Onassis
Reservoir

CENTRAL PARK WEST

WEST DRIVE

EAST DRIVE

86th
Street

86TH ST. TRANSVERSE

81st Street-
Museum of
Natural History

THE GREAT
LAWN

Delacorte
SHAKESPEARE Theater
GARDEN   Cleopatra's
Needle

79TH ST. TRANSVERSE   Turtle
Pond

Metropolitan
Museum of Art

Belvedere
Castle

PARK

The
Lake

THE RAMBLE

72nd
Street

STRAWBERRY
FIELDS

Bethesda
Fountain
and Terrace

Alice in
Wonderland

Hans Christian
Andersen   Conservatory
Water

Tavern
on the
Green

The
Pilgrim

72ND ST. TRANSVERSE

THE MALL

SHEEP
MEADOW

Robert
Burns

The Indian
Hunter

Mother
Goose

EAST
GREEN

FIFTH AVENUE

CENTRAL PARK WEST

WEST DRIVE

65TH ST
TRANSVERSE

Balto

HECKSCHER
SOFTBALL FIELDS

William
Shakespeare

CENTER DRIVE

59th Street-
Columbus Circle

COLUMBUS
CIRCLE

The
Dairy

Central Park
Wildlife Center
The
Arsenal

The
Pond

EAST DRIVE

5th
Avenue

CENTRAL PARK SOUTH

GRAND
ARMY
PLAZA

CENTRAL PARK

1 The Carousel
2 Children's Gate
3 Bow Bridge
4 Swedish Cottage

Charles A. Dana Discovery Center

110th Street-Central Park North

DUKE ELLINGTON CIRCLE

Harlem Meer

CONSERVATORY GARDEN

EAST MEADOW

CENTRAL PARK NORTH

EAST DRIVE

FIFTH AVENUE

Central Park, the first large public park in America, is a product of vision, revision, and compromise. Its inspiration were the great parks of London and Paris. Wealthy New Yorkers believed that a park in New York would add to the city's cachet, give them a place to drive their carriages, and provide the working classes with healthful recreation. Although the park has gone through periods of neglect and deterioration (a recent renovation ended one such cycle), it has consistently played an important role in city life. It is more than just greenery; critic Paul Goldberger has called it "the nonbuilding that could well lay claim to being New York's greatest work of architecture."

When you visit Central Park today, you will see it at its spanking best. Improvements, undertaken at the initiative of the Central Park Conservancy, a private fund-raising group that contributes substantially to the park's operating budget, have ranged from reseeding the Great Lawn to restoring the Swedish Cottage, a reproduction—recently renovated—of a typical Swedish schoolhouse of the 19th century that was shipped to this country for the 1876 Philadelphia Centennial Exposition. Other important park additions include the new nature center in the imposing, lakeside fortress known as Belvedere Castle.

GREENSWARD PLAN: AN URBAN VISION

Central Park's naturalistic landscaping successfully hides its mostly man-made origins. The area, now 843 acres, was filled with shanties and small farms when the state legislature, in 1853, authorized the city to seize a 700-acre parcel in the middle of Manhattan.

Four years later, the Central Park Commission held a contest to determine the design of the park. The winning entry, a "Greensward plan," based on romantic landscaping notions then popular in England, was submitted by Frederick Law Olmsted, who would oversee its construction as the park's superintendent, and his partner, Calvert Vaux. The plan stressed variety and contrast: open meadows, dense woods, and formal areas such as the Mall. The park's "one great purpose," Olmsted wrote, is "to supply to the hundreds of thousands of tired workers, who have no opportunity to spend their summers in the country, a specimen of God's handiwork …."

It took some 20,000 laborers 20 years to construct Central Park, which opened in 1859, before work was complete. In that time, they removed almost three million cubic yards of soil, blasted the rocky outcroppings to create the picturesque rifts the Olmsted-Vaux plan called for, planted four or five million trees and 816 varieties of other plants, drained marshlands, and dug the reservoir now named for Jacqueline Kennedy Onassis, which today is circumscribed by a popular 1.6-mile jogging track.

In its early years, the park was a preserve of the wealthy and their carriages; the strict rules discouraged others by prohibiting group activities such as picnics. Over the years, these rules were relaxed, then eliminated. At the same time, there were encroachments on the park's open space: wings added to the Metropolitan Museum of Art, the Tavern on the Green restaurant, two skating rinks, playgrounds, tennis courts, and other facilities, most of which were opposed by those who objected to any alteration of the original Greensward plan. (Proposals for a horse-racing track, an airstrip, and an underground garage were defeated.) The parks commissioner, Robert Moses, once tried to pave over a playground to enlarge the parking lot for the Tavern on the Green. His scheme was defeated by mothers pushing baby carriages, who blocked his bulldozers.

It was through this sort of give and take that Central Park became what it is today: a remarkable expanse of greenery in the midst of some of the most valuable real estate on Earth. ∎

Around Central Park

WHERE TO START? THE MAJOR ATTRACTIONS ARE SOUTH of 86th Street, so you might begin with a group of attractions near the Children's Gate (64th Street and Fifth Avenue) and work your way north. Descend the stairs off Fifth Avenue to the Arsenal, a redbrick fortress built in 1848 to house armaments, now the Parks Department headquarters.

Central Park information center
www.centralparknyc.org
- ✉ The Dairy, 65th St.
- ☎ 212/794-6564
- 🕐 Closed Mon.

Central Park Wildlife Center
- ✉ Children's Gate, 5th Ave. at E. 64th St.
- ☎ 212/861-6030 or 212/439-6500
- 🕐 Sea lions fed at 11:30, 2, 4
- 💲 $
- 🚌 Bus: M1-4 Subway: N, R to 5th Ave.; 6 to 68th St.

The walkway around the building will take you to the **Central Park Wildlife Center,** which offers its 450 residents natural settings instead of cages. Feeding time for the sea lions is a favorite with children, as is the adjacent **Tisch Children's Zoo.** West of the zoo is the **Dairy,** an 1870 building designed by Calvert Vaux, now a park information center. Contact the Dairy about free walking tours of the park, offered by the Central Park Conservancy.

Beyond is the Chess and Checkers Building (secure chess pieces at the Dairy with a deposit) and the **Carousel,** the latter a Coney Island transplant and, at a dollar a ride, one of the park's most popular attractions. Footpaths in the park meander, so do not worry if you begin to wonder where you are. There are signs, and local visitors can help with directions as well. Plus, it is fun to wander—as long as it is daytime.

Northwest of the Dairy, the **Sheep Meadow** is a huge expanse of lawn. Next to it on the east is the **Mall** (between 66th and 72nd Sts.), a formal promenade lined with American elms, which includes the sculpture-lined Literary Walk at its southern end. At the northern end are steps to the **Bethesda Fountain Terrace** (at 72nd St.). This two-level architectural space centers on the sculptured fountain, "Angels in the Water," by Emma

Central Park was not at all "central" when created, but has since been hemmed in by the city.

Carousel
- ✉ 64th St.
- ☎ 212/879-0244
- 🕐 Closed Mon.–Tues. Jan.–March
- 💲 $

Loeb Boathouse
- ☎ 212/517-3623
- 💲 $$$$ (plus refundable deposit)

Central Park Summerstage
- ✉ Rumsey Playfield
- ☎ 212/360-2777 or 212/360-2756
- 🕐 Summer only

Swedish Cottage
- ✉ Near West Drive
- ☎ 212/988-9093
- 🕐 Open summer only, call for hours
- 💲 $$. Reservations required.

Shakespeare in the Park
- ✉ Delacorte Theater
- ☎ 212/861-7277
- 🕐 Summer only
- 💲 Free, but tickets required.

Henry Luce Nature Observatory
- ✉ Belvedere Castle
- ☎ 212/772-0210
- 🕐 Closed Mon.

Stebbins. It overlooks the serpentine 18-acre body of water known as the **Lake.** Boats and bikes can be rented at the **Loeb Boathouse** on the Lake's eastern end *(74th St.)*, and there is a delightful open-air bar/café. Closer to Fifth Avenue *(at 74th St.)* is **Conservatory Pond,** where remote-controlled boats are raced and where there is an ice-cream café.

West of Bethesda Terrace are sites that honor musician John Lennon, who was killed in front of his Dakota Apartment home nearby in 1980. His widow, Yoko Ono, funded **Strawberry Fields** (named for Lennon's song "Strawberry Fields Forever"), a 2.5-acre, tear-shaped garden just off the entrance at Central Park West at 72nd Street. Naples, Italy, donated the nearby sidewalk mosaic, with the word "Imagine" (another Lennon song) at the center.

Throughout the summer, free events—from concerts to opera to readings, all with professional performers—happen daily at **Central Park Summerstage** at Rumsey Playfield. For the action-minded, there are free Rollerblading clinics at the West 72nd Street park entrance from April through October.

The cast-iron Bow Bridge (mid-park around 74th Street) across the Lake leads to the **Ramble,** a 37-acre, hilly maze of paths and foliage, a favorite with birds and bird-watchers. Near the park's West Drive *(around 79th St.)* is **Swedish Cottage.** Next door, the **Shakespeare Garden,** established in 1916 on the 300th anniversary of the Bard's death, contains half the plants mentioned in his plays. Shakespeare and other plays are performed at the open-air **Delacorte Theater** each summer by the New York Shakespeare Festival.

On Turtle Pond, formerly Belvedere Lake, picturesque Belvedere Castle nestles into the rock outcropping. The castle houses the **Henry Luce Nature Observatory.** The Wood and Water Discovery Room is at the center of the observatory's child-oriented educational programs.

To children especially, there is no better statue in Central Park than this bronze grouping of Alice and friends.

Sculpture in the park

The first statue in Central Park, a bronze bust of German dramatist and philosopher Johann Christoph Friedrich von Schiller, was placed in the Ramble in 1859. Other literary figures are represented on the Mall's southern end along Literary Walk, including Robert Burns and Walter Scott. The only American is Fitz-Greene Halleck, a minor but well-known poet and a member of the literary Knickerbocker Group. American sculptor John Quincy Adams Ward did the bronze statue of William Shakespeare, the realistic "Indian Hunter" (1886), located southwest of the Mall, and "The Pilgrim" (1884) on the 72nd Street transverse, just south of Conservatory Lake. Here, children climb over the bronze grouping, "Alice in Wonderland" (1959) by Jose de Creeft, and sit on the lap of "Hans Christian Andersen" (1956), rendered in bronze by Georg John Lober, with a book open on his lap and a duckling at his feet. ∎

Charles A. Dana Discovery Center

✉ Northern shore, Harlem Meer

☎ 212/860-1370

🕐 Closed Mon.

Lasker Rink

✉ Between 106th & 108th Sts.

☎ 212/534-5639

💲 $. Call for rental & lesson fees.

The Great Lawn, recently re-planted and reseeded, is where the Metropolitan Opera and the New York Philharmonic perform free summer concerts. It is behind the Metropolitan Museum of Art, where **Cleopatra's Needle,** the park's most prominent landmark, is also located. This 65-foot-tall, granite obelisk, dating from about 1475 B.C., was Egypt's gift to the U.S. in 1885.

The park north of here is wilder and less densely peopled. An exception is the jogging track, scheduled for restoration, around the 106-acre Jacqueline Kennedy Onassis Reservoir. The **Conservatory Garden** (5th

Ave. at 105th St.) is entered through the Vanderbilt Gate that once graced the Vanderbilt mansion on Fifth Avenue. The symmetrical formal garden with two sculptural fountains is noted for its seasonal plantings.

At the northern end of the park is the 11-acre Harlem Meer. On its northern shore, the **Charles A. Dana Discovery Center** offers nature programs for children and families. Here is some of the park's wildest scenery. If you are looking for a wintertime activity in a splendid outdoor setting, try the **Lasker Rink.** In the warmer months, it's a swimming pool. ∎

Spread out between two of the city's best parks, this is a lively area inhabited by people who are devoted to their neighborhoods. Since the advent of Lincoln Center, the performing arts have flourished here.

Upper West Side

Tyrannosaurus rex **in the American Museum of Natural History**

Upper West Side

BORDERED ON THE WEST BY RIVERSIDE PARK AND THE HUDSON RIVER AND on the east by Central Park, this popular residential neighborhood extends from West 59th Street north to 110th Street. Busy thoroughfares lined with shops and historic buildings cross quiet side streets with handsome brownstones. In this community the arts, commerce, and residential life peacefully coexist. The intimacy of the area, combined with the open-mindedness of its residents on any number of social and political issues, makes it a neighborhood where many people can feel at home. Upper West Siders also have demonstrated their respect for the past—practically everybody lives in an old building— and their willingness to battle to preserve it.

The Upper West Side has attractions that draw visitors, but not enough to turn it into a tourist attraction. Technically, since Fifth Avenue divides the East Side from the West Side, all of Central Park is part of the Upper West Side, although that particular asset truly belongs to the entire city. Along with the park's many visitors, West Siders make good use of its proximity, making it especially jammed on weekends.

The American Museum of Natural History (see pp. 184–86) is one of the great museums of its kind in the world. The New-York Historical Society (see pp. 182–83) is another estimable institution on Central Park West, but in a city with so many great museums, a visitor might well—and wrongly— decide to pass it by. Lincoln Center is the country's foremost performing arts center; any visitor interested in live orchestral or chamber music, ballet or opera must go there.

The surrounding area is filled with cafés, restaurants, and delightful small stores. Here you will find yourself among many resident New Yorkers. In fact, one of the main reasons to visit the Upper West Side is to see how most New Yorkers live—in a series of close-knit neighborhoods serviced by a wide variety of shops, stores, schools, and eateries.

THE DAKOTA LED THE WAY FOR SETTLEMENT

The major factor in developing the Upper West Side was access and transportation. Before the elevated line along Columbus Avenue, then called Ninth Avenue, was completed in 1879, the area was filled with shanties and squatters, many of them displaced by the development of Central Park. Still, the construction of the Dakota Apartments in 1884 in such an out-of-the-way wasteland was considered a rash and daring move—hence its name.

But others followed: In 1884 Isidor Straus, a merchant who would eventually take over R. H. Macy's, moved to 105th Street and West End Avenue to be near Riverside Park; William Tecumseh Sherman, the Union general famous for his rampage through the South during the Civil War, moved into a house on West 71st Street in 1886. That year the *New York Times* noted: "Thousands of carpenters and masons are engaged in rearing substantial buildings where a year ago nothing was to be seen but market gardens or barren rocky fields."

The arrival of the subway in 1904 prolonged the boom, which lasted into the late 1920s and early 1930s, years that saw the construction of the huge twin-towered apartment hotels on Central Park West.

Developers hoped that the Upper West Side would attract the city's social and business elite. Instead it tended to draw New Yorkers engaged in the arts or publishing or advertising and similar fields. One prestigious address, the Ansonia Hotel (1904), had as residents such diverse individuals as baseball star Babe Ruth, novelist Theodore Dreiser, composer Igor Stravinsky, impresario Florenz Ziegfeld, and tenor Enrico Caruso.

The Upper West Side still attracts stars and celebrities for its many amenities, the nearness of the park, the historical integrity of its buildings, and the fact that many other famous people live there as well. ■

Manhattan

Area of map detail

UPPER
WEST SIDE

UPPER WEST SIDE

1 Soldiers' and Sailors'
Monument
2 West End Collegiate
3 Ansonia Hotel
4 American Bible Society
5 Century Apartments
6 Hotel des Artistes
7 Shearith Israel Synagogue
8 Dakota Apartments
9 San Remo Apartments
10 Hayden Planetarium

American Museum
of Natural History

New-York
Historical Society

Lincoln
Center

American
Folk Art
Museum

0   600 yards
0   600 meters

Lincoln Center

**Lincoln Center
for the
Performing Arts**
www.lincolncenter.org

Map p. 175

65th St. at
Broadway

212/875-5000.
Information
& schedules:
212/546-2656.
Art & architecture
tours: 212/875-
5350.
Metropolitan Opera
House backstage
tours: 212/769-7020
(reservations
required).

Subway: 1, 9 to
66th St.-Lincoln
Center

NOW, MORE THAN 30 YEARS SINCE THE LINCOLN CENTER for the Performing Arts opened, there is no disputing its resounding success. As a public space, Lincoln Center, the country's largest performing arts complex, serves and pleases even those New Yorkers and visitors who have never been inside its theaters and concert halls. Some five million people a year attend performances there, but countless more simply wander through the spacious plaza, enjoy summer nights at the fountains, participate in open-air dances in the plaza, or attend free concerts and other events at the Guggenheim Bandshell in Damrosch Park on the center's southwest corner.

In addition to regular concerts and performances by the Metropolitan and New York City operas, the New York Philharmonic, and the American Ballet Theater, Lincoln Center is noted for featured events such as concerts at Alice Tully Hall, the summer Lincoln Center Festival, and the Mostly Mozart Festival.

In 1987, on the bicentenary of Mozart's death, the center's various concert stages were used to perform all of the composer's works in over 500 concerts. Concerts and operas are also televised on public television's *Live from Lincoln Center* series. Plays and musicals are staged at the Vivian Beaumont Theater. Various one-hour tours are offered.

NEW YORK PUBLIC LIBRARY OF THE PERFORMING ARTS

One of the New York Public Library's great collections—on music, dance, and theater—opened in Lincoln Center in 1965. The lending library, open to the public (*Tel 212/870-1630, closed Sun.– Mon.*), has more than 200,000 books, records, tapes, compact discs, videos, and music scores and materials suitable for children. Researchers can use the collections on the third floor. Four galleries hold rotating exhibits.

The **Dance Collection,** the world's largest archive on the subject, has more than 30,000 books as well as manuscripts, costume and set designs, and taped interviews with leaders in the field. It includes the Jerome Robbins Archive of Recorded Moving Image, a collection of videos and films of dance performances.

The **Music Division** comprises the Rodgers & Hammerstein Archives of Recorded Sound—nearly half a million recordings and videos—and the American Collection of jazz, pop, and imprints of colonial music. The **Billy Rose Theater Collection** includes thousands of clippings, programs, posters, and photos on theater, film, radio and TV, vaudeville, the circus, and magic. The **Theater of Film and Tape Archives** has more than 1,600 films and videos of live performances.

SCULPTURES

Lincoln Center has several pieces of modern sculpture, most notably Henry Moore's "Reclining Figure" (1965), a 30-foot-long, bronze abstract sculpture in two segments located in the reflecting pool in the plaza. After completing the work, Moore expressed the hope that "it will give contrast to the architecture, which, like all architecture, is rather geometric and static." Alexander Calder's spiderlike "Le Guichet" (1965), a 14-foot-high assemblage consisting of a large steel plate attached to four legs, is located in front of the library of the performing arts. In the park across from Lincoln Center formed by the crossing of Broadway and Columbus Avenue, there is a bronze bust by Milton Hebald of Richard Tucker, the Metropolitan Opera's leading tenor from 1945 until his death in 1975.

CONSTRUCTION

Robert Moses, the city's strong-willed master planner and builder, conceived of Lincoln Center as

At dusk, Lincoln Center glows with soft lighting. Below: A Chinese dancer an urban renewal project. Construction, its costs largely underwritten by the Rockefeller family, caused the demolition of several West Side landmarks and the dislocation of the tenement dwellers who had inhabited the neighborhood for years. High-rise housing for 10,000 people was built along West End Avenue, but the construction of Lincoln Center irrevocably changed the area from a working-class to a middle-class neighborhood. Ironically, just before they were demolished, the tenements had one last moment of

Lincoln Center's production of *The Nutcracker* **has become a traditional part of a New York Christmas.**

glory—as the street setting for the film version of the musical, *West Side Story.*

The first building in the complex to be completed was the 19.7-million-dollar concert hall designed by Max Abramovitz, which opened on September 23, 1962. Philharmonic Hall, as it was called then, was plagued from the beginning with acoustical problems, which were finally solved in 1976 after several major readjustments. The auditorium, seating over 2,700 people, was renamed

Avery Fisher Hall in 1973, after the philanthropic manufacturer of high-fidelity equipment, who donated ten million dollars to Lincoln Center. Some of the funds went toward the acoustics.

Architect Wallace K. Harrison, head of the Lincoln Center's board of architects, designed the **Metropolitan Opera** house, the largest hall (nearly 4,000 seats) and most costly (46.9 million dollars) in the complex. Philip Johnson was the architect of the third largest building, the **New York State Theater** (1964), the one building in the complex constructed with state and city funding. It, too, had poor acoustics, a problem that was remedied in 1982. These three principal buildings, wrote architectural critic Ada Louise Huxtable, "are lushly decorated, conservative structures that the public finds pleasing and most professionals consider a failure of nerve, imagination and talent."

The **Lincoln Center Theater,** a building housing both the Vivian Beaumont and the Mitzi E. Newhouse Theaters, and the New York Public Library of the Performing Arts were both completed in 1965 in an unusual collaboration between architects: Eero Saarinen & Associates did the theater, while Skidmore, Owings & Merrill designed the library, which is cantilevered out over the theater at the plaza level. **The Juilliard School** *(144 W. 66th St.)* was completed in 1968. It houses the thousand-seat Alice Tully Hall, home to the Chamber Music Society of Lincoln Center. In 1991 the 28-story Samuel B. and David Rose Building was completed. This most recent addition to the complex houses offices, rehearsal studios, dormitories, a library branch, and a fire station. ■

American Folk Art Museum

FOLK ARTISTS SPEND MANY A LIFETIME BUILDING castles out of old bottles or whittling their fantasies into whirligigs. These are among 4,000 objects the American Folk Art Museum has amassed in the past 40 years—a much larger collection than could be shown. Providing much-needed exhibition space, the new Midtown building (see p. 126) opened as the main location in 2001. The Lincoln Square space in the Upper West Side now operates as a branch museum.

When the museum was chartered in 1963, folk art was known as the people's art. Since then, there has been considerable discussion about what constitutes folk art. The museum takes a broad view. It showcases decorative arts; decorative pieces that serve a practical purpose—quilts, trade signs, gravestones, decoys, and the like; religious and patriotic items; and household objects, such as carved cookie boards or painted tin. It also includes work by individual artists, including Grandma Moses.

Exuberant works are found at both AFAM locations. For a sampler, visit the **Upper West Side branch,** where admission is free. Creations here include the 12-foot-high "St. Tammany Weather Vane," a molded copper Native American. Changing exhibits hang in the Eva and Morris Feld Gallery. A recent show featured scroll-like paintings, drawings, and books by renowned artist Henry Darger (1892–1973).

At AFAM's **Midtown branch** on 53rd Street, an exhilarating experience awaits: seven floors of outstanding works, including those from the preeminent Esmerian Collection. Recently donated to the museum, it includes more than 400 paintings, sculptures, watercolors, weather vanes, carvings, pottery, *fraktur* (keepsake documents), furniture, and more. Many works are icons of American folk art, including "Girl in Red Dress with Cat and Dog" (1834–36) by Ammi Phillips; and one of 62 versions of "The Peaceable Kingdom" by Edward Hicks. ■

American Folk Art Museum
www.folkartmuseum.org
 Map p. 175
Upper West Side:
✉ 2 Lincoln Sq. & Columbus Ave., between 65th & 66th Sts.
☎ 212/595-9533
🚇 Subway: 1, 9 to 66th St.-Lincoln Center
Midtown:
✉ 45 W. 53rd St.
☎ 212/265-1040
🕐 Closed Mon.
🚇 Subway: E, V to 53rd & 5th

**Above:
St. Tammany, namesake of a notorious political organization, adorns a weather vane.
Left: Quilts on display at the Upper West Side branch**

Walk from park to park

The Upper West Side once boasted some of New York's finest hotels and residences. This walking tour visits those bygone days, beginning with grand old buildings at Central Park West and West 70th Street. It ends on the relaxing greenery of Riverside Park, with its view of the Hudson River and the Palisades and spaces for jogging, baseball, cross-country skiing, or just taking it easy. As you walk be prepared for an area of exhilarating contrasts and tempting places to stop: One minute you can be buying a rare book at a bargain price from a street bookseller, the next peering skyward at an awesome structure. You will pass assorted shops and restaurants, and may also choose to pick up some delicious gourmet takeout and picnic at Riverside Park at the end.

Begin at the **Shearith Israel Synagogue ❶** *(W. 70th St. at Central Park West, tel 212/873-0300)*, a Spanish and Portuguese synagogue built in the classical revival style in 1897 by the oldest Jewish congregation in New York. The Sephardic Jews arrived in New York from Brazil in 1654. One block north, at 115 Central Park West, the **Majestic Apartments** were built by developer Irwin S. Chanin in 1930–31. It is one of four twin-towered apartment buildings facing the park. Go left on West 71st Street.

The area between Central Park West and Columbus Avenue has a fine selection of 1890s brownstones with high stoops and balustrades; note the cupids on the cornice of No. 24. The Roman Catholic **Church of the Blessed Sacrament ❷** *(W. 71st St., between Columbus Ave. and Broadway)* is a neo-Gothic landmark designed in 1917 by Gustave Steinback, a prominent church architect. At No. 171 (northeast corner of Broadway), the beaux-arts **Dorilton,** nine floors topped by a two-and-a-half story mansard roof, is today a landmarked apartment building. When it opened in 1902, however, a critic complained that "the sight of it makes strong men swear and weak women shrink affrighted," and it was condemned for the same multiplicity of details that are today described as handsome.

The square nearby, at the intersection of Amsterdam Avenue and Broadway at West 73rd Street, is **Verdi Square ❸**, named for a statue of Giuseppe Verdi unveiled in 1906, five years after the Italian composer/patriot's death. The statue sits on a cylindrical pedestal; figures of four of his characters surround the base—Falstaff, Aida, Otello, and Leonora. An ornate **subway kiosk,** designed in 1904, graces the island formed by the intersection of Amsterdam Avenue and Broadway. This bustling intersection is the heart of shopping and a convenient subway stop. At 2100 Broadway, the **former Central Savings Bank** building (1928) provides an imposing backdrop for the Verdi statue.

Proceed north (uptown) along Broadway. The beaux-arts **Ansonia Hotel,** at No. 2109 *(between W. 73rd and W. 74th Sts.),* is one of New York's most acclaimed apartment buildings. Architect Paul E. M. Duboy gave the highly ornamented building its Parisian flair. Solid construction for fireproofing made its apartments soundproof, a feature that appealed to its tenants and guests.

Turn left on West 77th Street to No. 250. The beaux-arts **Hotel Belleclaire** (1901) is the first known design of apartment-house architect Emery Roth, Sr.

Continue on West 77th Street to West End Avenue, a street lined with stylish apartment houses. The **West End Collegiate Church ❹** *(245 W. 77th St.)* is an 1893 Dutch-Renaissance structure marked by stepped gables. It is a direct descendant of New Amsterdam's first church (a Dutch Reformed church built in 1628); Number 312 was for many years home to jazz musician Miles Davis. Walk west, to curving Riverside Drive, and turn right to an area lined with stunning town houses and mansions, with a historic district of 1890s row houses between West 80th and 81st Streets. Those by architect Clarence F. True are Nos. 103, 104, 105, and 107–109.

At 140 Riverside Drive (the northeast corner of West 86th Street), the 19-story

Normandy Apartments by Emery Roth combine art deco touches such as the rounded corners with details borrowed from the Italian Renaissance. One of two freestanding mansions remaining on Riverside Drive, the **Isaac L. Rice House** ❺, at the southeast corner of 89th Street, was designed by Herts and Tallent, theatrical designers. The impressive 100-foot-tall **Soldiers' and Sailors' Monument,** honoring the Civil War dead, is opposite in **Riverside Park** ❻, Paul E. M. Duboy collaborated on its design.

Riverside Drive and Riverside Park are both designated scenic landmarks. The land was set aside in 1865 to enhance real estate values and in 1873 Frederick Law Olmsted

designed the park, which slopes down toward the Hudson River, a place to relax after your long walk. ∎

- 🗺 Map inside front cover
- ► Shearith Israel Synagogue
- 🔄 Nearly 2 miles
- 🕐 About an hour
- ► Riverside Park

NOT TO BE MISSED
- Church of the Blessed Sacrament
- Verdi Square
- West End Collegiate Church
- Soldiers' and Sailors' Monument

New-York Historical Society

FOUNDED IN 1804, THE NEW-YORK HISTORICAL SOCIETY IS the oldest museum in the city and the second oldest in the country. The society's name proudly retains the hyphen in New-York that was in use when the society was founded. Known for its vast and varied collection, its holdings include the country's largest collection of Tiffany lamps, John James Audubon's original watercolors for his *Birds of America,* and millions of books and manuscripts. The museum has taken a leadership role in establishing an archive of objects and information related to the events of September 11.

New-York Historical Society

www.nyhistory.org
- Map p. 175
- 2 W. 77th St.
- 212/873-3400
- Closed Mon.
- $$
- Subway: 6, 4, B, C to 81st St.

The museum moved to its present neoclassic building in 1908. The entrance on West 77th Street leads into an elegant hall, with several galleries and a gift shop. Pick up a brochure upon admission to see what temporary exhibits are showing. There are many: Having survived a financial crisis in the early 1990s, the society is now back on its

Dexter Hall, with 19th-century masterpieces from the society's permanent collection, some being shown for the first time in 25 years. Among the artists represented are Thomas Cole and John Trumbull. The new **Luce Center,** on the fourth floor, houses nearly 40,000 museum objects covering 400 years of American history.

MORE HIGHLIGHTS

The **Luman Reed Gallery,** named for a 19th-century collector and patron of the arts, is a re-creation of the picture gallery at Reed's 13 Greenwich Street residence, where he lived in the 1830s. Reed believed that art was important to the development of the nation and commissioned Thomas Cole, the founder of the Hudson River school of landscape painting, to create a five-part allegory. "The Course of Empire" is the focal point of the gallery here, but it also holds Dutch, Flemish, German, and Italian paintings and engravings and other treasures.

The granite-faced exterior of the society's austere neo-classic home

feet with a vigorous program. Recent exhibits of note have included "The Tumultuous Fifties: A View from the New York Times Photo Archive."

There are more galleries on the next three floors. The second floor holds the **Department of Prints and Photographs,** with rare materials such as Audubon originals (access by appointment). Also here is the recently reopened

In the **Lowlight Gallery** lights are dimmed. Here one can view rare documents, books, and correspondence, such as British Gen. John Burgoyne's articles of surrender ending the American Revolution, the authorization in 1674 from Charles II for the British takeover of New Netherland from the Dutch, or a piece of ticker tape from the day the stock market crashed. Items are frequently rotated.

Finally, the society's library is well worth visiting, and no appointment is needed. Its scope is immense, with 600,000 volumes and more than a million manuscripts, including the first printing of Lincoln's Second Inaugural Address, and an outstanding collection of 18th-century newspapers, including the city's earliest, the *New-York Gazette* (1725–1744) and John Peter Zenger's *New-York Weekly Journal.*

SPECIALIZED COLLECTIONS

The silver collection, with objects from the colonial through Victorian periods, includes work by New York silversmith Myer Myers, and flatware that belonged to such important families as the Roosevelts and the Schuylers. The **Neustadt Collection** of Tiffany lamps was compiled by a New York physician in the latter half of the 20th century. The **Bella C. Landauer Collection of Business and Advertising Art** contains more than one million items.

HISTORY

The society has its roots in a collection of "everything and from whatever clime," assembled by John Pintard, one of its founders, and briefly displayed in City Hall in 1791. The historical society is also an art museum, the city's first, and the only one until the Metropolitan Museum of Art opened in 1870. In 1858 the society received the collection of Luman Reed, a wealthy grocer; when he died in 1836, friends and associates arranged for his art collection to be displayed to the public on a paying basis—an enterprise they called the New York Gallery of Fine Arts—in the Rotunda in City Hall Park. When the Rotunda closed, the collection was given to the historical society. ∎

An 1826 oil painting by Thomas Cole depicts a scene from James Fenimore Cooper's *Last of the Mohicans.*

American Museum of Natural History

WITH ITS HUGE SKELETONS OF DINOSAURS AND DIORAMAS of cavemen, the American Museum of Natural History is a great place to take children. But, make no mistake, it is not primarily a museum for them. It is a complex scientific and educational institution and one of the largest and most important museums in the world. Sprawled out over four square blocks, the museum owns nearly 40 million specimens (including 96 percent of all known species of birds).

American Museum of Natural History
www.amnh.org
- Map p. 175
- Central Park West at 79th St.
- 212/769-5000
- $$ (donation)
- Subway: C to 81st St.; 1, 9 to 79th St.

Opposite: Dinosaurs command the entrance to the American Museum of Natural History.

Visitors—more than three million a year—must decide what and how much to see in the museum's maze of buildings. There are guided tours of certain exhibits, but many people solve the problem by heading straight for something they know. Often this is the dinosaurs; there is a reproduction of the 55-foot *Barosaurus* in the first-floor Rotunda and the entire fourth floor is given over to prehistoric beasts. For others, it may be the Hall of Minerals and Gems, or the North American Indian exhibits, or the Hall of Ocean Life, with its giant blue whale immersed in a virtual ocean, or one of the newest areas, the Hall of Biodiversity, featuring an African rain forest: There is much from which to choose.

The first floor of the museum includes halls and exhibit spaces devoted to birds, invertebrates, North American mammals, fish, forests, and the environment of

New York State. The **Hall of the Northwest Coast Indians** has two imposing lines of totem poles running down the center of the room. The **Hall of Mollusks and Our World** includes items from a collection of 50,000 shells that the museum acquired in 1874, when shell collecting and decorating was a popular pastime. A 34-ton piece of a meteorite discovered in 1897 in Greenland and excavated by explorer Robert Peary is a highlight of the **Hall of Meteorites. The Hall of Gems** includes the 563-carat "Star of India" sapphire that J. P. Morgan donated to the museum in 1901.

Gertrude Vanderbilt Whitney gave the second-floor **Whitney Hall of Oceanic Birds** on the death of her husband, Harry Payne Whitney, who supported the museum's ornithological research and collecting expeditions in the 1920s and 1930s.

On the third floor is the **Hall of Pacific Peoples,** reflecting the studies of anthropologist Margaret Meade, who worked in the museum's Anthropology Department until her death in 1978. Other halls on the floor include ones devoted to reptiles and amphibians, eastern Woodland and Plains Indians, primates, and North American birds.

The fourth floor is all dinosaurs. Here you can follow 500 million years of development from

primitive vertebrates to such colossal mammals as mammoths and mastodons. The **Hall of Saurishian Dinosaurs** (those that could walk upright) include mounted skeletons of *Tyrannosaurus rex* and *Apatosaurus*, the latter sporting a longer tail after a recent reinstallation. The **Hall of Ornithischian Dinosaurs** includes the armored *Stegosaurus*, discovered in Wyoming, and *Styracosaurus*, with a spiked neck and nose. The **Halls of Mammals and Their Extinct Relatives** draws on the museum's collection of fossils, the largest in the world, and includes fossilized ancestors of armadillos, cats, dogs, bears, seals, whales, camels, and other modern-day creatures.

The museum is aware of current trends in museum activity, and offers opportunities for shopping, dining, and entertainment: the Dino Store, the Junior Store, and the Main Shop; the Naturemax Theater featuring IMAX films; the punnily named Diner Saurus cafeteria; and the Garden Café.

The museum moved to its present site in 1874. President Ulysses S. Grant laid the cornerstone for the first building, a high Victorian Gothic structure designed by Vaux and Mould, which has been almost completely swallowed up by additions to the museum.

The equestrian statue at the museum's main entrance is by James Earle Fraser and shows a vigorous Roosevelt, flanked by two native guides, one African, the other American Indian. Roche, Dinkeloo & Associates did the museum's library in 1992.

In its beginnings, the museum consisted mostly of mounted birds and fishes; in the modern era, however, the museum has actively pursued ways to exhibit its specimens in the most educational and compelling manner. Thus, the **Hall of Human Biology and Evolution** contains dioramas of our hominid ancestors in action that capture the drama inherent in the story of man. Similarly, the dioramas in the **Akeley Memorial Hall of African Mammals** (second floor) are startlingly realistic in their attention to detail and their presentation of animals in lifelike positions. The hall is named for Carl Akeley, one of many great scientists and taxidermists associated with the museum over the years. From 1909 until his death on an African expedition in 1926, he developed methods to mount animals in natural poses and habitats.

The museum's staff continues to find imaginative ways to present the vast collection to an ever expanding audience. ∎

Rose Center for Earth and Space

✉ Central Park West at 81st St.

☎ 212/769-5100; advance tickets for Hayden Planetarium 212/769-5200

🕐 Closed Mon.

💲 $$$–$$$$$

🚇 Subway: C to 81st St.

Rose Center for Earth and Space

Described both as a metaphorical tour de force and one of the city's newest architectural icons, the center provides a dramatic portal into a multisensory experience of the universe.

Its heart is a gleaming glass cube enveloping the four-million-pound Hayden Sphere. In the re-created Hayden Planetarium, visitors experience outer space via the world's largest and most powerful virtual reality simulator. Other areas include the Hall of Planet Earth (HoPE), the Hall of the Universe, the Scales of the Universe, and the dynamic Cosmic Pathway, a spiraling ramp that ushers visitors through 13 billion years of cosmic evolution. ∎

Central Park West

CENTRAL PARK WEST IS A GRAND COUNTERPART TO THE Upper East Side. The East Side has its millionaires' mansions, but the West Side is graced by the dramatic silhouette of four twin-towered apartment buildings and a fifth with three towers. These monumental structures, the Century, the Majestic, the San Remo, the Beresford (with three towers), and the Eldorado, were constructed between 1929 and 1931. They are found at intervals between West 62nd and West 91st Streets.

Several of the buildings were either built or commissioned by the Irwin Chanin Company. Chanin first encountered art deco at the 1925 Paris Exposition and, on his return, introduced the style in his New York buildings, including the 1931 **Century Apartments** *(25 Central Park W. at 62nd to 63rd Sts.).* The **New York Society for Ethical Culture** *(2 W. 64th St., tel 212/874-5210)* is an austere art nouveau building of 1910. This humanist religious organization was instrumental in the founding of the ACLU and the NAACP. The heavily ornamental art deco brick building at 55 Central Park West (corner of 66th Street) was the setting for the 1980s film *Ghostbusters.*

At 1 West 67th Street, the **Hotel des Artistes** opened in 1918. Residents of the kitchenless apartments ordered their meals from the **Café des Artistes** on the ground floor. Although the apartments now have kitchens, the café has remained one of the city's most popular restaurants *(Tel 212/877-3500).* Architect Henry J. Hardenbergh's **Dakota Apartments** *(1 W. 72nd St.)* were completed in 1884. The German Renaissance-style structure was named after the Dakota Territory, in response to criticism of the building's then remote location. Its many celebrity occupants have included actress Lauren Bacall, singer Roberta Flack, and Yoko Ono and John Lennon, who was shot out in front in 1980. The **San Remo** (1930), between 74th and 75th Streets, features neoclassic trim and circular Roman towers. Past the beaux-arts New-York Historical Society (see pp. 182–83) and the American Museum of Natural History (see pp. 184–86), the **Beresford** *(211 Central Park W. at 81st St.),* another Emery Roth

apartment building, has three baroque towers. In the 1950s, resident Alan Jay Lerner wrote the lyrics for *My Fair Lady* here. The 1931 **Eldorado** *(300 Central Park W. between 90th and 91st Sts.)* has art deco trim. Novelist Sinclair Lewis lived here in the 1940s in what he described as a "gaudy flat, a cross between Elizabeth Arden's Beauty Salon and the horse-stables at the Ringling Circus Winter Quarters." ■

The Dakota Apartments were built in 1884.

Some small Upper West Side museums

CHILDREN'S MUSEUM OF MANHATTAN

Four floors are devoted to educational activities and hands-on exhibits for children, including a room of children's books and a television studio.

✉ 212 W. 83rd St. ☎ 212/721-1234 ⊕ Closed Mon.–Tues. ⑤ $$ ⊞ Subway: 1, 9 to 86th St., B to 81st St.

MUSEUM GALLERY OF THE AMERICAN BIBLE SOCIETY

The society was founded in 1816 to disseminate the Bible without involving doctrine or creeds, The second-floor gallery includes a full-size reproduction of the Gutenberg printing press and Helen Keller's Braille Bibles. There is also a large library and archive.

✉ 1865 Broadway at 61st St. ☎ 212/408-1200 ⊕ Closed Sun. ⊞ Subway: A, B, C, D, 1, 9 to 59th St.-Columbus Circle

NICHOLAS ROERICH MUSEUM

This museum is dedicated to the works of Russian-born Nicholas Roerich (1874–1947), a mystic, Theosophist, philosopher, stage designer, painter, and writer. He was nominated for a Nobel Peace Prize for his proposal (passed as the Roerich Pact in 1935) that important cultural, scientific, and religious sites be protected by treaty in wartime as in peacetime. The museum contains about 200 of his paintings, examples of his writings, and art objects from his collection.

✉ 319 W. 107th St. at Riverside Drive ☎ 212/864-7752 ⊕ Closed Mon. & a.m. daily ⑤ $$ ⊞ Subway: 1, 9 to 110th St. ■

Above: Learning through play at the Children's Museum
Below: The Nicholas Roerich Museum

U neven terrain here provides a dramatic setting for some of the city's greatest assets—among them a medieval cloister, a renowned university, and an immense cathedral. The area is also a melting pot of different races and ethnic groups.

The Heights & Harlem

**Through a window
at The Cloisters**

The Heights & Harlem

AS THE ISLAND OF MANHATTAN NARROWS AT ITS NORTHERN END, IT ALSO rises in an undulating and disorderly sequence of rocky outcroppings, escarpments, ridges, plateaus, and bluffs until it reaches its greatest elevation—267.75 feet—near where Fort Washington once stood. Here, during the Revolution, American troops made a last stand against the British before they were driven from the island.

Northern Manhattan, once the exclusive territory of the landed gentry, is made up of a number of historic neighborhoods. At the northernmost tip is ethnically diverse Inwood, where, some believe, Peter Minuit might have purchased Manhattan Island from the Indians.

To the south is Washington Heights, today home to immigrants from the Dominican Republic, since the mid-1960s the fastest growing ethnic group in the city. Here the streets teem with life, shops are called bodegas, and Spanish is the preferred language.

Farther south is Hamilton Heights, home to Ecuadoreans, Chinese, Dominicans, and African Americans, among others. Within Hamilton Heights is Sugar Hill (W. 141st St to W. 145th St.), since early in the 20th century a neighborhood of well-to-do African Americans.

Finally, between 125th and 110th Streets, is Morningside Heights, where Columbia University—nearly 20,000 students enrolled in its 16 schools—and its women's affiliate, Barnard College, are at the heart of a lively, student-oriented neighborhood.

The eastern section of northern Manhattan is Harlem, world-famous in the 1920s as a vital center of African-American culture. Harlem was Jewish, German, and Irish until 1905, when an African-American realtor, Philip A. Payton, rented apartments to African Americans in a building on West 133rd Street. A few years later there were so many African Americans in Harlem that the *Harlem Home News* warned against "black hordes that stand ready to destroy homes and scatter fortunes of the whites living and doing business in the very heart of Harlem." By 1930, Harlem had a high concentration of African Americans. Today, national chains that previously skipped over Harlem are now anxious to invest in this prime marketplace.

When northern Manhattan was truly the hinterlands, Manhattanites such as Alexander Hamilton and John James Audubon owned large tracts of land there. Today their names live on: in Hamilton Heights, where Hamilton's House still stands, and the Audubon Ballroom, remembered as the place where the African-American nationalist leader, Malcolm X, was assassinated in 1965. On the northern edge of Harlem is onetime Coogan's Bluff, a turn-of-the-20th-century neighborhood on the Harlem River between 155th and 160th Streets. Here the revered Polo Grounds once stood, home of the New York Giants from the 1890s until the baseball team moved to San Francisco in 1957.

Fort Tryon Park, with its splendid view of the Hudson River, is the location of The Cloisters Museum, a branch of the Metropolitan Museum of Art and the best assemblage of medieval art and architectural elements in America. Near Columbia in Morningside Heights is the Cathedral Church of St. John the Divine, the largest Gothic cathedral in the world. In Riverside Park, the General Grant National Memorial (restored in 1997) was once one of the city's premier attractions.

Audubon Terrace is an enclave of buildings housing cultural institutions, such as the American Academy and Institute of Arts and Letters, which celebrated its centennial in 1998. At 112th Street and Broadway, the Goddard Institute for Space Studies is an affiliate of the National Aeronautics and Space Administration (Tel 212/678-5500). The Union Theological Seminary (Tel 212/662-7100), a nondenominational institution, is located in a Gothic quadrangle north of Columbia; since its founding in 1836, it has had some of the country's most distinguished theologians on its faculty.

Even today northern Manhattan's distance from the city's center makes many reluctant to explore its unfamiliar streets and neighborhoods. A certain caution about the area is advisable; some parts are unsafe. On the other hand, this section of the city contains some of its great treasures, and no one should hesitate to seek them out—the many available tours make this easy to do. ■

THE HEIGHTS & HARLEM

❶ Dyckman Farmhouse Museum
❷ Morris-Jumel Mansion ❸ Mother African Methodist Episcopal Zion Church
❹ Studio Museum in Harlem

Manhattan

Area of map detail

Begun in 1892, St. John the Divine remains unfinished.

Cathedral Church of St. John the Divine

BECAUSE IT HAS TAKEN MORE THAN A CENTURY TO BUILD, the Cathedral Church of St. John the Divine in Morningside Heights has had, for many years, the distinction of being both a historic landmark (not an official one) and a work in progress.

Cathedral Church of St. John the Divine (Episcopal)

www.stjohndivine.org

- Map p. 191
- Amsterdam Ave. at W. 112th St.
- 212/316-7540
- Donation
- Subway: 1, 9 to Cathedral Parkway (110th St.)

The cornerstone was laid on St. John's Day, December 27, 1892. The construction of the choir and crossing was begun in the Byzantine-Romanesque style. In 1911, architect Ralph Adam Crams took over; his nave and west front were in French Gothic style. Construction ceased during World War II, resuming in 1979. Although damaged by fire in 2001, the cathedral continues to evolve and extend its social activism mission.

A CHURCH FOR ALL

The Episcopal bishop at the time construction began was Henry Codman Potter, the "people's bishop," who believed the cathedral should serve all creeds, nations, and levels of society. St. John's today lives up to this philosophy, engaging in community service and work among the poor, even making it a priority over the completion of the cathedral. The church also reaches out to the larger population through its many events, from concerts to art exhibits, lectures, theater, and special holiday offerings. The main attraction, however, remains the incredible structure itself. You can marvel at the beauteous interior—the nave alone is 248 feet long and 124 feet high; more than 10,000 pieces of glass are in the 40-foot-diameter Great Rose window. ■

Columbia University

AS A LEADING MEMBER OF THE ELITE BAND OF EAST COAST universities known as the Ivy League, Columbia University, located in upper Manhattan's Morningside Heights, is both an integral part of New York City and its history and apart from it.

But Columbia is no ivory tower isolated from the general population. While there is a large distinct quad, there are many places in its seven-block campus (between Amsterdam Avenue and Broadway) where you can pass between the campus and the city streets without knowing it. The **Wallach Art Gallery** has changing exhibits, curated by faculty and students, in the fields of art history and visual arts. Visitors enjoy the adjacent streets, especially the secondhand bookstores and the coffeehouses along Broadway and Amsterdam, including the West End (*2911 Broadway*).

FROM DOWNTOWN TO UPTOWN

Chartered in 1754 as King's College, the school first met in the schoolhouse of Trinity Church in Lower Manhattan. Colonial-era graduates included Alexander Hamilton, John Jay, and De Witt Clinton. Renamed Columbia after the American Revolution, it moved to Madison Avenue and 49th Street in 1857, to land it had received in 1814 as a windfall from the legislature. Formerly the Elgin Botanical Gardens, this tract of land on Fifth Avenue between 47th and 51st Streets (which Columbia owned until 1985) eventually became home to Rockefeller Center. The school moved to its Morningside Heights campus in 1897.

At its heart was domed **Low Library,** modeled on the Roman Pantheon, which sits at the head of an expanse of stairs. It is named for Seth Low, donor of the library,

Columbia's president from 1890 to 1901, and a key figure in Columbia's development. He moved the university to Morningside Heights, added the School of Nursing and Teachers' College, and strengthened ties with Barnard, the women's college affiliated with Columbia. In 1934, Low Library was turned into administrative offices. However, it remains—together with Daniel Chester French's larger-than-life bronze statue, "Alma Mater" (1903),

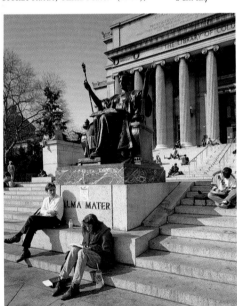

at the foot of the library's steps—a symbol of a great university.

Among other campus buildings, **St. Paul's Chapel** on the main quad, and McKim, Mead & White's 1927 **Casa Italiana** on Amsterdam Avenue, stand out. ∎

Columbia University
www.columbia.edu

⬛ Map p. 191
✉ Broadway & W. 116th St.
☎ 212/854-1754. Visitor center and tours: 212/854-4902
🕐 Closed Sat.–Sun.
🚇 Subway: 1, 9 to 116th St.

Wallach Art Gallery
✉ Schermerhorn Hall
☎ 212/854-7288
🕐 Closed Sun.–Tues. & a.m. daily

Daniel Chester French sculptured the "Alma Mater" on the steps of Columbia University's Low Library.

General Grant
National Memorial

www.nps.gov/gegr

 Map p. 191

Riverside Dr. &
W. 122nd St.

212/666-1640

Subway: 1, 9 to
116th St.-Broadway

General Grant National Memorial

GRANT'S TOMB, THE LARGEST MAUSOLEUM IN THE UNITED States, was until World War I one of the most popular sights in New York City. A former President of the United States, a native of the Midwest, and victorious commander of Union forces in the Civil War, Ulysses S. Grant (1822–1885) moved to New York in 1884.

The tomb of Ulysses S. Grant, the only U.S. President buried in New York City, overlooks the Hudson River.

Grant was immensely popular when he died. One million people observed his funeral procession in 1885. Mayor William R. Grace donated the land for the tomb, and the Grant Memorial Association raised $600,000 (from about 90,000 contributors) to build it. President Benjamin Harrison laid the corner-stone in 1892, and President William McKinley attended the dedication on April 27, 1897.

Architect John H. Duncan, designer of the Brooklyn Soldiers' and Sailors' Memorial Arch, won the competition to design Grant's

Tomb, which he based on such classical models as the Mausoleum at Halicarnassus. The 150-foot-tall granite tomb consists of a domed rotunda ringed by Doric columns atop a square base. Over the entrance carved figures representing Victory and Peace flank a plaque inscribed with Grant's famous words, "Let Us Have Peace."

The interior of the tomb, a cruciform in Carrara marble, is based on Napoleon's Tomb in Paris. Grant's military victories and Lee's surrender at Appomattox

are the subjects of mosaics above the windows. A double staircase leads down to the crypt where Grant and his wife, Julia Dent Grant, are interred. Bronze busts along the wall depict Grant's generals, among them William Tecumseh Sherman and Philip Sheriden. The tomb was taken over by the National Park Service in 1959 and restored in 1997. Grant is the only American President buried in New York City. ■

Inside Grant's tomb, mosaics depict Robert E. Lee surrendering to Grant at Appomattox to conclude the Civil War.

Audubon Terrace

This distinguished beaux-arts cultural complex was far from the center of the city when it was built in 1908 and, unfortunately, it remains remote today. Its development began in 1904, on land that once belonged to John James Audubon. In addition to monumental statuary including "El Cid" by Anna Hyatt Huntington, today the complex also houses the American Academy of Arts and Letters, and the American Numismatic Society.

The **American Academy of Arts and Letters,** an organization of artists and writers, limited to 250 living members, is housed in two buildings designed by McKim, Mead & White, and Cass Gilbert. Original members included Henry Adams, William and Henry James, Theodore Roosevelt, Augustus Saint-Gaudens, John La Farge, and Mark Twain. A current member is John Updike. Exhibitions are based on works of candidates for membership,

new and deceased members, and exhibits of new additions to the collection.

Founded in 1858, the **American Numismatic Society** maintains a coin museum that includes a gallery of American money. There are some 750,000 numismatic items in its collection and 70,000 volumes in its library. You will see on permanent display Spanish doubloons and the plaster cast of the Lincoln penny. Changing exhibits in the East Gallery are often linked to academic programs sponsored by the society.

The **Hispanic Society of America** has more than 200,000 books and manuscripts in its library. Addressing the cultures of Spain, Portugal, Latin America, and the Philippines, its museum's permanent collection includes works by Goya and El Greco, antique furniture, tiles and mosaics, and a noted collection of Spanish ceramics. The interior is designed like a Spanish courtyard. ■

Audubon Terrace
🅰 Map p. 191
✉ Broadway, between 155th & 156th Sts.
🚇 Subway: 1 to 157th St.; B to Washington Heights

American Academy of Arts and Letters
☎ 212/368-5900
🕐 By appt. only

American Numismatic Society
☎ 212/234-3130
🕐 Closed Mon.
💲 Donation

Hispanic Society of America
☎ 212/926-2234
🕐 Closed Mon.; by appt. only
💲 Donation

The Cloisters Museum & nearby

WHAT BETTER LOCATION FOR A MEDIEVAL CLOISTER THAN a high and wooded point of land. In just such a place, on the far northern end of Manhattan, stands The Cloisters, devoted to art of the Middle Ages. Looking remarkably authentic, the building is actually from the 20th century, designed in a style evocative of medieval architecture and incorporating columns and stonework from French medieval abbeys. It opened to the public in 1938 as a branch museum of the Metropolitan Museum of Art. Many find a visit to The Cloisters a uniquely contemplative experience.

The Cloisters Museum

🅰 Map p. 191

✉ Fort Tryon Park, W. 190th St. at Fort Washington Ave.

☎ 212/923-3700

🕐 Closed Mon.

💲 $$ (donation)

🚇 Subway: A to 190th St.-Overlook Terrace

The arcades of four different medieval cloisters have been integrated into the modern Cloisters to create a sympathetic context for the exhibition of sculpture, tapestry, stained glass, metalwork, paintings, and manuscripts. Cloister denotes a covered walkway surrounding a large open courtyard with access to other monastic buildings. In similar manner, the museum's cloisters are passageways to galleries.

The nucleus of The Cloisters' collection, including large sections of four medieval cloisters, was gathered by American sculptor George Grey Barnard (1863–1938) while living in France. In 1925, John D. Rockefeller, Jr., purchased the collection for the Metropolitan Museum of Art. He also provided the building and its Fort Tryon setting, and donated works from his own collection.

FOUR CLOISTERS

The main level, where one enters, contains a number of gallery areas enclosing two cloisters. The capitals of the 12th-century **Cuxa**

Cloister have robust Romanesque carvings of double bodied animals with a single head, a design that fits corners well. In the **St. Guilhem Cloister,** built about 804 by a peer of Charlemagne's court, drill holes in a honeycomb pattern embellish the capitals. On the lower level, **Tri Cloister** is from a 16th-century convent destroyed by Huguenots. And encompassing a medieval herb garden, the **Bonnefont Cloister** is from the late 13th or early 14th century. Its naturalistic floral decorations were a reaction to grotesque Romanesque carvings.

The museum is organized in roughly chronological manner, beginning with art from the Romanesque period, continuing through the Gothic eras, and ending with the flowering of medieval art around 1520. Although every space contains superb art, especially popular on the main floor are the 15th-century stained-glass panels in the **Boppard Room;** the idealized funerary monument in the **Gothic Chapel,** of a crusader knight portrayed as young man, eyes open and hands joined in prayer; and the **Unicorn Tapestries Room,** where six woven tapestries (circa 16th century, Brussels) tell an allegorical story of the Incarnation of Christ. Downstairs, the **Treasury** displays small objects, such as a 12th-century walrus ivory cross; while the **Glass Gallery** contains glass, sculpture, and tapestries.

You will also want to visit the excellent gift shop and bookstore, try out the café, and take advantage of the spectacular views of the Hudson River from the grounds. Be forewarned; some bus tours leave you at the base of the hill, so expect a walk.

NEARBY SITES

Built in 1765 by a British military officer, Roger Morris, the **Morris-Jumel Mansion** was George Washington's headquarters for a month in 1776 before the British took it over. A French merchant, Stephen Jumel, and his American wife, Eliza Bowen, restored it in 1810. After Jumel's death, the former prostitute was married briefly to Aaron Burr, formerly vice president. The house, a museum since 1904, is noted for its Palladian portico, an octagon room, and Georgian interiors.

The **Dyckman Farmhouse Museum,** a Dutch colonial house, with gambrel roof and overhanging eaves, belonged until 1871 to the Dyckman family. They were owners of Manhattan's largest farm in colonial times, some 300 acres

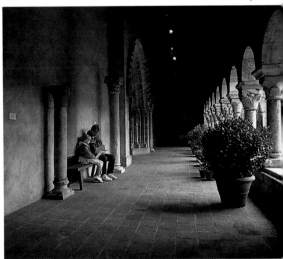

surrounding the house. The house was rebuilt in 1783 after the British destroyed it before evacuating the city. Early in the 20th century two Dyckman descendants purchased the house, furnished it in period style, and then donated it to the city. Manhattan's only remaining farmhouse, it opened as a museum in 1916. There is a formal garden in the rear. ■

Morris-Jumel Mansion
🗺 Map p. 191
✉ 65 Jumel Terrace
☎ 212/923-8008
🕐 Closed Mon.–Tues.
💲 $
🚇 Subway: C to 63rd St.

Dyckman Farmhouse Museum
🗺 Map p. 191
✉ 4881 Broadway at W. 204th St.
☎ 212/304-9422
🕐 Closed Mon.
💲 $
🚇 Subway: A to 104th St.

Visitors resting in a cloistered walkway

In & around Harlem

Abyssinian Baptist Church

- Map p. 191
- 132 Odell Clark Pl. W. at 138th St.
- 212/862-7474
- Subway: 2, 3 to 135th St.

Harlem Heritage Tours

- 212/280-7888
- $–$$$. Reservation required.

STRETCHING FROM 110TH TO 168TH STREET, HARLEM IS one of the city's most vibrant neighborhoods. New York City's nickname "The Big Apple" came from a jazz club here, and many know Harlem as home to the Apollo Theater and the Harlem Renaissance (see pp. 200–201). Of great excitement now is a second renaissance underway, in commerce, culture, property redevelopment, and tourism. Former residents are returning, and new ones—even a former U.S. President, Bill Clinton—are moving in. There are plans for both the National Jazz Museum and the National Black Sports & Entertainment Hall of fame.

Signs of regeneration in the heart of Harlem

The **St. Nicholas Historic District,** a late 19th-century development of four blockfronts along West 138th and 139th Streets, is the work of three prominent architects—James Brown Lord, Bruce Price, and Stanford White. During the 1920s the development, known as Striver's Row, was home to many prominent blacks, including surgeon Louis T. Wright, architect Vertner Tandy, and bandleader Fletcher Henderson. Redevelopment between 134th and 136th Streets is introducing boutiques, restaurants, and jazz clubs.

Close by is the **Abyssinian Baptist Church,** known for its prominent minister, Adam Clayton Powell, Jr. (1908–1972), the first black congressman from New York City. Founded in 1808, its church building dates from 1923. **Mother African Methodist Episcopal Zion Church** *(140 W. 137th St.)* is the oldest black congregation in New York. George W. Foster, Jr., one of the country's first black architects, designed the neo-Gothic building, completed in 1925. Foster collaborated with Vertner Tandy on the 1911 neo-Gothic

St. Philip's Episcopal Church
(214 W. 134th St.).

Hamilton Heights Historic District, on Harlem's western edge, includes the fine collection of row houses known as Sugar Hill, built in 1886–1906 on land once belonging to Alexander Hamilton. To the south is the **North Campus of City College** *(Convent Ave. between W. 138th and W. 140th Sts.),* a collection of Gothic buildings constructed in the early 20th century.

The **Mount Morris Park Historic District,** which contains a number of landmark churches and some of the city's finest brownstones, received government and private rehabilitation funding in the late 1990s. The neighborhood takes its name from the park in its center (renamed Marcus Garvey Park in 1973, after the black nationalist leader), which has the city's only remaining fire watchtower. The 1888 **St. Martin's Episcopal Church & Rectory** has been called the finest Romanesque Revival religious complex in the city; it also possesses the smaller (42 bells) of the city's two carillons (the other is at Riverside Church in Morningside Heights). The **Greater Metropolitan Baptist Church** *(147 W. 123rd St.)* was built in the late 19th century.

New businesses and revitalization efforts are enriching Harlem's main east–west thoroughfare, 125th Street (Martin Luther King Boulevard). Upscale stores, multiplex cinemas, and a rejuvenated **Apollo Theater** attract droves of visitors. Built in 1914, the Apollo began featuring black entertainers, such as Bill "Bojangles" Robinson, in the 1930s. Since then, virtually every top black performer has appeared here. Whoopi Goldberg recently drew raves.

Also on 125th Street—at Adam Clayton Powell, Jr., Boulevard

The famed Apollo Theater in Harlem, where stars are born

(Seventh Avenue)—**Hotel Theresa,** known in its heyday as the Waldorf of Harlem, still stands, although it is now an office building called Theresa Towers. Built in 1913 when 125th Street was a white area, the Theresa did not admit blacks until 1940; by 1946, it was celebrated as "social headquarters for Negro America." Heavyweight champion Joe Louis, and musicians and singers Duke Ellington, Lena Horne, and Paul Robeson were among the celebrity guests. From 1948 to 1953, the hotel was the childhood home of late Secretary of Commerce Ron Brown, whose father was manager. By the mid-1950s the Theresa's popularity was declining. In the early 1960s the hotel housed Malcolm X's Organization of Afro-American Unity.

Though Harlem's main street changes, its authenticity remains—in historic sites, sidewalk vendors, and proprietor-run shops, clubs, and restaurants. ∎

St. Martin's Episcopal Church & Rectory
- Map p. 191
- 230 Lenox Ave.
- 212/534-4531
- Bells are still played on Sundays and for special occasions such as weddings
- Subway: 2, 3 to 135th St.

Apollo Theater
- Map p. 191
- 253 W. 125th St.
- Tours: 212/531-5337 (**$$**); tickets: 212/749-5838
- Subway: A, B, C to 125th St.

Harlem Renaissance

The cultural flowering of black New York, a period known as the Harlem Renaissance, took place in the liberating years of the 1920s. The black artists, writers, and musicians who gathered in Harlem shared the belief that black culture had the power to improve the status of their race. It was also the first time that black intellectuals looked to Africa, folk culture, and black heroes as a source of racial pride.

Author Zora Neale Hurston

The roots of the renaissance have been traced back to *The Souls of Black Folks* (1903), a collection of essays by writer and civil rights leader W.E.B. Du Bois. In it he wrote the oft-quoted: "The problem of the twentieth century is the problem of the color-line." Du Bois was also editor of *The Crisis: A Record of the Darker Races,* a magazine published in 1910 by the National Association for the Advancement of Colored People (NAACP). In its pages, he encouraged blacks to relate to their common African heritage—a philosophy known as Pan-Africanism. Du Bois was an elitist, who pinned his hopes for blacks on what he called the "New Negro" and the "Talented Tenth," the privileged group that "rises and pulls all that are worthy of saving up to their vantage ground."

An all-black musical revue, *Shuffle Along,* which opened on Broadway in 1921, giving, in the words of African-American poet Langston Hughes (1902–1967), "a scintillating sendoff to that Negro Vogue in Manhattan," is often cited as the beginning of the Harlem Renaissance. The revue was written by songwriters Eubie Blake and Noble Sissle. Although the production, which starred Florence Mills, was not much more than a sophisticated minstrel show, it paved the way for other black shows on Broadway and made black entertainers the rage with whites, who flocked to Harlem to hear the likes of Fletcher Henderson, Cab Calloway, and Duke Ellington at the Cotton Club and other nightspots.

It was in literature that the spirit of the Harlem Renaissance was best expressed. An early work was "If We Must Die," a sonnet written in 1919 by Claude McKay, a Jamaican immigrant who has been called the Harlem Renaissance's first celebrity. A response to violence against blacks, the poem ended: "Like men we'll face the murderous, cowardly pack, Pressed to the wall, dying, but fighting back!" Other literary highlights included the mid-decade publication of poetry by Countee Cullen and Langston Hughes by mainstream publishing houses.

Zora Neale Hurston published her first short story in 1925, in *Opportunity, A Journal of Negro Life,* a publication edited by African-American sociologist Charles Johnson. Johnson, a literary mentor to many young African Americans, organized a dinner in 1924 to introduce the cream of the Harlem writers to the white publishing establishment. As a result of the dinner, the editors of a white magazine, *Graphic Survey,* invited Alain Locke, a Phi Beta Kappa graduate of Harvard (1907) and the first African-American Rhodes Scholar, to put together a special issue on "the progressive spirit of contemporary Negro life." The issue became a landmark book, *The New Negro.*

In 1926 white author Carl Van Vechten (a "Negrotarian," as whites attracted to Harlem were called) published a best-selling novel about Harlem. His book increased interest in Harlem among whites, although it was controversial among blacks.

Harlem's Cotton Club in its heyday

Artists are probably the least remembered from the decade, with the exception of photographer James VanDerZee, who documented the movement and whose work is well represented at the Studio Museum in Harlem (see p. 202). Illustrator Aaron Douglas did covers for the journal *Opportunity*. Painter William H. Johnson specialized in primitive style paintings of religious themes. Augusta Savage was the Harlem Renaissance's best-known sculptor and ran the Savage Studio of Arts and Crafts, which reached out to younger artists.

The crash of 1929 and the ensuing Depression effectively killed the Harlem Renaissance. During the 1930s, unemployment in Harlem was five times that of the rest of the city. Looking back on that time, most participants realized that cultural ferment in Harlem had failed to benefit blacks as a whole.

As Langston Hughes succinctly put it: "The ordinary Negroes hadn't heard of the Negro Renaissance. And if they had, it hadn't raised their wages any." ■

Langston Hughes (1902–1967)

Duke Ellington (1899–1974)

Schomburg Center for Research in Black Culture
www.schomburgcenter.org
- Map p. 191
- 515 Lenox Ave.
- 212/491-2200
- Closed Sun.
- Subway: 2, 3 to 135th St.

Studio Museum in Harlem
- 144 W. 125th St.
- 212/864-4500
- Closed Mon.–Tues.
- $
- Subway: 2, 3 to 125th St.

"Midsummer Night in Harlem," a painting by Palma Hayden (1883–1973), at the Schomburg Center

Schomburg Center for Research in Black Culture

NAMED FOR ARTHUR A. SCHOMBURG (1874–1938), A BLACK Puerto Rican bibliophile, collector, and scholar, the center is one of the best research facilities in the world for the study of the black experience. Among more than five million items in the collection are 125,000 books, 400 black newspapers, and 1,000 periodicals. Rare books include early editions of the poetry of Phyllis Wheatley, an American slave, and Richard Wright's *Native Son*, in the original manuscript. Its facilities include a theater, art galleries, and a well-stocked bookstore/gift shop.

The center's collection is based on material Schomburg compiled after moving to New York from Puerto Rico in 1891. In 1911 he co-founded the Negro Society for Historical Research. In 1926, the Carnegie Foundation purchased his collection—described as "the most extensive collection of Afro-American history and culture in America" (5,000 books, 3,000 manuscripts, 2,000 etchings, and several thousand pamphlets)—for $10,000 and gave it to the New York Public Library. Shortly afterward, the library moved the collection to Harlem to the 135th Street Branch Division of Negro Literature, where Schomburg served as its curator from 1932 until his death in 1938. The branch library was housed in a 1905 building where renaissance writers often met. In 1980, the collection was moved to a new adjacent building; the original building was redone as gallery space for exhibits. ∎

STUDIO MUSEUM IN HARLEM

Founded in 1967 to provide studio space for Harlem artists, the Studio Museum soon developed into a leading museum of black culture housed, since 1982, in its present spacious quarters. Its permanent collection includes paintings by Romare Bearden, Jacob Lawrence, and Faith Ringgold and photography by James VanDerZee (1886–1983) and Gordon Parks. In the late 1970s the museum merged with the James VanDerZee Institute—named for the well-known Harlem photographer and founded to promote the photography of young blacks—and acquired a large collection of his work. The museum sponsors workshops, lectures, artists-in-residence, and films, and has a shop selling books and African crafts. ∎

New York's four vast
outer boroughs—
Brooklyn, Staten Island, the
Bronx, and Queens—offer
museums, parks, and open
space, along with rich ethnic
communities and some of the
oldest buildings in the city.

The Outer Boroughs

Brooklyn Bridge detail

The Outer Boroughs

GONE ARE THE DAYS WHEN A VISIT TO THE OUTER BOROUGHS WAS a maybe on the list of things to do in New York. Today your top ten destinations will likely include at least one borough. There is something for everyone, from the new "Artloop" of museums in Queens; to Arthur Avenue, the Little Italy of the Bronx; to Brooklyn's historic Prospect Park. For those drawn to water, nothing can beat the Staten Island Ferry.

Leading the list of family attractions, the Bronx Zoo, part of the Wildlife Conservation Society, is among the world's best—and free to all on Wednesdays. If you are interested in gardening, a trip to the equally renowned Bronx Botanical Garden is a required stop on any New York itinerary.

Brooklyn also has outstanding cultural institutions. The Brooklyn Academy of Music, known as BAM, is a preeminent performing arts center that sponsors unique avant-garde events. Housed in a neo-Italianate building, it has three major performance spaces. The Brooklyn Museum of Art (see pp. 210–212) is an institution that would be the pride of any city, and its excellent collection is large and varied.

Some people believe that Staten Island is the city's undiscovered treasure, though Staten Islanders know this, and many have wanted to secede from the city for decades. Along with a number of unique museums, Staten Island has more colonial-era buildings than anywhere else in the city.

Queens, the largest borough, is presently generating tremendous excitement. The fact that many immigrant populations choose it as their new home gives it a vital ethnic flavor, especially in its restaurants. But it is the continuing influx of cultural organizations that has caused a spike in tourism. P.S.1 Contemporary Art Center broke new ground when it opened its vast exhibit space in 1997, and the 2002 opening of MoMA Queens firmly established the borough's place in the arts. And these are just two of its many art venues. To facilitate your trip, the Queens Council of the Arts (718/647-3377) offers a free illustrated map to the Artloop in western Queens.

For sports and outdoor recreation, the

boroughs are a paradise. Baseball fans flock to Shea Stadium in Queens or Yankee Stadium in the Bronx; horse-racing enthusiasts to Aqueduct to Belmont in Queens. Queens also hosts the U.S. World Tennis Open. There are beaches from Brooklyn's Coney Island to the Long Island Rockaways, while Staten Island, and Brooklyn's Jamaica Bay, hold excellent nature preserves. ■

Brooklyn Heights walk

Brooklyn Heights was developed in the early 1800s as the city's first suburb; many of its streets—Pierrepont, Hicks, Middagh, Remsen, Joralemon—are named for early landowners. Today it is a living museum of residential architecture, and the city's first historic district. Just a brief distance from Wall Street by subway, or a quick walk across the Brooklyn Bridge, this is a cohesive, well-kept neighborhood, where such well-known writers as Walt Whitman and Truman Capote lived and where many prominent people still reside. Go there to escape busy Manhattan, to enjoy views from the Brooklyn Promenade, and to absorb the atmosphere of 19th-century privilege and contentment its tranquil streets exude.

Start at **Borough Hall ❶** *(209 Joralemon St.)*—a subway stop—a highly regarded marble Greek Revival building constructed in 1845–48 as the Brooklyn City Hall, and renamed Borough Hall after the 1898 consolidation with Manhattan and the other boroughs. Continue west on Joralemon Street to No. 170. The colleges of Oxford and Cambridge were the model for Minard Lafever's Gothic Revival **Packer Collegiate Institute** (1853–56), among the city's oldest private schools.

Turn right onto Henry Street and head north toward Remsen Street. The (Congregational) Church of the Pilgrims (1844–46) here was designed by Richard Upjohn in the Romanesque Revival style with typical rounded arches. A Victorian addition was made in 1869. In 1994, the church merged with Plymouth Church (see p. 207), and the building was sold to the **Our Lady of Lebanon Cathedral ❷**. Continue on Henry Street to Montague Street and turn right to the Holy Trinity Church (Episcopal), on Clinton at Montague Street. Now **St. Ann and the Holy Trinity Episcopal Church ❸** *(Tel 718/875-6960)*, this church was also designed by Lafever. When built in 1844–47, it was the largest church in Brooklyn. The red sandstone exterior and the stained-glass windows by William and John Bolton have been restored.

Turn left on Clinton Street, and left on Pierrepont Street to No. 128, the **Brooklyn Historical Society ❹** *(Tel 718/222-4111, closed Tues.–Wed. & Sun.)*, where many unusual Brooklyn artifacts are exhibited. (The society will be undergoing extensive renovation until late 2003. Research facilities will be closed until then; the museum remains open.) The Renaissance-style exterior has terra-cotta ornamentation, and its interior is a designated landmark. Built between 1842 and 1844 at Pierrepont Street and Monroe Place, the **First Unitarian Church of Brooklyn, Church of the Saviour ❺** *(Tel 718/624-5466)* is considered one of Lafever's masterpieces.

Continue on Pierrepont to Willow Street and turn right. This pleasant street has fine examples of residential architecture. Note Nos. 108, 110, and 112 on the west side, whose bay windows, dormers, towers, and doorways make them examples of the 1880s shingle style. Across the street, an earlier stable at Nos. 151 and 155–59 Willow Street was, according to legend, linked by a tunnel used for the Underground Railroad.

Turn left on Clark, and then right, which places you on the romantic **Brooklyn Promenade ❻**, or Esplanade, a parklike, cantilevered walkway completed in 1950 over the Brooklyn Queens Expressway. Running between Remsen and Orange Streets, it has incomparable views of the harbor, Brooklyn Bridge, and Lower Manhattan, and is a frequent film location. You may remember it from the film *Saturday Night Fever*.

With the water on your left, pass Pineapple Street, turning right onto Orange Street, left on Willow, and right on Middagh to **No. 24 Middagh Street ❼**. The beautifully proportioned, federal-style, clapboard house at the corner of Willow is the former Eugene Boisselet residence. Built in 1829, it is one of Brooklyn Height's oldest and most cherished houses. **Number 30 Middagh Street** is even older—1824—but not as well preserved.

Continue to Hicks Street and turn right, then left on Orange Street. If you get a bit lost on any of these turns, just wander. Between Hicks and Henry Streets, the famous Plymouth Church, now **Plymouth Church of the Pilgrims ❽** *(Tel 718/624-4743),* is a simple, barnlike brick structure designed by

---

▣   Map inside front cover
▶   Borough Hall
⬌   2 miles
🕒   2 hours
▶   Plymouth Church of the
      Pilgrims

NOT TO BE MISSED
- Cathedral of Our Lady of Lebanon
- Brooklyn Historical Society
- Brooklyn Promenade
- Plymouth Church of the Pilgrims

Joseph C. Wells and completed in 1849. The parish house and connecting arcade at 75 Hicks Street are 1914 additions. From 1847 to 1887, Henry Ward Beecher (brother of Harriet Beecher Stowe, the author of *Uncle Tom's Cabin*) was the church's pastor. Beecher was a spellbinding preacher and an ardent abolitionist. To demonstrate the horrors of the slave trade, he once auctioned off a slave girl from the pulpit, and then used the proceeds to buy her freedom. Beecher was later publicly accused of improper relations with a married woman. Although exonerated, the widely publicized scandal was damaging to his career. The tour ends here, and you can stroll to the corner of Henry, turn right, wander down to **Montague Street,** the heart of the Heights, where there are plenty of shops and restaurants. ■

The well-kept row houses of Brooklyn Heights make the neighborhood one of the most desirable in the city.

Prospect Park & environs

LANDSCAPE ARCHITECTS CALVERT VAUX AND FREDERICK Law Olmsted thought that Prospect Park (1866–67) was their best effort; today many agree, including some Manhattanites who consider it their favorite park. Unlike Central Park, which is confined in a rectangular box, Prospect Park's 526-acre area is irregularly shaped, a configuration that makes it seem more a natural part of the urban landscape.

Prospect Park
www.prospectpark.org
🅰 205 C2
✉ Boathouse Visitor
Center, Lincoln Rd.
entrance, Brooklyn
☎ 718/965-8999
🚇 Subway: 2, 3 to
Grand Army Plaza

Victory in a chariot drawn by four horses streaks across the top of the triumphal arch at Grand Army Plaza.

A short distance from the Brooklyn Public Library is the northern entrance to the park, **Grand Army Plaza.** Designed by Olmsted and Vaux in 1870, the statuary here makes this indeed grand and memorable. Take a look at the plaza. It is centered on the Soldiers' and Sailors' Memorial Arch, erected in 1892 to honor the Union dead in the Civil War. The 80-foot-high arch is topped by a bronze group done by sculptor Frederick W. MacMonnies at the turn of the 20th century. Since 1981 there has been a small art gallery inside the arch that shows changing exhibits.

By the park entrance is a detailed standing park map for orientation. First, you enter the enormous 75-acre **Long Meadow,** usually filled with clusters of people—barbecuing, playing catch, sunning, drumming, playing guitars—having a good time. From here, the park unfolds in a succession of open spaces alternating with intimate ones.

Olmsted and Vaux also designed **Eastern Parkway,** today a designated scenic landmark, running between Grand Army Plaza and Ralph Avenue. The partners envisioned it as a first link in a tree-lined boulevard that would connect Prospect and Central Parks. Later in the century, architects McKim, Mead & White added more formal elements to the park, such as gates, pavilions, and the Corinthian templelike **Croquet Shelter** at Parkside Avenue on the park's southern end near Prospect Lake.

One of the favorite park attractions is the **Prospect Park Carousel,** a reminder of the days when Brooklyn was a center of carousel manufacturing, from 1875 to 1918. Nearby, located in an 18th-century structure, **Lefferts Historic House** (Flatbush Ave., tel 718/789-2822) offers period rooms, workshops, and crafts demonstrations. Another popular children's destination is the 14-acre Prospect Park Zoo, now the **Prospect Park Wildlife Center** (450 Flatbush Ave., tel 718/399-7339). Throughout the year, the park is used by joggers, skaters, and hikers, plus there are sponsored celebrations and musical and performing arts events; many are held at the Prospect Park Bandshell (Prospect Park W. at 9th St., tel 718/965-8999 for weekly schedules). ∎

Park Slope Historic District

PROSPECT PARK IS BORDERED TO THE NORTHWEST BY THE Park Slope Historic District, a residential area developed after the opening of the Brooklyn Bridge in 1883, which facilitated the commute to downtown Manhattan.

The row houses in the district are outstanding, especially those designed by C.H.P. Gilbert on Carroll Street and Montgomery Place. The **Montauk Club** *(25 8th Ave. and Lincoln Pl., closed to the public)* has terra-cotta detailing that mixes Venetian style with sculptural representations of the Montauk Indians. At St. John's Place and Seventh Avenue await three exceptional Gothic-style churches: **St. John's Episcopal** (1889), **Grace Methodist** (1883), and **Memorial Presbyterian** (1883).

Southwest of the park, the 478-acre **Greenwood Cemetery,** which opened in 1840, became popular when Gov. De Witt Clinton's body was moved there in 1844. There are 20 miles of paths winding about wooded glades, streams, lakes, and hills. "Boss" Tweed, Peter Cooper, Samuel F.B. Morse, and Horace Greeley are among the notables buried there.

The **Pieter Claesen Wyckoff House Museum** is the oldest building in New York City and one of the oldest wooden houses in the country. It was built in 1652—with additions in 1740 and 1819—by a Dutch indentured servant who became a wealthy farmer. The one-story, shingled house has overhanging eaves typical of Dutch vernacular architecture. It remained in the Wyckoff family until 1902. The city restored it using period materials and building techniques in 1982. After exploring here, go to **Seventh Avenue,** the main thoroughfare for shopping and places to eat. ■

St. John's Episcopal Church
☎ 718/783-3928

Grace Methodist Church
☎ 718/638-1165

Memorial Presbyterian Church
☎ 718/638-5541

Pieter Claesen Wyckoff House Museum
www.wyckoffassociation.org
✉ 5816 Clarendon Rd. at Ralph Ave., Brooklyn
☎ 718/629-5400
🕐 Open Tues.–Sun., by appt. only

The quaint row houses of Park Slope

Brooklyn Museum of Art

Brooklyn Museum of Art

www.brooklynmuseum.org

🅐 205 C2

✉ 200 Eastern Parkway, Brooklyn

☎ 718/638-5000

🕐 Closed Mon.–Tues.

💲 $$

🚇 Subway: 2, 3 to Eastern Parkway; D, Q to Prospect Park

AS ORIGINALLY DESIGNED, THE BROOKLYN MUSEUM OF Art was to have been six times larger than it is today. After Brooklyn was annexed to Manhattan in 1898, museum construction was scaled back. Even so, today the museum is the second largest in New York, seventh largest in the United States, and among the country's most prestigious institutions. It is housed in a stunning beaux-arts landmark with allegorical statuary, designed by architects, McKim, Mead & White as a temple grand enough to house the museum's treasures.

In addition to the areas devoted to collections, the first floor has a café, museum shops, and space for large-scale installations by contemporary artists. The "Dame of the Narrows" by Red Grooms turned the **Lobby Gallery** into a delightful version of New York Harbor for several years (1992–95). A popular spot in summer is the outdoor sculpture garden, where there is live jazz amid the sculptures rescued from demolished houses.

MUSEUM HIGHLIGHTS

A pioneer in the collection and study of non-Western art, in 1923 Brooklyn Museum was the first to exhibit African objects as art. Visit the **African Art Gallery** on the first floor to view such outstanding pieces as the *Karanse* mask, a dance mask with a six-foot-high top, made by the Mossi people to honor the dead. Nearby, the arts of Central America and South America includes the 2,000-year-old "Paracas Textile." Exquisitely created, its border has 90 male figures in ritualistic dress. A must-see on the third floor is the museum's extensive Egyptian collection, one of the world's most famous,

with everything from immense wall sculptures to delicately sculptured jewelry. On the fourth floor, visit the 28 superb American period rooms, including the **Moorish Smoking Room** (complete with bronze *hookah*) from John D. Rockefeller's 1880s West 54th Street home. Before leaving the fourth floor, enjoy the view from above of the third-floor beaux-arts court.

On the fifth floor, primarily devoted to painting and sculpture, the **Iris and B. Gerald Cantor Gallery** holds 58 Rodin sculptures given to the museum by the Cantors in the 1980s. East of this gallery, the **Gallery of Old Masters and French Impressionists** includes a strong collection of 19th-century French art, with works by Cézanne, Degas, Matisse, Toulouse-Lautrec, and others. Also on this floor see the American Paintings Collection.

AMERICAN PAINTINGS COLLECTION

Displayed around the central courtyard on the fifth floor, this collection of 18th- and 19th-century American art is superb. Portraits include two of George Washington by Charles Willson Peale and Gilbert Stuart; and "Portrait of Betsey Beckwith" by the itinerant portraitist Ammi Phillips (1788–1865). Among the religious paintings are Benjamin West's "The Angel of the Lord Announcing the Resurrection to the Three Marys at the Sepulchre" (1805). One gallery displays works by Henry Inman, George Caleb Bingham, Williams Sidney Mount, and Asher B. Durand. The Hudson River school and American impressionism are well represented, and there are fine works by John Singer Sargent, Winslow Homer, and Thomas Eakins. Especially popular is "Storm

George Caleb Bingham's "Shooting for the Beef" (1850)

in the Rocky Mountains" (1866) by Albert Bierstadt, and "Brooklyn Bridge" by Georgia O'Keeffe.

EGYPTIAN COLLECTION

Covering four millennia, and displayed in six galleries in the renovated west wing, this collection is based on the bequest of Charles Edwin Wilbour (1833–1896). A journalist turned Egyptologist, Wilbour conducted extensive excavations in the Nile Valley. His widow gave his library and collection to the museum, and in 1932 their children provided an endowment to establish the Department of Egyptology. The Egyptian galleries hold more than 500 objects, in two exhibits, one chronological and one of the theme of tombs and temples. In gallery one of the chronological exhibition, covering the Late Dynasty 18 and Armana Period (1347–1334 B.C.), is one of Wilbour's more famous finds; a plaque depicting King Akhenaten, who became pharoah in 1352 B.C., and his wife Nefertiti. The second gallery covers the Late 18th Dynasty to the start of the Roman Period (circa 1336 B.C. to circa 30 B.C.). It includes material from the reign of King Tutankhamun (circa 1336–1327 B.C.), and the extraordinary "Coffin for an Ibis," made to contain a mummified bird believed to be a manifestation of the god Thoth. Highlights of the thematic exhibit are a funeral monument of Ramesses II (1279–1213 B.C.) and thirty limestone blocks with finely carved reliefs, some still in progress, from the tomb of Nespeqashuty (664–610 B.C.).

DEVELOPMENT OF THE MUSEUM

Walt Whitman was among the early directors of the Brooklyn Apprentices Library, founded by citizenry in 1823 to aid youths "in learning the mechanic arts and … becoming useful and respectable members of society." After various phases, the library grew to become the Brooklyn Institute of Arts and Sciences—which along the way acquired a fine arts gallery—later renamed the Brooklyn Museum.

In 1893 architects McKim, Mead & White won a competition to design a new building. The firm's plan, calling for four wings, each with a glass-covered central court, would have made the Brooklyn Museum the world's largest, surpassing the Louvre. Only the west wing and one court were ever finished.

In 1986, a new master plan for the museum's growth and modernization was devised and the redesign of the West Wing galleries and the Egyptian collection was completed in 1993. ∎

**Brooklyn
Childrens Museum**

✉ 145 Brooklyn Ave.,
Brooklyn
☎ 718/735-4400
🕐 Closed Mon. & Tues.
💲 Donation
🚇 Subway: 2 to
Kingston Ave.

Brooklyn Childrens Museum

This museum, several blocks west of the Brooklyn Museum, is entered under a 1907 trolley kiosk, located below ground in Brower Park. Founded in 1899, the museum is the world's oldest children's museum. It moved to its new underground facility in 1976 from two brownstones. Its interior, approached through a culvert, is an intriguing maze of passageways on different levels. The museum led the way in creating interactive exhibits for children. One permanent exhibit, "Night Journeys," offers children the opportunity to stretch out on beds from different cultures. The museum also has a popular large doll collection. ∎

Brooklyn Botanic Garden

The unruffled waters of a reflecting pool at the Botanic Garden

FROM THE AROMATIC FRAGRANCE GARDEN TO THE winding Japanese Garden, the Brooklyn Botanic Garden is a triumph of the garden designer's art. With a seemingly endless succession of formal and informal landscapes and different specialized areas, the garden seems much larger than its mere 52 acres.

The Brooklyn Institute of Arts and Sciences founded the Botanic Garden, next to the museum, in 1910. Architects McKim, Mead & White designed the **Victorian Palm Conservatory** and the administration building, and landscape architect Harold Caparn did the layout of the grounds.

Two early additions to the garden, both in 1914, were the children's garden, the first of its kind in the world—where schoolchildren learn the techniques of vegetable and flower gardening—and the **Japanese Hill and Pond Garden,** north of the main entrance. Designed by a Japanese artist living in New York, the garden borders an irregularly shaped pond that is overlooked by a shrine to the Shinto god of the harvest. Nearby is the rectangular **Cherry Esplanade,** planted with double rows of Kwanzan cherry trees, a gift from Japan. The trees begin to blossom in early May, an unforgettable sight that draws many visitors.

The garden's latest addition is the 1988 **Steinhardt Conservatory,** housing the Bonsai Museum, with over 750 species of bonsai, and an exhibit called the "Trail of Evolution," illustrating four billion years of plant development. The conservatory also includes the Aquatic House, with displays of water lilies and other water plants and, on the lower level, three sections devoted to tropical, desert, and warm temperate plantings. ∎

Brooklyn Botanic Garden
www.bbg.org
🅰 205 C2
✉ 1000 Washington Ave., Brooklyn
☎ 718/623-7200
🕐 Closed Mon.
💲 $
🚇 Subway: 2, 3 to Eastern Parkway

Coney Island

BROOKLYN'S CONEY ISLAND IS AN ETHNICALLY DIVERSE and complex neighborhood of some 50,000 people—and home to its claim to fame today, the historic and world-famous amusement park, Coney Island. The park flourished early in the 20th century, then declined after World War II, but the glamour and fantasy of it all seized the American imagination and has hung on to this day. In fact, there is serious talk of restoring what little is left of Coney Island.

Coney Island
205 CI
Subway: B, D, F, N
to Coney Island
718/946-1353

Go there regardless; let your imagination sweep away the tawdriness and take you back to when Coney Island was vibrant with lights and color and packed with people in pursuit of nothing more than a good time. Though diminished from its former size, there is enough left in the way of history and thrills to

Still an attraction after nearly 80 years—the Wonder Wheel at Coney Island

make your trip to Brooklyn's outer reaches worthwhile. Three attractions have landmark status, the most famous of these being the **Cyclone,** one of the few gravity-ride, wooden track roller coasters left in the world. Built in 1927, it hits speeds of 68 miles an hour as it races

through nine drops and six curves. The **Wonder Wheel,** a 150-foot-high Ferris wheel, opened on Memorial Day in 1920. It has 24 passenger cars that not only rock but slide along tracks as the wheel turns. The **Parachute Jump,** near the Coney Island Boardwalk, came to Coney Island from the New York World's Fair of 1939–1940. Although long closed, the steel tower remains a beckoning landmark. And, if the sea air makes you hungry, there is the original **Famous Nathan's,** a hot dog stand opened in 1916, still a fixture on Surf Avenue.

CONEY ISLAND'S THREE PARKS

Coney Island was actually three amusement parks that have blended into one in memory. George Tilyou opened Steeplechase Park at West 17th Street in 1897; here patrons could race on mechanical horses attached to iron rails or try to hold on to a fast-spinning wooden disk called the Human Roulette Wheel. Luna Park (1903) was a fantasyland of minaret towers, its buildings outlined by more than a million light bulbs. The third park, Dreamland, quieter and more tasteful, featured reproductions of the Tower of Seville and Venetian canals. Of the three, it was the least successful. Fire ended it in 1911. Luna Park burned in 1944, and Steeplechase Park closed in 1964. ■

In & around Staten Island

A FERRY RIDE FROM MANHATTAN TO THE ISLAND LEAVES you at the St. George Ferry Terminal, in an area you can explore on foot. There are buses right at the terminal that will take you directly to nearby attractions, including the Snug Harbor Cultural Center, the Alice Austen House, Fort Wadsworth, and the zoo. For more distant attractions, a car is recommended because public transportation will involve many connections.

Leaving the terminal on Richmond Terrace, you'll find **Borough Hall,** which has historical exhibits. Behind the police station, the **Staten Island Institute of Arts and Sciences** (75 Stuyvesant Place, tel 718/727-1135, closed Sun.) dates from 1881. It has more than two million items, including 55,000 photos and a collection of 19th-century painting, sculpture, and decorative arts.

On the island's northern end (but just a few minutes from the terminal by bus), the **Snug Harbor Cultural Center** is located in the impressive Greek Revival buildings founded in 1831 as a retirement home for "aged, decrepit, and worn out sailors."

The former Administration Building (also called Building C) houses the **Newhouse Center for Contemporary Art** (Tel 718/448-2500, closed Mon.–Thurs.), a community gallery. Other organizations in the center include the **Staten Island Children's Museum** (Tel 718/273-2060, closed Mon.), with interactive, hands-on exhibits, and the **Staten Island Botanical Garden** (Tel 718/273–8200), which maintains specialized gardens and collections.

Farther inland, the eight-acre **Staten Island Zoo,** founded in 1936, is known for its Serpentarium with its many North American rattlesnakes. ∎

From the ferry you get an unforgettable view of Staten Island. On the return, the view of Manhattan is even better.

Snug Harbor Cultural Center
- 204 B2
- 1000 Richmond Terrace
- 718/448-2500
- Bus: S40 from the ferry terminal

Staten Island Zoo
- 204 B2
- 614 Broadway
- 718/442-3100
- $ (free Wed.)

Staten Island Ferry
- Manhattan to Staten Island
- 718/815-BOAT

Alice Austen House

Alice Austen House

www.aliceausten.org

🅰 205 C2

✉ 2 Hylan Blvd., Staten Island

☎ 718/816-4506

🕐 Closed Mon.–Wed., & Jan.–Feb.

💲 $

🚌 Bus: S51 from the ferry terminal

THIS UNIQUE MUSEUM IS LOCATED AT THE VERY EDGE OF Staten Island, overlooking the Narrows. The onetime home of Alice Austen (1866–1952), the museum is dedicated to the life and work of one of America's finest early women photographers. The Austen house was originally built as a cottage in the early 18th century. Austen's grandfather purchased it in 1844 and enlarged and remodeled it in the Gothic Revival style, naming it Clear Comfort. A visit here provides an opportunity not only to view some of Austen's work, but to savor the lifestyle of Staten Island's middle class at the turn of the 20th century, when travel was as much by water as by foot—hence the waterfront location of the better homes.

Much of Austen's extant work consists of scenes from the photographer's pleasant surroundings and lifestyle—picnics, the interiors of friends' homes, motor racing, and parties. One sequence done for a woman's "how-to" book on bicycling illustrated the art of mounting, pedaling, and dismounting in a long skirt. More daring, and difficult to achieve, given the size and weight of the large format equipment she used, was her street photography. Austen ventured into the midst of New York City to photograph such subjects as immigrants arriving at the Battery and at the Quarantine Station on Staten Island. Her work on the

Photographer Alice Austen lived at Clear Comfort on Staten Island until 1945.

Lower East Side includes the well-known 1896 photograph of an egg peddler on Hester Street. In this body of work, Austen has been cited alongside photographers Jacob Riis and Lewis Hine, who focused on social issues of the time.

An inheritance from her father enabled Austen to live comfortably for most of her life, until losses in the 1929 stock market crash forced her to mortgage the house, which she lost in 1945. By the time a researcher for *Life* magazine came across some of her photographs in 1951, she was an indigent resident at the Staten Island Farm Colony. *Life* did an article on her that gave her the funds to spend the last six months of her life in a private nursing home. The article also spurred the Staten Island Historical Society to acquire what remained of her work—some 4,800 negatives, many of them glass. The Friends of Alice Austen House are gradually restoring the residence, which was declared a city landmark in 1971. Although Austen's rediscovery came too late to do her much good, today the Alice Austen House preserves her home, her place in the history of American photography, and, most importantly, her work, a fascinating female perspective on turn-of-the-century New York. ∎

Historic Richmond Town

HISTORIC RICHMOND TOWN (1611) IS PROOF THAT NEW York City has everything—even a restored rural village. In this Staten Island complex, you can browse through a late 19th-century general store (in the Stephens-Black House) or watch craftsmen make woodsplint baskets in the Basketmaker's House (1810), or throw pots in the basement of the Guyon-Lake-Tysen House, an exquisite Dutch Colonial-style house built about 1740 (with later additions).

The restoration has some of the oldest restored buildings in the city. The wood-and-stone Britton Cottage (central section: circa 1670) predates the founding of the settlement in 1690. The house was moved to Richmond Town in 1967. Because Richmond Town was located at the center of the island, it became the seat of government about 1730.

Eleven of the 28 buildings in the restoration are original to the site, including the circa 1695 Voorleezer House—also the oldest surviving elementary school in the country. The settlers, members of the Dutch Reform Church, built the house for their lay reader, or *voorleezer,* who was also the schoolteacher. More than a century and a half later, in 1855, the congregation built the Parsonage for the Dutch Reformed minister, but by then their church was in decline.

The Greek Revival Third County Courthouse (1837) is now the Visitor Center and the first stop on a tour of the restoration to see craftsmen and costumed staff re-enacting life in the 17th century. The historical museum is also located in a government building: the Richmond County Clerk's and Surrogate's Office (1848). The museum's permanent exhibit examines the economy and history of the island. ∎

Historic Richmond Town
www.historicrichmondtown
.org

🅐 204 B1

✉ 441 Clarke Ave., Staten Island

☎ 718/351-1611

🕐 Closed Mon.–Tues. Hours vary with season

💲 $

🚌 Bus: S74 from the ferry terminal

Some of Richmond Town's earliest settlers are buried in the Reseau-Van Pelt Cemetery, located near the present-day Visitor Center.

More Staten Island sites

CONFERENCE HOUSE

One of the oldest houses in the city, the two-and-a-half-story Billop House, named for Christopher Billop who built it about 1680, is located in a park on the southern tip of Staten Island. Its current name refers to an unsuccessful peace conference that took place in the early days of the American Revolution—on September 11, 1776—between American patriots Benjamin Franklin, John Adams, and Edward Rutledge and British Vice-Admiral Lord Richard Howe. The house is open for guided tours and the grounds are a pleasant spot to picnic.
204 A1   7455 Hylan Blvd.
718/984-2086   Closed winter (call for details) & Mon.–Tues. $ Bus: S78 to Craig Ave., walk one block south into the park

GARIBALDI-MEUCCI MUSEUM

Inland from the Alice Austen House, this is a circa 1845 farmhouse known for its two famous residents. One of them, Antonio Meucci (1808–1889) was an Italian-born immigrant with a plausible claim to having invented the telephone several years before Alexander Graham Bell; the other was the Italian hero, Giuseppe Garibaldi (1807–1882). Meucci moved to Staten Island in 1850. His attempts to take out a patent on his invention failed because of his poverty and poor English. When Garibaldi fled to New York after the defeat of the republican forces in Italy, Meucci took him in. Garibaldi lived there for almost a year until becoming a sea captain, his original occupation, and finally returned to Italy in 1853 to resume his struggle. Throughout the house are exhibits on the men's lives, including a prototype of Meucci's telephone and his death mask.
204 B2   420 Tompkins Ave. 718/442-1608   Closed Mon. $ Bus: S52, S78 to Tompkins Ave.

JACQUES MARCHAIS MUSEUM OF TIBETAN ART

Not far from the Richmond Town restoration, built in the style of Tibetan monasteries, this

An example of the beautiful items of Tibetan art exhibited in the Jacques Marchais Museum

museum houses the art collection of a Madison Avenue art dealer, Edna Coblentz, who devoted her life to studying and collecting Tibetan art.
204 B2   338 Lighthouse Ave.
718/987-3500   Closed Mon.–Tues.
$ Bus: S74 to Lighthouse Ave.

PIERRE BILLIOU HOUSE (BILLIOU-STILLWELL-PERINE HOUSE)

This is the oldest building surviving on Staten Island and also one of the oldest house museums, having been opened to the public in 1919. The original stone farmhouse was built in the 1660s; additions were added, extending the house in every direction, over the next century and a half.
204 B1   1476 Richmond Rd., Dongan Hills 718/351-1611   Open by appointment, call caretaker ■

In & around the Bronx

WHEN THE NATIONAL CIVIC COUNCIL DESIGNATED the Bronx as an All-American City in 1997, it symbolized this community's turnaround from its economic plight of the late 1970s.

Ever popular attractions include the Bronx Zoo (see p. 221) and Botanical Garden (see p. 220), but a tour with the Bronx County Historical Society *(718/881-8900)* offers a more intimate experience. The choices are varied, covering neighborhoods, ethnic areas, and historic sites, from Riverdale, with its views of the Hudson, to the seaside area of City Island, to the art deco homes along the Grand Concourse. Tours by bicycle and horse are also possible.

The **Museum of Bronx History** *(3309 Bainbridge Ave., tel 718/881–8900)* offers unique artifacts relating to the borough's past and a research library. It is housed in the Valentine-Varian House, a circa 1758 fieldstone residence built by blacksmith Isaac Valentine.

The Bronx Community College campus boasts two architectural treasures designed by Stanford White: Gould Memorial Library (1887–99) and the **Hall of Fame for Great Americans** *(University Ave. and W. 181st St., tel 718/289-5161)*. The latter, a 630-foot-long semicircular arcade, holds portrait busts of 97 famous Americans (Franklin D. Roosevelt was the most recently added, in 1992).

Among the 300,000 interred in the 400 acres of the pastoral 1863 **Woodlawn Cemetery** *(Jerome Ave. at Webster Ave. & E. 233rd, tel 718/920-0500)* are such luminaries as Herman Melville, Miles Davis, and F. W. Woolworth, in an Egyptian Revival mausoleum.

A rickety wooden bridge connects the mainland to 2-mile-long **City Island,** a picturesque fishing village rich in nautical history. Its

blend of boatyards, seafood restaurants, galleries, and antique shops overlook Eastchester Bay and Long Island Sound—to some it resembles a New England fishing village. Boatmakers here have built five America's Cup winners. Don't miss the quaint Victorian architecture along Schofield Street.

Home to the New York Yankees (the Bronx Bombers) and known as the House That Ruth Built, **Yankee Stadium** *(River Ave. at 161st St., tel 718/293-6000)* was the first ballpark called a stadium, because of its size. On opening day, April 18, 1923, Babe Ruth hit a game-winning homer. The city of New York bought the stadium in 1972, the same year George Steinbrenner bought the Yankees. When it reopened after renovation in 1976, it had a new name: the House Steinbrenner Rebuilt. ∎

On Opening Day for the New York Yankees, Yankee Stadium is filled to capacity.

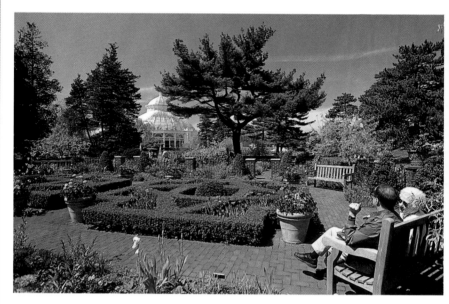

New York Botanical Garden

**New York
Botanical Garden**
www.nybg.org
🅰 205 D5
✉ 200th St. &
Kazimiroff Blvd.,
Bronx
☎ 718/817-8700
🕐 Closed Mon.
💲 $$
🚇 Subway: 4, D to
Bedford Park Blvd.
Bus: Shuttle from
Manhattan (Tel
718/817-8700)
Train: Metro North
from Grand Central
Terminal
(Tel 212/532-4900)

UNLIKELY AS IT MAY SEEM, NEW YORK CITY IS A MECCA FOR
garden lovers; all four outlying boroughs have outstanding botanic
gardens. Anyone here on a garden tour, however, must make the New
York Botanical Garden in the Bronx a priority.

The Bronx garden is distinguished
architecturally by the **Enid A.
Haupt Conservatory** (1902),
based on London's Crystal Palace of
1851. The palm court, 100 feet in
diameter, is located under the 90-
foot-high glass dome; there are ten
other galleries in the wings, includ-
ing two rain forest displays that can
be viewed from various heights on
an elevated catwalk. When the con-
servatory was renovated in 1978,
17,000 glass panes were replaced by
hand. It has been renamed for the
philanthropist who gave five mil-
lion dollars for the restoration.

Some of the newer additions to
the grounds include the **Jane
Watson Perennial Garden**
and the **Peggy Rockefeller
Rose Garden,** installed in 1988.
The rose garden is based on plans

that the well-known garden design-
er Beatrix Farrand drew up in 1916.
A unique garden for children, the
nine-million-dollar, 12-acre
**Everett Children's Adventure
Garden,** opened in 1998. Here,
among many different activities,
children can look for frogs in
a pond, explore the "kids only"
meadow path, and examine their
findings through a microscope in
a laboratory located inside an
Adirondack-style cottage.

The Royal Botanical Gardens at
Kew outside London were the
original inspiration for the Bronx
garden, which opened in 1891 on an
estate that the city had purchased.
The three-and-a-half-story, field-
stone **Snuff Mill** (circa 1840) from
the Lorillard estate has been restored
and is now the garden's restaurant. ■

**Visitors relax
on a garden
bench with the
Enid Haupt
Conservatory in
the background.**

Bronx Zoo

WHATEVER NAME YOU CHOOSE TO CALL IT—BRONX ZOO (official), New York Zoological Park (earlier), or Wildlife Conservation Society (parent organization)—it is, for viewing wild animals in natural surroundings, unsurpassed in the country. Situated on 265 acres, with some 4,500 animals representing more than 500 species, it is also the country's largest urban zoo.

From JungleWorld to Himalayan Highlands to World of Darkness, you can visit habitats of all seven continents, each filled with native animals. What the zoo has been most famous for since its inception in 1899, however, is its innovative approaches to zookeeping. The use of natural settings surrounded by moats rather than cages and a dedicated breeding center for endangered species are just two examples instigated early on. Successful breeding programs have helped restock the West with bison around the turn of the 20th century, and were part of the designs of **Himalayan Highlands** (1986) for snow leopards; and the **Congo Gorilla Forest** (1999), a 6.5-acre African rain forest habitat with 23 lowland gorillas.

The latest exhibit is **Tiger Mountain,** featuring endangered Siberian tigers in a re-created environment where visitors can observe the big cats' natural behavior (including underwater as they swim in a pool).

Consult the zoo map and strategize your visit—there's much to see! Several transportation options are available for an additional fee, including a zoo shuttle, the Safari Train, and the Skyfari aerial tramway. The 40-acre, large-scale outdoor exhibit, **Wild Asia,** is visible only from the Bengali Express, a 25-minute guided tour on a monorail. ∎

Bronx Zoo
www.bronxzoo.com
🅰 205 D5
✉ Fordham Rd. & Bronx River Parkway, Bronx
☎ 718/367-1010
💲 $$ (free Wed.)
🚇 Subway: 2 to Pelham Parkway
Bus: Liberty Lines (private bus service) from Madison Ave. (Tel 718/652-8400)
Train: Metro North from Grand Central

Tiger Mountain re-creates a corner of the Amur Valley, between China and Russia, for Siberian tigers.

Historic houses of the Bronx

BARTOW-PELL MANSION

Thomas Pell purchased land on Long Island Sound from Indians in 1654, but this mansion was not built until 1842. Ten rooms of the classical revival mansion are filled with period furniture, much of it on loan from city museums. The spiral staircase has been attributed to Minard Lafever, a friend of the family. The city purchased the house and the stone carriage house (1840) in 1888; it opened as a museum in 1915.

205 E5 895 Shore Rd. N., Pelham Bay Park 718/885-1461 Open p.m. Wed. & Sat.–Sun. $

EDGAR ALLAN POE COTTAGE

Shortly after he moved to the Bronx in 1846, Edgar Allan Poe described his home as "a snug little cottage." He wrote *Ulalume* and *The Bells* here. The house became a museum in 1917. Three downstairs rooms have been restored to the period Poe lived here; upstairs is an exhibit on his life and an audiovisual presentation.

205 D5 East Kingsbridge Rd. & Grand Concourse 718/881-8900 Closed weekdays $ Subway: D to Kingsbridge Rd. or 4 to Kingsbridge

VAN CORTLANDT HOUSE MUSEUM

Built in 1748, this elegant Georgian-style manor house was briefly used by George Washington during the Revolution. Today it is filled with antiques that span the history of this remarkable family, which lived in the house until 1889. Included are a painted cupboard made in the Hudson Valley in the early 18th century and a Gilbert Stuart portrait of John Jacob Astor, who was related to the Van Cortlandts by marriage.

205 D5 Van Cortlandt Park, West 246 St. & Broadway 718/543-3344 Closed Mon. $ Subway: 1, 9 to 242th St.

WAVE HILL

The two mansions on this 28-acre estate were built in the mid-19th and early 20th centuries. Theodore Roosevelt, Mark Twain, and Arturo Toscanini lived here at different times. Today, Wave Hill is a cultural center, but most visitors come to tour the stunning gardens overlooking the Hudson River and New Jersey Palisades.

205 D5 West 249th St. 718/549-3200 Closed Mon. $ (free during winter months) Subway: A to 207th Street and then No. 7 bus northbound. ∎

Sunshine highlights the fall beauty of Wave Hill.

In & around Queens

THE TEMPORARY MOVE OF THE MUSEUM OF MODERN ART
to Queens in 2002 (see pp. 122–126) has sparked an arts boom in this
typically snubbed outer borough. In addition to bringing crowds to
admire world-famous tableaus of modern art, it has also focused
attention on several art venues here that are more than Manhattan
worthy: among them, the P.S.1 Contemporary Art Center (see
p. 224); the American Museum of the Moving Image (see p. 225); the
Isamu Noguchi Garden Museum (see p. 226); and the Museum of
African Art (see p. 226).

Beyond the arts scene, Queens is a
uniquely multiethnic neighborhood with much to offer. Thanks to
its hosting of two world fairs, in
1939–1940 and 1964–65, the
**Flushing Meadows-Corona
Park** area is today the site of many
of the borough's leading attractions. With 1,255 acres, it is the
city's second largest park. Several
fair structures remain, most promi-
nently the **Unisphere**, the largest
globe in the world, built by U.S.

Steel as the symbol of the 1964–65
World's Fair. Another refurbished
structure, the New York City
Building (used for fairs in both
1939–40 and 1964–65), is now
the **Queens Museum of Art**
(*Tel 718/592-5555, closed Mon.*). It
houses contemporary art and the
world's largest architectural scale
model, a 9,335-square-foot panorama of New York City.

Also in the park, the 1964–65
World's Fair Space Center was

Note: The Artlink shuttle
takes visitors from
the Manhattan
MoMA to MoMA
QNS; tel 212/708-
9750. The shuttle
also offers a circuit
linking seven
cultural sites in
Queens.

**The Unisphere,
an imposing relic
of the 1964–65
World's Fair**

The Bowne House, the oldest in Queens, is also a monument to the colonial struggle for religious tolerance.

converted into the **New York Hall of Science** *(Tel 718/699-0005)* in 1986. It features a variety of interactive displays on physics, biology, and technology, including one titled "Hidden Kingdoms—the World of Microbes"—a 14-foot sewing needle on which scale models of microbes are displayed.

Queens's major league baseball park, and home of the New York Mets, **Shea Stadium** *(Tel 718/507-8499)* was another project related to the 1964–65 fair.

MORE QUEENS SITES

East of the park, the 1661 **Bowne House** *(37–01 Bowne St. at 37th Ave., tel 718/359-0528)* is the oldest in Queens; it was built by John Bowne, a convert to Quakerism, whom Peter Stuyvesant arrested in 1662 for holding Quaker meetings in the house. By ordering Stuyvesant to free him, the Dutch West India Company established the principle of religious tolerance in the colony (see p. 20). The house was occupied until 1945 by nine generations of Bownes, when it became a museum.

Close by, the **Friends Meeting House** *(Tel 718/358-9636)* was built by Bowne and other Quakers in 1694. It has been used for Quaker services almost continu-ously since. Another Quaker, Charles Doughty, built the nearby Kingsland Homestead about 1785. It is now the **Queens Historical Society** *(143–35 37th Ave., tel 718/939-0647)*, which exhibits memorabilia from the residents, including its second owner, Joseph King, Doughty's son-in-law. There is a Victorian parlor and changing exhibits on Queens history.

The 38 acres of the **Queens Botanical Gardens** *(43–50 Main St., tel 718/886-3800, closed Mon.)* in Flushing include the 4,000-plant rose garden donated by Oregon-based Jackson and Perkins, which started in Queens. There is also a Wedding Garden for marriage ceremonies' photographs, and an ethnic garden, with plants from various countries represented in an ethnically diverse community.

P.S.1 CONTEMPORARY ART CENTER

Located in what was an abandoned public school (P.S. 1), the P.S.1 Contemporary Art Center *(22–25 Jackson Ave., tel 718/784-2084)* reopened in late 1997 after a three-year, 8.5-million-dollar renovation. Now, with 125,000 square feet of exhibit space, it is the world's largest museum for contemporary art. ■

American Museum of the Moving Image

THE AMERICAN MUSEUM OF THE MOVING IMAGE (AMMI) IS America's only museum devoted to the art, history, and technology of motion pictures, television, and video. It's located in one of 13 buildings that comprise the 14-acre studio where production first began in the Silent Era and, after a hiatus, is now back in full swing. From Rudolph Valentino, Gloria Swanson, and the Marx Brothers, to films including *All That Jazz* and *Hair,* to Al Pacino, Meryl Streep, and the resident cast of *Sesame Street,* the parade of movie triumphs and stars lives on.

Famous Players/Lasky (later Paramount Pictures) were first to film at Astoria Studios, starting in 1920. The property transferred to the U.S. Army in 1942, which used it for its own productions until 1971. Falling into disrepair, the studio was saved by the Astoria Motion Picture and Television Foundation in 1977 and soonafter obtained landmark status. In 1982, realizing that additional resources would be needed to return the studio to its feature-film production abilities, the city awarded its redevelopment to George Kaufman, who renamed it Kaufman-Astoria Studios. The city also set aside one building, which opened as AMMI in 1988.

Nostalgia buffs will gravitate to the stunning memorabilia: Shirley Temple dolls, Don Johnson's designer suits from the TV series *Miami Vice,* and even the yellow-brick road from *The Wizard of Oz.* Interactive programs let you become part of moviemaking: Graft your voice onto famous film scenes, insert sound effects into film clips, and piece together moving images in a digital scrapbook.

A permanent exhibit, "Behind the Screen," surveys the history of making, marketing, and exhibiting motion pictures, from 19th-century optical devices to computer animation. Vintage serials play in the whimsical re-creation of a 1920s Egyptian Revival-style movie palace.

Retrospectives, screenings, and special events are offered year-round in the museum's Riklis Theater. ∎

American Museum of the Moving Image
www.movingimage.us

🅰 205 D3
✉ 35th Ave.
    at 36th St., Queens
☎ 718/784-0077
🕐 Closed Mon.
💲 $$
🚇 Subway: R to
    Steinway St.

Nearly a century of motion picture memorabilia and technology are presented in innovative ways at AMMI.

Noguchi's Indoor/Outdoor Garden, in the process of renovation

Isamu Noguchi Garden Museum

Isamu Noguchi Garden Museum

- 205 D4
- Temporary: 36-01 43rd Ave. (at 36th St.), Long Island City; Permanent: 32–7 Vernon Blvd. (at 33rd Rd.)
- 718/204-7088
- Closed Mon.–Tues.
- Donation
- Subway: N to Broadway in Queens

There is something stoic about sculpture that neutralizes or at least calms the restless energy of a big city. The works of world-renowned sculptor Isamu Noguchi (1904–1988) have that affect on New York. His specialty is sculpture for public places, and this indoor/outdoor museum displays it to perfection (he himself designed the space).

Since the museum's permanent location, at 32–7 Vernon Blvd. (at 33rd Rd.), is currently undergoing restoration, it is in temporary nearby space until 2004. Shows are drawn from the permanent collection, including 250 stone, bronze, and wood sculptures,

dance sets for choreographer Martha Graham, models for public projects, and Noguchi's well-known Akari light sculptures, derived from traditional Japanese paper lanterns.

Noguchi was born in Los Angeles, his father a Japanese poet and his mother an American writer. He moved to New York in 1923 to study medicine, but turned instead to art. In 1968 the Whitney Museum mounted a retrospective of his work. The permanent Noguchi museum and garden grew from the artist's studio, which he established in the Queens neighborhood in the 1960s. ■

Nearby sites

Punu face mask, from Gabon

Recently relocated from SoHo to the Noguchi museum's temporary site, the **Museum for African Art** (*36–01 43rd Ave., Long Island City, tel 718/784-7700, closed Tues.–Wed.*) has produced more than 40 shows in its 20-year history, with objects loaned from collections around the globe. "Facing the Mask," for example, provided a family-friendly introduction to African art and culture.

Performances and workshops complement exhibits. The museum plans to move to 119th 5th Ave. in 2006.

The **Socrates Sculpture Park** (*Vernon Blvd. at Broadway, tel 718/956-1819*) is on a four-acre site facing the East River, with a Manhattan skyline view. Here you can see changing exhibits of large-scale sculpture by establishing and emerging artists. ■

You do not have to go far to escape the city. Nearby western Long Island is easy for day trips. The Hudson River Valley—offering military sites, riverside estates, and scenery of incomparable grandeur—is another destination. It can take several days to see it all.

Excursions

Bear Mountain Bridge, Hudson River Valley

The map labels, reading by region:

Hudson River Valley (New York)

Hudson
Catskill
Olana S.H.S.
Germantown
Clermont S.H.S.
Saugerties
Tivoli
West Hurley
Montgomery Place
Rhinebeck
Senate House S.H.S.
Ashokan Reservoir
Kingston
Kerhonkson
West Park
Vanderbilt Mansion N.H.S.
New Paltz
F.D. Roosevelt N.H.S.
Poughkeepsie
Modena
Marlboro
Wappingers Falls
Walden
NEW
Washington's Headquarters S.H.S.
Newburgh
YORK
Lake Carmel
Washingtonville
West Point U.S. Military Academy
Goshen
Monroe
Peekskill
Stony Point Battlefield S.H.S.
Warwick
Croton-on-Hudson
Stony Point
Van Cortlandt Manor
Greenwood Lake
New City
Suffern
Philipsburg Manor
Kykuit
Ramsey
Tarrytown
CONN.
Lyndhurst
Wyckoff
Sunnyside
Port Chester
NEW
JERSEY
Yonkers
Paterson
Paramus
Sagamore Hill N.H.S.
Stony Brook
Museums
Coram
Passaic
Fort Lee Historic Park
Planting Fields Arboretum S.H.P.
Huntington
Centereach
Walt Whitman Birthplace
Old Westbury House & Gardens
Plainview
Brentwood
Medford
Shirley
Newark
Jersey City
NEW YORK CITY
BRONX
Old Bethpage Village
Patchogue
Sayville
Mastic Beach
Bayonne
BROOKLYN
QUEENS
Levittown
Bay Shore
Elizabeth
Hempstead
Massapequa
Lindenhurst
STATEN ISLAND
J.F.K. Airport
Long Beach
JONES BEACH STATE PARK
FIRE ISLAND NATIONAL SEASHORE
Long

Scale:
0 — 20 miles
0 — 30 kilometers

A   B   C   D

Excursions

SOONER OR LATER, EVEN THOSE who thrive on New York's intensity feel the need to put the city behind them. For any so inclined, there are many outstanding choices within shouting distance of the city, some less than a day away. There are beaches, mountains, rivers, lakes, and, because much early history occurred in the region, an abundance of historic sites.

Getting out of the city is another matter, and the difficulty of travel will depend upon your destination. There are subways, buses, trains, and rental cars from which to choose. Of these, driving your own vehicle may be the most difficult, particularly if you are unfamiliar with routes and unaccustomed to the city's renowned traffic jams. But it can be done—just know what to expect. Train travel can be pleasant, though crowds can make traveling during commuter hours stressful, especially to Long Island.

This chapter covers the Hudson River Valley and the western end of Long Island, two nearby regions rich in attractions and quite different in topography, scenery, and character. The Hudson River Valley was home to Rip Van Winkle, Washington Irving's famous character; Long Island lives eternally in literature as the land of F. Scott Fitzgerald's Gatsby. The robber barons of the Gilded Age constructed their ostentatious mansions and gardens on the exclusive North Shore of Long Island. In colonial times, patroons built their magnificent estates along the Hudson. The descendants of Cornelius Vanderbilt constructed houses in both places.

HUDSON RIVER VALLEY

In 1807 inventor Robert Fulton built a steam-powered boat, the *Clermont*. Its inaugural run—along the Hudson River, from New York to Albany in 32 hours—signaled the first profitable venture in steam navigation and ushered in a whole new era in commercial transportation. But it was the 1825 opening of the Erie Canal, from Albany to Buffalo, that made the

Hudson River even more important commercially to Manhattan, as a link between the city and the Great Lakes via the canal. More than Long Island, the Hudson River Valley has retained its historic flavor. There are also stretches, particularly where the mountains descend to the water, that are, to the eye, as unspoiled as they were in the early 19th century, when the Hudson River artists created a school of landscape painting based on the river's incomparable scenery.

LONG ISLAND

One hundred and twenty miles long, and 23 miles across at its widest point, Long Island is mostly flat. Its North Shore is graced by picturesque harbors and inlets. On its southern side, the Atlantic Ocean rolls into its beaches and barrier islands. Farms once covered the entire island; today they are only found on its eastern end. During the Revolution, General Howe drove off Washington and his troops in the Battle of Long Island, August 26–31, 1776, and the island remained in British hands for the rest of the war. Industries that rose there—whaling, shipbuilding, and shipping—are completely gone. Long Island waters are now used more for sport than for commerce. America's newly rich industrialists began building their mansions on Long Island's North Shore—the Gold Coast— at the turn of the 20th century. During the roaring 1920s, Long Island became notorious as a playground for the wealthy, who indulged themselves in fast cars, illegal liquor, polo ponies, and lavish parties. F. Scott Fitzgerald perfectly portrayed the era in *The Great Gatsby*. After World War II, developers turned large tracts into housing developments and shopping malls (the eventual fate of Roosevelt Field). Today, heavily populated western Long Island blends seamlessly into New York City. But there are places where you can step back into the past—into a horticultural paradise of the very rich at Old Westbury Gardens, for example, or into the simple life of an earlier farm at Old Bethpage Village. ■

Hudson River Valley

THIS VISIT TO THE HUDSON RIVER VALLEY PROCEEDS north along the west bank, crosses the river at Catskill, and returns down the east side. Although it only covers some 200 miles, it would take several days to thoroughly see and do everything along the way. However, any combination of sites would make an interesting trip. Those wanting a shorter journey can use any of the several bridges across the Hudson River to return to New York.

Antique artillery pieces guard the Hudson River on heights overlooking West Point.

Start in New Jersey at **Fort Lee Historic Park** *(Hudson Terrace, Palisades Interstate Park),* south of the George Washington Bridge, a reconstruction of a Revolutionary War artillery post. On November 16, 1776, from this vantage point, George Washington watched Fort Washington in northern Manhattan fall to the British. Proceeding north,

enter New York State and detour to the **Stony Point Battlefield S.H.S.** *(Park Road off US 9W).* Here, Gen. Anthony Wayne vanquished the British in a surprise attack on July 16, 1779. There is a small museum *(Tel 845/786-2521, call for hours)* and tours of the battlefield.

Continue on US 9W to **West Point,** where the United States

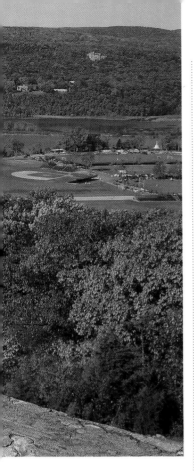

Military Academy overlooks a spectacular and unsullied bend in the Hudson River. Try to visit in the spring or fall when the cadets parade. West Point has trained Army officers since 1802; its four-year course is famous for its rigor and discipline. Before it was a school, West Point was a fortification, designed and built in 1778 by Thaddeus Kosciuszko, the Polish officer who fought for the Americans during the Revolution. Most famous American generals graduated from West Point, but not all excelled. Ulysses S. Grant finished near the bottom of his class; Dwight Eisenhower was a mediocre student. **West Point Museum** has an extensive collection of weapons, military art, uniforms, and diora-

mas explaining historic battles. The **Old Cadet Chapel** (1836) is in the post cemetery and inside, battle flags line the walls. Bertram Grosvenor Goodhue designed the 1910 **Cadet Chapel** in the neo-Gothic style. Near the parade ground rises a monument to Thaddeus Kosciuszko.

After leaving West Point on US 9W, stop in Newburgh at **Washington's Headquarters State Historic Site.** George Washington spent more than a year, 1782–83, in the Hasbrouck House, a small stone dwelling furnished as when he stayed there. There is also a museum of Revolutionary War artifacts on the grounds. The next stop going north is the town of **New Paltz,** founded by French Huguenots in 1677. Six stone houses (1692–1717) remain on Huguenot Street. Tours are conducted from the Historical Society *(Deyo Hall, 18 Broadhead Ave., tel 845/255-1889, May only).*

From New Paltz continue north on US 9W to **Kingston,** the Revolutionary War capital of New York. The first state constitution was adopted in 1777 at the **Senate House S.H.S.** *(296 Fair St., tel 845/338-2786).* Here are exhibits on early state government and paintings by the Hudson River school's John Vanderlyn. Maps of walking tours through Kingston's Stockade Historic District are available at the Urban Cultural Park Visitor Center *(20 Broadway, tel 845/331-7517).*

Leaving Kingston, cross the Hudson at Catskill on the Rip Van Winkle Bridge. Take N.Y. 9G south a mile to **Olana S.H.S.,** the villa overlooking the Hudson River. Its owner, painter Frederic Church (1826–1900), designed it in a style he called "personal Persian." Church, who began living there in 1872, belonged to the Hudson River school of painting.

West Point
www.usma.edu
🅰 228 B4
Visitor information
✉ Building 2110, West Point
☎ 845/938-2638

Washington's Headquarters S.H.S.
🅰 228 B4
✉ Liberty & Washington Sts., Newburgh
☎ 845/562-1115
🕐 Closed Oct.–April
💲 $

Olana S.H.S.
🅰 228 B6
✉ N.Y. 9G, Hudson
☎ 518/828-0135
🕐 Closed Nov.–March
💲 $

Clermont S.H.S.

- 🅰 228 B5
- ✉ 1 Clermont Ave., Germantown
- ☎ 518/537-4240
- 🕐 Closed Mon. April–Oct., & Mon.–Fri. Nov.–mid-Dec.
- 💲 $

Montgomery Place

- 🅰 228 B5
- ✉ North of Kingston-Rhinecliff Bridge
- ☎ 845/758-5461
- 🕐 Closed Tues. April–Oct.
- 💲 $$

Philipsburg Manor and a reconstructed mill

Vanderbilt Mansion N.H.S.

- 🅰 228 B5
- ✉ 519 Albany Post Rd., Hyde Park
- ☎ 914/229-9115
- 🕐 Closed Mon.–Tues. in Nov.–March
- 💲 $

Continue south on N.Y. 9G to the **Clermont State Historic Site** in Germantown. Clermont was the home of Robert R. Livingston, a member of the Continental Congress and chancellor of New York who administered the first presidential oath of office to George Washington. The house (named after the steam-powered boat of his partner, Robert Fulton) was burned by the British in 1777 and rebuilt after independence. A short distance off N.Y. 9G, in Annandale-on-Hudson, is **Montgomery Place,** a meticulously restored mansion. It was built in 1805 by Janet Montgomery, the widow of Gen. Richard Montgomery.

For a great family outing, visit the **Old Rhinebeck Aerodrome** (*Off N.Y. 9 on Stone Church Rd., tel 845/758-8610 or 845/752-3200 for information about tours, rides, and airshows*).

North of Poughkeepsie on N.Y. 9 you will find the **Vanderbilt Mansion,** a lavish two-million-dollar pile built for Frederick W. Vanderbilt in 1899 by McKim, Mead & White.

Continuing south, US 9 will bring you to the **Franklin D.**

Roosevelt National Historic Site (*Tel 845/229-9115*) in Hyde Park, an 1826 house that remains much as it was when Roosevelt died in 1945. Roosevelt and his wife, Eleanor, are buried in the rose garden. Also on the grounds is the Franklin D. Roosevelt Museum and Library, probably the first presidential library. Two miles east is the **Eleanor Roosevelt National Historic Site.** After her husband died, Eleanor lived in the cottage, Val-Kill, until her death in 1962. The **Culinary Institute of America** (*Tel 845/471-6608*) is also located in Hyde Park. Advance reservations are needed for its excellent four student-run restaurants.

Off US 9 in Croton-on-Hudson, is the **Van Cortlandt Manor,** the home (until 1945) of the Van Cortlandt family, once patrons of an 86,000-acre domain. Van Cortlandt Manor is operated by Historic Hudson Valley (*Tel 914/631-8200*), as is **Philipsburg Manor,** an early 18th-century manor house, a working farm, and mill in Sleepy Hollow.

Kykuit (*Tel 914/631-9491*), a 40-room mansion built by John D. Rockefeller, with Rockefeller's collection of modern art, is open to the public (reservations are necessary) and reachable by shuttle bus from Philipsburg Manor.

In Tarrytown, **Lyndhurst** (*US 9, tel 914/631-4481*) was the summer home of railroad baron Jay Gould. Designed by Alexander Jackson Davis, it is one of the best Gothic Revival-style mansions in the country. Also in Tarrytown is **Sunnyside** (*Historic Hudson Valley, tel 914/631-8200*). Author Washington Irving purchased the stone cottage in 1836 and rebuilt it as a cozy but eccentric house.

From here you can continue to explore or head toward Long Island to visit its sights. ■

Long Island

MANY OF LONG ISLAND'S HISTORIC AND OTHER POINTS OF interest are located on its North Shore, near New York City, and recall earlier days when Long Island was farms and seaports and millionaires' estates.

Having promised his English bride that he would create an estate for her similar to her child-hood home, John Jay Phipps, son of Andrew Carnegie's partner, built **Old Westbury House and Gardens** *(71 Old Westbury Rd., Old Westbury, tel 516/333-0048, closed Tues.)*, a 105-acre manor house and estate in 1907. The manor house contains antique fur-niture and paintings by Reynolds, Gainsborough, and Sargent.

The landscaped gardens that surround the mansion include a two-acre, brick Walled Garden with flower borders in bloom from spring to fall. The grounds also include a demonstration garden, rose and boxwood gardens, an allée of European lindens and hemlock hedge, and a Primrose Walk. In May the 2,000 tulips are the attraction; in June it's the arrangement of 300 giant pink and blue delphinium.

The 409-acre **Planting Fields Arboretum State Historic Park** *(Planting Fields Rd., Oyster Bay, tel 516/922-9200, ext. 13 for assistance)* was once the estate of English-born William Coe, an insurance executive who completed his Elizabethan-style manor house in 1921.

The gardens contain more than 600 species of plants, including an ever growing collection of rhododendrons and azaleas and more than 300 camellias grown in a small conservatory. Planting Fields is the translation of the Indian name for the once agricultural North Shore of Long Island.

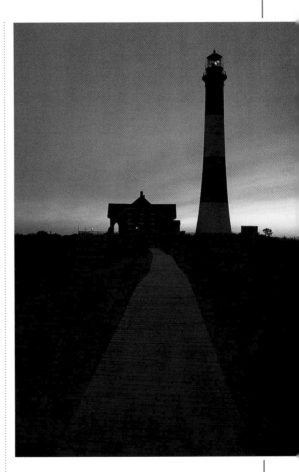

After he graduated from Harvard, Theodore Roosevelt helped to design **Sagamore Hill National Historic Site** *(20 Sagamore Hill Rd., Oyster Bay, tel 516/922-4447, by guided tour only, house closed Mon.–Tues. in winter)*. A rambling 23-room mansion, this was a place he con-sidered home—and used as the

On Long Island's Fire Island, a lighthouse and keeper's cottage stand out against a darkening sky.

The simple parlor in the house where Walt Whitman, perhaps America's greatest poet, began life.

summer White House while he was President—and where he indulged himself in "hard work and the joy of life." The interior, decorated with hunting trophies and mementoes of his travels, reflects Roosevelt's vigorous lifestyle. In 1938 his son built the Old Orchard House next door, now a museum with exhibits on Roosevelt and an introductory film.

In the early 19th century, Long Island was agricultural, and the 50 buildings in the **Old Bethpage Village** *(Round Swamp Rd., Old Bethpage, tel 516/572-8400, closed Mon.–Tues.)* restoration re-create a village of this era. The Powell Farmhouse is on its original site, but the others, including a church, country store, tavern, and houses, were moved here from elsewhere on Long Island. The restoration is also a working farm with interpreters in period costume demonstrating agricultural techniques and crafts.

Walt Whitman (1819–1892) spent the first four years of his life in this early 1800s farmhouse, now the **Walt Whitman Birthplace** *(246 Old Walt Whitman Rd., South Huntington, tel 631/427-5240, closed Tues.).* Nineteenth-century furnishings in the newly restored home

and an interpretive center with 130 Whitman portraits, Whitman's voice on tape, manuscripts, and artifacts, illume the life of America's greatest poet.

Founded in 1939, **Museums at Stony Brook** *(1208 N.Y. 25A, Stony Brook, tel 631/751-0066)* is a historical complex noted for its Carriage Museum. There are more than 300 horse-drawn vehicles, including a 23-foot-long omnibus painted with still lifes, people, and animals. The Art Museum owns many works by genre painter William Sydney Mount, born in nearby Setauket in 1807, who did scenes of rural Long Island. Mount's family home, the Hawkins Mount House (1725), is on the museum grounds, which also has a History Museum and a number of period buildings, including a 1794 barn and a one-room schoolhouse.

If you venture south, you will reach the South Shore, with its remarkable barrier beaches: **Fire Island National Seashore** *(Tel 631/289-4810)* and the 2,413-acre **Jones Beach State Park** *(Tel 631/785-2420)* with undeveloped areas for nature lovers and an outdoor concert stadium. ■

Travelwise

Ever busy New York taxicabs

TRAVELWISE INFORMATION

There is really no bad time to visit New York, and although the weather is usually nicest in spring or fall, special events take place year-round. During summer's high heat and humidity, there are many outdoor festivals, often free, as well as indoor events in museums and galleries (always air-conditioned). Conventions often block-book hotels, so always check room availability before making travel reservations.

PLANNING YOUR TRIP

There are several key sources of information to help you. The New York City's Official Visitor Information Center (tel 212/484-1222) or any of the theater and entertainment hotlines listed in the entertainment section of this book (see pp. 261–264) will yield useful information. For a personalized introduction to a neighborhood, contact Big Apple Greeter (tel 212/669-8159). This nonprofit volunteer group matches knowledgeable New Yorkers with visitors, based upon visitor request applications.

USEFUL WEBSITES

Internet websites can provide up-to-date information, right down to giving street maps and finding addresses. The New York Public Library (tel 212/930-0747) offers Internet access.

www.nycvisit.com
New York Convention & Visitors Bureau
www.bigapplegreeter.org
Big Apple Greeter, available in several languages
www.panix.com/clay/nyc
New York City reference index
digitalcity.com
Manhattan User's Guide

NOTABLE EVENTS & FESTIVALS

JANUARY
Winter Antiques Show, Seventh Regiment Armory, tel 212/472-1180.
FEBRUARY
Westminster Kennel Club Dog Show, Madison Square Garden, tel 212/465-6741.

Grammy Awards, Madison Square Garden, tel 212/465-6741.
MARCH
St. Patrick's Day Parade, along Fifth Avenue.
Macy's Flower Show, tel 212/695-4400.
New Directors/New Films, Museum of Modern Art (based in Queens until 2005), tel 212/708-9400.
APRIL
Easter Parade, along Fifth Ave.
Opening day at Yankee and Shea Stadiums. Yankee Stadium, tel 718/293-6000, Shea Stadium, tel 718/507-8499.
New York International Auto Show, Jacob Javits Center, tel 212/216-2000.
MAY
Bike New York, The Great Five Borough Bike Tour (42-mile recreational bike ride), tel 212/932-0778.
New York Armory Antiques Show, Seventh Regiment Armory, tel 212/472-0590.
Ninth Avenue Food Festival, from 37th to 57th Streets.
Washington Square Outdoor Art Exhibition, tel 212/982-6255.
JUNE
Lesbian and Gay Pride Week (parade on Fifth Ave).
JULY
Fourth of July (tall ships in New York Harbor and fireworks on the East River), tel 212/695-4400.
Rockefeller Center Flower and Garden Show, tel 212/632-3975.
Midsummer Night's Swing, Lincoln Center (outdoor dance lessons, bands), tel 212/875-5766.
AUGUST
U.S. Open, Flushing Meadows Park, Queens, tel 718/760-6200.
SEPTEMBER
West Indian Labor Day

Parade, Crown Heights, Brooklyn (a Mardi Gras-like celebration), tel 718/625-1515.
New York Film Festival, Lincoln Center, tel 212/875-5610.
OCTOBER
Greenwich Village Halloween Parade.
Next Wave Festival, Brooklyn Academy of Music, tel 718/636-4100.
NOVEMBER
New York City Marathon, tel 212/860-4455.
Macy's Thanksgiving Parade, along Central Park West and Broadway, tel 212/695-4400.
Big Apple Circus, in a tent, Damrosch Park, Lincoln Center, tel 212/268-2500.
DECEMBER
Tree-lighting, Rockefeller Center, tel 212/632-3975.
New Year's Eve, Times Square (see the ball drop to bring in the New Year, live).

GETTING AROUND

FROM THE AIRPORTS

Air-Ride provides recorded information on transportation to and from all airports, tel 800/247-7433.

Buses New York Airport Service has regular buses to/from JFK, LaGuardia, and Newark Airports to/from Grand Central Station and Port Authority, tel 212/564-8484 or 718/707-9658. SuperShuttle for JFK and LaGuardia to/from most hotels, tel 212/315-3006 or 800/451-0455. Olympia Trails between Newark and three New York City destinations, tel 212/964-6233.
Car services Try to book 24 hours in advance or earlier. A variety of vehicles are available, but basic sedans are cheapest, reliable, and at reasonable rates. Tel-Aviv, tel 212/777-7777 or 800/222-9888; Allstate, tel 212/741-7440 or 800/453-4099.
Taxis JFK: Fixed rate of $35

excluding tolls and tip to Manhattan. LaGuardia: By the meter, $20–$25. Newark: Dispatcher-determined flat rate of $30–$45, depending on destination, excluding tolls and tip.

NYC TRANSPORTATION

If you can, walk, and as you stroll through a neighborhood or to your destination, enjoy a new food experience along the way. If you drive, park you car in a garage ($20–$40 per day), because traffic is always heavy and on-street parking hard to find.

MASS TRANSIT

Information: tel 718/330-1234, www.mta.nyc.ny.us
Buses & subways These cover most of the city and cost $1.50 per ride (half price for seniors and disabled, free for children under 3'8"), including a transfer. Subways are generally safe and the most efficient way to get around. They are a good choice for long distances and during rush hour. Buses can be scenic and relaxing but unbearably slow. They stop every two blocks, except "limited" ones (ask). A free map, showing all bus and subway routes, is usually available at token booths in subway stations, and one is posted on the wall and in each subway car and bus.
Lost & Found Buses and subways, tel 212/712-4500; Taxis, tel 212/692-8294.
MetroCards Available at many stores and newsstands and at all subway stations; cards can be purchased in whatever amount you choose (you get a free ride if you purchase $15 or more), and are debited each time you enter the subways or ride a bus. They allow for a free transfer from subway to/from connecting bus within a two-hour period. You can also use tokens ($1.50) for subways and buses, or exact change on buses.

TAXIS

Widely available and fairly reasonable, taxis can get you wherever you wish. Hail them from anywhere, though you may have better luck finding one on major avenues. Take only yellow cabs with the medallion numbers on the roof and the rates on the door. They are available if the medallion number is lit (and not the off-duty sign). The base fare is $2, with a 50-cent 8 p.m.–6 a.m. surcharge, and then 30 cents for every fifth mile (4 blocks) and 20 cents for every minute in stopped or slow traffic. There is no charge for other passengers (taxis can take four) or luggage, but unusually large items are extra, and tips are expected to be 15 percent.

OTHER

Rollerblading and biking are a fun way of getting around in parks and traffic-free places. Many bike/skate shops rent: For bikes, try the Loeb Boathouse in Central Park, tel 212/517-3623. For skates, try the various Blades locations throughout the city.

PRACTICAL ADVICE

Although New York City's crime rate has steadily declined in the past few years, and the most trafficked areas and subways are well-patrolled by police, one should be alert and exercise caution. The following personal safety tips should help you to have an incident-free trip:
•Do not give your bags to anyone in an airport or train/bus station other than authorized personnel, or your yellow-taxi driver while loading the trunk.
•Avoid abandoned or badly lit streets.
•Know where you're going in areas of Manhattan north of 96th St., west of 8th Ave., east of Ave. A, the financial district at night, and in all of the other boroughs.
•Avoid all parks after dark, except for crowded special events.
•Do not make eye contact or get drawn into conversation with suspicious characters.
•Do not use cash machines when there's no one around, and do not count cash on the street.
•Carry your wallet in an inaccessible place, and keep your handbag securely across your body, clasp facing in.
•Avoid the subway after 11 p.m. (buses are fine), and stay with the crowd.
•If you are robbed, hand over your wallet and whatever else is requested without resistance and call 911 from the nearest phone (free call).

TRAVELERS WITH DISABILITIES

Asser Levy Park is a playground designed for disabled children (E. 23rd at Asser Levy Place near the East River).
Big Apple Greeters is a clearinghouse for information for disabled travelers and offers neighborhood visits led by volunteers, reserve three days in advance. Tel 212/669-8159; TTY 669-8273.
HAI (Hospital Audiences Inc.) publishes a guide to access in New York's cultural institutions and offers services for the blind for theater performances. Tel 212/575-7676.
Lighthouse International has events by and for visually impaired; and Braille subway maps. (111 E. 59th St., tel 800/334-5497 or 212/821-9200).

EMERGENCIES

Helpful phone numbers and addresses:
•Emergencies of any kind, tel 911.
•Crime Victims Hotline, tel 212/577-7777.
•Poison Control Center, tel 800/221-1222.
•Medical Emergencies: Proceed to nearest hospital emergency room (call 411 or check Yellow Pages for nearest hospital) or call 911 for an ambulance.
•New York Healthcare Immediate Care, 55 E. 34th St., tel 212/252-6001, walk-in clinic.
•Dental Referral Service, tel 800/917-6453.

HOTELS & RESTAURANTS

The variety and price range of places to stay in the city is remarkably varied, with options sure to meet every taste and budget. In fact, one will find that there are as many bargains available in New York as in any other place—if not more, with low-cost options that include comfortable bed-and-breakfasts and small older hotels in some of the city's most interesting neighborhoods. One might also opt to spend a few days in an inexpensive accommodation and then splurge on something exquisitely fine, the kind of metropolitan luxury one finds only in New York. When it comes to food, one can eat well in a historic Lower East Side deli, an ornate Chinese banquet hall, a cozy French bistro that seats only twelve, or savor delectable fare by a world-class chef in the most extravagant of settings. While roaming the streets sight-seeing or shopping, there is nothing more satisfying than sampling the offerings of sidewalk vendors or noshing the entire length of an avenue during one of the city's many food festivals.

HOTELS

Once you determine your total room budget, decide what neighborhood or area appeals to you and then research in depth. From Lower Manhattan to the Upper East and West Sides, the city teems with shopping, sight-seeing, cultural, and historic attractions. If you are drawn more to Broadway or other West Side attractions, then a place in the Times Square or Lincoln Center area may be best. Taxis are usually available, but a ride from the West Village to the Upper East Side, for example, can be quite expensive and also—depending on traffic—slow. Be sure to calculate transportation in your budgets of money and time. Choosing lodging for its convenience and accessibility is usually best for those with limited time to spend exploring the Big Apple. Once you pick your location, then you can explore the many options.

For disabled access, it is recommended you check with the hotel to establish the extent of their facilities. Also verify parking or access to parking spaces. All hotels are air-conditioned.

RESTAURANTS

New York may well be the world's best fed city. The variety of restaurants—from the hautest French to the simplest Asian, and absolutely everything in between—is unsurpassed. At all levels, value is generally good because everyone wants to take a bite of the Big Apple. The challenge is getting a reservation.

Included in the listings below are restaurant closings, though you should always check times when making a reservation, which is recommended when possible. Verify access for those with disabilities; facilities vary, depending on how old the restaurant is as well as its size. If you can't get through to a place by phone, it is likely to be so popular reservations are impossible to come by. Prices at lunch can be expected to be lower than at dinner at the more upscale establishments, and many of these restaurants offer a special prix-fixe menu that can be a real bargain. All restaurants are air-conditioned unless otherwise noted, and all establishments have non-smoking areas.

ORGANIZATION

Hotels and restaurants listed here have been grouped first according to neighborhood, then listed alphabetically by price range.

ABBREVIATIONS

L = lunch
D = dinner
Credit card abbreviations are: AE (American Express), DC (Diner's Club); MC (Mastercard); and V (Visa).

LOWER MANHATTAN

HOTELS

🏨 MILLENNIUM HILTON
$$$$$
55 CHURCH ST.
TEL 212/693-2001
FAX 212/571-2317
Top-end corporate destination. High-tech style with a fax in each room, and some beautiful views of New York Harbor. Lower rates available weekends.
🛈 561 🚇 1, 9 to Cortlandt St.; C, E to World Trade Center 🚫 🎭 🚫 All major cards

🏨 SOHO GRAND
$$$$$
310 W. BROADWAY (BET. GRAND & CANAL STS.)
TEL 212/965-3000 or 800/965-3000
FAX 212/965-3141
Striking design and a fashion-able destination for those who enjoy the downtown vantage point. Endless interesting stores and galleries are within walking distance.
🛈 367 + 4 suites 🚇 A, C, E to Canal St. 🎭 🚫 All major cards

⊞ SOHO B&B
$$$
CROSBY ST. (AT BLEECKER ST.)
TEL 212/925-1034
Carriage house and high-ceilinged loft with exotic decor. Rates vary according to number of guests.
🚻 2 🚇 B, D, F to Broadway-Lafayette Ave.
⊗ Not accepted

RESTAURANTS

🍴 ALISON ON DOMINICK STREET
$$$$
38 DOMINICK ST. (BET. HUDSON & VARICK STS.)
TEL 212/727-1188
Romantic, out-of-the-way SoHo destination, with fine French country cuisine that changes seasonally.
🍽 60 🚇 1, 9 to Houston St. or C, E to Spring St.
🕐 Closed L
⊗ All major cards

🍴 BAYARD'S
$$$$
1 HANOVER SQ. (BET. PEARL & STONE STS.)
TEL 212/514-9454
Featuring a French cuisine-based menu that includes seasonal dishes such as celery root soup and rack of lamb.
🍽 80 🚇 4, 5 to Wall Street
🕐 Closed Sun.
⊗ All major cards

🍴 BOULEY BAKERY
$$$$
120 WEST BROADWAY AT DUANE ST
TEL 212/964-2525
Understated and elegant French restaurant by David Bouley, emphasizing seasonal ingredients and breads.
🍽 80 🚇 1, 2, 3, A, C to 9 Chambers St.
⊗ All major cards

🍴 CHANTERELLE
$$$$
2 HARRISON ST. (AT HUDSON ST.)
TEL 212/966-6960
Lovely, formal dining room

with TriBeCa flavor. Here you will find impeccable service, wines, and cheeses.
🍽 17 tables 🚇 1, 9 to Franklin St. 🕐 Closed all day Sun., Mon. L, July 2–16
⊗ All major cards

🍴 THE GRILL ROOM
$$$$
2 WORLD FINANCIAL CENTER, 225 LIBERTY ST. (AT WEST ST.)
TEL 212/945-9400
Visit great American chef Larry Forgione's downtown outpost with a view. House specialties are roast lobster and lamb chops.
🍽 200 🚇 1, 9 to Cortlandt St.; N, R to World Trade Center 🕐 Closed Sat., Sun.
⊗ All major cards

🍴 MONTRACHET
$$$$
239 W. BROADWAY (BET. WALKER & WHITE STS.)
TEL 212/219-2777
Superb food and award-winning wine list in sedate French bistro setting. Good service, fine roasted vegetable terrine, truffle-crusted salmon, foie gras dishes. Very nice for Friday lunch.
🍽 85 🚇 1, 9 to Franklin St. 🕐 Closed Sat.–Thurs. L
⊗ All major cards

🍴 NOBU
$$$$
105 HUDSON ST. (AT FRANKLIN ST.)
TEL 212/219-0500
A deservedly popular Nobu Matsuhisa–Drew Nieporent venture with exciting Japanese cuisine and dramatic design. Specialties include black cod with miso and *tiradito*. Reservations almost impossible, but there's always the sushi bar.
🍽 100 🚇 1, 9 to Franklin St. 🕐 Closed Sat. & Sun. L
⊗ All major cards

🍴 14 WALL STREET RESTAURANT
$$$
14 WALL ST., 13TH FL. (BET. BROADWAY & BROAD ST.)
TEL 212/233-2780
Dine on French cuisine in J. P. Morgan's former penthouse, overlooking the financial district. Specialties include citrus-marinated salmon baked on an oak plank and sea scallops in porcini broth.
🍽 150 🚇 2, 3, 4, 5 to Wall Street 🕐 Closed Sat. & Sun.
⊗ All major cards

🍴 BALTHAZAR
$$$
80 SPRING ST. (AT CROSBY ST.)
TEL 212/965-1414
A beautiful SoHo brass-erie with matching menu, upbeat tempo, breakfast, lunch and dinner, late nights and weekend brunch. The oysters and cold seafood platter are particularly impressive.
🍽 160 🚇 6 to Spring St.
⊗ All major cards

🍴 BLUE RIBBON
$$$
97 SULLIVAN ST. (BET. PRINCE & SPRING STS.)
TEL 212/274-0404
Minimalist setting with excellent raw bar (ask for Alonso's sauce) and eclectic menu. They even have fondue and *pupu* platters.
🍽 45 🚇 C, E to Spring St. 🕐 Closed L & Mon.
⊗ All major cards

🍴 DELMONICO'S
$$$
56 BEAVER ST. (NEAR WILLIAM ST.)
TEL 212/509-1144
A classic dating from 1827, birthplace of eggs Benedict and lobster Newburg.
🍽 130 🚇 2,3,4,5 to Wall Street 🕐 Closed weekends
⊗ All major cards

🍴 ECCO
$$$
124 CHAMBERS ST. (BET.
CHURCH ST. & BROADWAY)
TEL 212/227-7074
Savory Italian cooking well
worth the steep price. Try
the veal scallopine with
artichokes, penne *arrabiata*,
or assorted grilled fish.
🛏 75 🚇 A, C, 1, 2, 3, 9 to
Chambers St. ⏱ Closed L
Sat. & all Sun.
💳 All major cards

🍴 HONMURA AN
$$$
170 MERCER ST. (BET. PRINCE
& HOUSTON STS.)
TEL 212/334-5253
Zenlike soba noodle
experience. Pricey but
exquisite.
🛏 50 🚇 N, R to Prince St.
⏱ Closed Sun.–Tues. L
💳 All major cards

🍴 LE MARAIS
DOWNTOWN
$$$
5-17 JOHN ST. (BET. BROADWAY
& NASSAU ST.)
TEL 212/285-8585
A French brasserie gone
kosher offering steak and
more.
🛏 210 🚇 2, 3, 8, C to
Fulton, Nassau St. ⏱ Closed
Sat. in summer
💳 All major cards

🍴 ODEON
$$$
145 W. BROADWAY
(AT THOMAS ST.)
TEL 212/233-0507
Hip downtown eatery
with reliable French and
American food, good late-night
scene. Recommended dishes
are steak au poivre, steak frites,
and other classic bistro fare.
🛏 140 🚇 1, 9 to Chamber
St. 💳 All major cards

🍴 RAOUL'S
$$$
180 PRINCE ST. (BET. SULLIVAN
& THOMPSON STS.)
TEL 212/966-3518
Always happening, lively

French bistro/bar, garden in
season, good late at night. The
steak au poivre and foie gras
terrine are recommended.
🛏 200 🚇 1, 9 to Houston
or C, E to Spring St.
⏱ Closed L
💳 All major cards

🍴 ROY'S NEW YORK
$$$
130 WASHINGTON ST. (BET.
ALBANY & CARLISLE STS.)
TEL 212/266-6262
Skewered coconut shrimp
and individual pizzas in an
upbeat and cheerful setting.
A refreshing change of pace
in the stately Wall Street
neighborhood.
🛏 195 🚇 1, 9, N, R to
Rector St. ⏱ Closed L
Sat.–Sun. 💳 All major cards

🍴 SAMMY'S ROUMANIAN
STEAKHOUSE
$$$
157 CHRYSTIE ST.
(AT DELANCEY ST.)
TEL 212/673-0330
Unbelievable only-in-New York
option for schmaltz-laden
Jewish meal in old-fashioned
Lower East Side location. Go
for the classics: brisket,
chopped liver, along with a
bottle of vodka in an ice block.
🛏 110 🚇 F to Delancey
St.-Essex St. ⏱ Closed L &
some Jewish holidays 💳 All
major cards

🍴 SAVOY
$$$
70 PRINCE ST. (AT CROSBY ST.)
TEL 212/219-8570
Cozy setting with inventive,
well-executed menu. New
upstairs dining with rotating
prix-fixe menus, fireplace
cooking. A house specialty is
salt-crusted baked duck.
🛏 65 🚇 N, R to Prince St.
⏱ Closed Sun. L 💳 All
major cards

🍴 SOHO STEAK
$$$
90 THOMPSON ST. (BET.
PRINCE & SPRING STS.)
TEL 212/226-0602

Well-priced, reliable, and lively.
Treat yourself to the $9 slab
of foie gras to start and, what
else, the steak.
🛏 50 🚇 C, E to Spring
St.-6th Ave. ⏱ Closed
Mon.–Fri. L 💳 Not
accepted

🍴 BRIDGE CAFE
$$
279 WATER ST. (AT DOVER ST.)
TEL 212/227-3344
Casual, charming spot next to
Brooklyn Bridge for good
American food. Sautéed soft-
shell crabs and pan-roasted
chicken are specialties.
🛏 63 🚇 A, 2, 3, 4, to Fulton
St. ⏱ Closed Sat. 💳 All
major cards

🍴 JOE'S SHANGHAI
$$
9 PELL ST. (BET. BOWERY &
MOTT STS.)
TEL 212/233-8888
Often a wait but worth it for
broth-filled crab or pork
dumplings and a large selection
of other Shanghai savories. The
eggplant with garlic sauce and
bean curd wrapped in spinach
are very good.
🛏 85 🚇 6 to Canal St.
💳 Not accepted

🍴 NEW YORK NOODLE
TOWN
$$
28 BOWERY (AT BAYARD ST.)
TEL 212/349-0923
No-frills Chinatown setting
with great dishes: salt-baked
seafood, duck with flowering
chives, noodles with ginger
scallion sauce.
🛏 60 🚇 6 to Canal St.
💳 Not accepted

🍴 THAILAND
RESTAURANT
$$
106 BAYARD ST. (AT BAXTER ST.)
TEL 212/349-3132
Low-key spot with some hard-
to-find, good Thai food. The
grilled beef salad and green
curry dishes are delicious.
🛏 55–60 🚇 6 to Canal St.
💳 All major cards

KEY   🏨 Hotel   🍴 Restaurant   ⓘ No. of guest rooms   🛏 No. of seats   🚇 Subway   ⏱ Closed

SOMETHING SPECIAL

🍴 COWGIRL HALL OF FAME

A theme restaurant that rings absolutely authentic, with Western decor, lots of wood, antlers, barbed wire, cowboy trappings, and a re-created 1950s-era motel room where you can wait to be seated. Definitely casual and for those with hearty appetites, good for families too: There is a special children's menu. A small gift shop sells collectibles and Western items.

$
519 HUDSON ST.
TEL 212/633-1133
🍴 283 🚇 1,9 to Franklin St. 💳 AE, MC, V

🍴 BO-KY
$
80 BAYARD ST. (BET. MOTT & MULBERRY STS.)
TEL 212/406-2292
Dozens of inexpensive Vietnamese soups served in plain Chinatown setting with communal tables. The favorite is curried chicken, and they do a decent roast duck.
🍴 100 🚇 6 to Canal St.
💳 Not accepted

🍴 BUBBY'S
$
120 HUDSON ST.
(AT N. MOORE ST.)
TEL 212/219-0666
Casual but popular spot for all meals. Weekend breakfasts, brunch, and homemade baked goods.
🍴 120 🚇 1, 9 to Franklin St. 💳 All major cards

🍴 JING FONG
$
20 ELIZABETH ST. (BET. BAYARD & CANAL STS.)
TEL 212/964-5256
Overwhelming and unforgettable dim sum paradise in the late morning/lunchtime hours. Don't miss the Chinese chive

dumplings and the taro leaf-wrapped packages of sticky rice, chicken, and sausage. Huge and bustling.
🍴 1000 🚇 6 to Canal St.
💳 AE, MC, V

🍴 KATZ'S DELICATESSEN
$
205 E. HOUSTON ST.
(AT LUDLOW ST.)
TEL 212/254-2246
Classic Lower East Side destination for hot dogs, the best pastrami, corned beef, pickles, Dr. Brown's soda.
🍴 340 🚇 F to E. Houston St. 💳 AE, MC, V

🍴 LOMBARDI'S
$
32 SPRING ST. (BET. MOTT & MULBERRY STS.)
TEL 212/941-7994
Try one of the city's best pizzas in the first New York City pizza-parlor location.
🍴 100 🚇 6 to Spring St.
💳 Not accepted

🍴 NHA TRANG
$
87 BAXTER ST. (BET. BAYARD & CANAL STS.)
TEL 212/233-5948
No-nonsense setting for Vietnamese fare. Try pork chops and hot and sour shrimp soup, then sweet Vietnamese coffee for dessert.
🍴 80 🚇 6 to Canal St.
💳 Not accepted

🍴 PITA EXPRESS
$
15 ANN ST. #4 (AT BROADWAY)
TEL 212/571-2999
Not-too-spicy Middle Eastern menu serving hummus, baba gannouj, and tabbouleh.
🍴 30 🚇 4, 5 to Ann St.
🕐 Closed Sun. 💳 All major cards

THE VILLAGES

HOTELS

🏨 ABINGDON GUEST HOUSE
$$$
13 8TH AVE. (BET. 12TH ST. & JANE ST.)
TEL 212/243-5384
FAX 212/807-7473
Unhosted B&B with nicely decorated rooms, two of which share a bathroom.
🛏 9 rooms 🚇 A, C, E to 14th St. 💳 All major cards

🏨 LARCHMONT
$$$
27 W. 11TH ST. (BET. 5TH & 6TH AVES.)
TEL 212/989-9333
FAX 212/989-9496
Tiny but pleasant rooms in excellent location, quaint touches. Shared bathrooms.
🛏 50 🚇 F to 14th St.
💳 AE, MC, V

🏨 WASHINGTON SQUARE HOTEL
$$$
103 WAVERLY PLACE (AT MACDOUGAL ST.)
TEL 212/777-9515 or 800/222-0418
FAX 212/979-8373
Good location in the heart of Greenwich Village, off park. Functional but well-furnished rooms.
🛏 180 🚇 A, B, C, D, E, F to W. 4th St. 🏋
💳 All major cards

RESTAURANTS

🍴 BABBO
$$$$
110 WAVERLY PL.
TEL 212/777-0303
Mario Batali's excellent, adventurous Italian restaurant has been a sensation since opening day. Getting reservations can be challenging.
🍴 126 🚇 A, B, C, D, F to West 4th St. 🕐 Closed L
💳 All major cards

HOTELS & RESTAURANTS

🍴 GOTHAM BAR & GRILL

In this spacious multilevel Gramercy-area eatery, the architecture, as well as the food, stands out: One reviewer called this award-winning, postmodern warehouse conversion "an awesome dining temple." Chef Alfred Portale serves up specialties such as grilled rack of lamb and seared yellowfin tuna, and whimsical creative desserts. Gotham is consistently voted a favorite.

$$$$
12 E. 12TH ST. (BET. 5TH AVE. & UNIVERSITY PLACE)
TEL 212/620-4020 or 212/620-0181
🛏 150 🚇 4, 5, 6 to Union Sq. 🕐 Closed Sat. & Sun. L 🚫 All major cards

🍴 DA SILVANO
$$$$
260 6TH AVE.
(AT HOUSTON ST.)
TEL 212/982-2343
Since opening in 1975, this cozy trattoria, with a sidewalk café, has transformed into a popular celebrity haunt. Ever changing pastas, entrées such as osso buco, and owner Silvano Marchetto's hospitality are the reasons behind all the fuss.
🛏 190 🚇 A, C, E, B, D, F, Q, W to 4th St. 🚫 All major cards

🍴 JAMES BEARD HOUSE
$$$$
167 W. 12TH ST. (BET. 6TH & 7TH AVES.)
TEL 212/627-2308
Gastronomic Carnegie Hall featuring the world's best chefs, a different one performing nightly. Call for monthly calendar. Advance reservations only.
🛏 90 🚇 1, 2, 3 to 14th St. 🚫 All major cards

🍴 FIRST
$$$
87 1ST AVE. (BET. 5TH & 6TH STS.)
TEL 212/674-3823
Lively upscale East Village spot for sophisticated filling food with an emphasis on fish, martinis, and lava lamps. Open late night weekends.
🛏 90–100 🚇 6 to Astor Place 🕐 Closed Mon.–Sat. L 🚫 All major cards

🍴 LUCKY CHENG'S
$$$
24 1ST AVE. (BET. 1ST & 2ND STS.)
TEL 212/473-0516
A veritable transvestite sideshow with passable pan-Asian food; go for the fun and late-night cocktails.
🛏 200–350 🚇 F to 2nd Ave. 🕐 Closed L 🚫 All major cards

🍴 MI COCINA
$$$
57 JANE ST. (AT HUDSON ST.)
TEL 212/627-8273
Rich and varied authentic Mexican regional cuisine. A specialty is *conchinita pibil*, shredded pork in a banana leaf. Unlike the rest.
🛏 42 🚇 A, C, E to 14th St. 🕐 Closed Mon.–Sat. L 🚫 All major cards

🍴 PÒ
$$$
31 CORNELIA ST.
(BET. BLEECKER & W. 4TH STS.)
TEL 212/645-2189
Well-priced contemporary Italian cuisine by Lee McGroon. The chef's tasting menu is a delicious deal.
🛏 12 tables 🚇 A, B, C, D, E, F to W. 4th St. 🕐 Closed Mon., & Tues. L 🚫 AE

🍴 DANAL
$$
90 E. 10TH ST. (BET. 3RD & 4TH AVES.)
TEL 212/982-6930
Eclectic cuisine in charming storefront setting. Garden seating available. Serves afternoon tea (reservations only) and brunch. Wine bar.
🛏 50 🚇 6 to Astor Place 🕐 Closed Mon. 🚫 All major cards

🍴 FLORENT
$$
69 GANSEVOORT ST.
(BET. GREENWICH & WASHINGTON STS.)
TEL 212/989-5779
Open 24 hours on weekends and until 5 a.m. Amazingly diverse clientele. Boudin, steak frites, and gratins are the best bet.
🛏 70 🚇 A, C, E to 14th St. 🚫 Not accepted

🍴 JAPONICA
$$
100 UNIVERSITY PL.
TEL 212/243-7752
Popular sushi and Japanese fare. You can get good deals on prix-fixe lunches and dinners.
🛏 84 🚇 4, 5, 6 to Union Sq. 🚫 AE

🍴 JOHN'S PIZZERIA
278 BLEECKER ST. (BET. 6TH AVE. & 7TH AVE. S.)

🍴 CENT'ANNI

An unpretentious, friendly storefront restaurant in West Village's heart. Chef Gary Devincez serves up generous portions of Northern Italian fare, including excellent pastas; his veal and pork dishes are also popular. It's usually full of patrons who revel in the atmosphere, summed up in the translation of the restaurant's name "May you live one hundred years!"

$$
50 CARMINE ST.
(BET. BLEECKER & BEDFORD STS.)
TEL 212/989-9494
🛏 60 🚇 A, B, C, D, E, F to W. 4th St. 🚫 AE, MC, V

TEL 212/243-1680
Brick-oven pizza and 50s
decor in a perennially favorite
spot for locals, celebs, and
tourists.
🍴 100 🚇 A, B, C, D, E, F to
W. 4th St. 💳 Not accepted

🍴 SECOND AVENUE DELI
$$
156 2ND AVE. (AT 10TH ST.)
TEL 212/677-0606
One of New York's finest,
with chopped liver and
matzoh ball soup to write
home about, along with other
classic deli fare.
🍴 175 🚇 6 to Astor Place
🕐 Closed some Jewish
holidays 💳 All major cards

🍴 TEA & SYMPATHY
$$
108 GREENWICH AVE. (BET.
12TH & 13TH STS.)
TEL 212/807-8329
Tiny storefront serving
delicious, hearty British fare,
like Welsh rarebit, and
bangers and mash. Afternoon
tea. Be prepared to wait.
🍴 22 🚇 A, C, E to 14th St.
💳 Not accepted

🍴 CORNER BISTRO
$
331 W. 4TH ST. (AT 12TH ST.)
TEL 212/242-9502
Bar for burgers and fries on
paper plates. Get the Bistro
burger, with cheese, bacon,
lettuce, and tomato, all for $5.
Open late.
🍴 34 🚇 A, C, E to 14th St.
💳 Not accepted

🍴 LITTLE BASIL
$
39 GREENWICH AVE.
(AT CHARLES ST.)
TEL 212/645-8965
Thai food in the West Village
with wonderful tasting and
looking food.
🚇 1, 2, 3, 9 to 14th St.
💳 All credit cards

🍴 POMMES FRITES
$
123 2ND AVE. (BET. 7TH ST. &
ST, MARKS PL.)

🍴 ONE IF BY LAND, TWO IF BY SEA
Located in a 1786
landmark stone carriage
house that was once the
home of Aaron Burr, this
elegant restaurant on two
levels overlooks a private
garden with festive lights.
Inside, candles, live piano
music, flowers, and four
fireplaces create an ambience
perfect for a romantic
intimate meal or a large
celebration. Menu favorites
are beef Wellington,
American specialties, and
contemporary interpretations
of classic dishes. And, if you
are one of the lucky, you may
dine there on a night when
the ghost of Aaron Burr,
victorious after his duel with
Alexander Hamilton, appears.
$$$$
17 BARROW ST.
TEL 212/228-0822
🍴 150 🚇 A, B, C, D, E, F
to W. 4th St.
💳 All major cards

TEL 212/674-1234
Not quite a meal, but a nice,
big snack of Belgian-style fries
in a paper cone and even a
bench to sit on. Try the
especia sauce for dipping, and
the malt vinegar.
🍴 2 tables 🚇 6 to Astor
Place 💳 Not accepted

🍴 TAQUERIA DI MEXICO
$
93 GREENWICH AVE.
(BET. BANK & 12TH STS.)
TEL 212/255-5212
Authentic casual Mexican
food. Good tortilla soup and
taquitos al pastor.
🍴 14 tables 🚇 A, C, E to
14th St. 💳 Not accepted

🍴 VESELKA
$
144 2ND AVE. (AT 9TH ST.)
TEL 212/228-9682
Casual neighborhood hangout

with Ukrainian specialties,
especially soups, and timeless
murals. Try buckwheat pan-
cakes or challah French toast.
🍴 60 🚇 6 to Astor Place
💳 All major cards

🏨 INN AT IRVING PLACE
$$$$$
56 IRVING PLACE (BET. 17TH
& 18TH STS.)
TEL 212/533-4600 or
800/685-1447
FAX 212/533-4611
Intimate, romantic,
Victorian-style hotel
with four-poster beds
and fireplaces in
every room.
🛏 5 + 7 suites 🚇 4, 5, 6
to Union Sq. 💳 All major
cards.

🏨 MORGANS
🍴
There's no sign out front
and design is minimalist in
this hotel, its colors subdued
grays, black, and white. But this
peaceful retreat, opened in 1984
by Studio 54 creators Ian
Schrager and Steve Rubell, now
packs a punch: Asia de Cuba,
the first-floor restaurant.
Designed in the 1990s by
Phillipe Starck, it is pristine
white but flashy, its focus a
long share-table in the center,
with a picture of a waterfall
above. When you get closer, the
water moves, revealing itself
as a hologram. Celebrities
flock here.
$$$$$
237 MADISON AVE.
TEL 212/686-0300 or
800-334-3408
FAX 212/779-8352
🛏 113 🚇 6 to 33rd St.
🚕 Nearby 💳 All major
cards

TRAVELWISE

no**HOTELS & RESTAURANTS**

🏨 W NEW YORK–THE TUSCANY
$$$$
120 E. 39TH ST.
TEL 212/686-1600 or 877/946-8357
FAX 212/779-7822
Large rooms with Italian marble bathrooms.
🛈 110 + 12 suites 🚇 4, 5, 6 to Grand Central 🅿 🃏 All major cards

🏨 CHELSEA HOTEL
$$$
222 W. 23RD ST. (BET. 7TH & 8TH AVES.)
TEL 212/243-3700
Historic home of famous artists and writers, with a cozy lobby filled with art. Definitely worth a look even if no rooms are available.
🛈 400 🚇 1, 9 to 23rd St.; C, E to 23rd St. 🅿 Nearby 🃏 All major cards

🏨 GRAMERCY PARK HOTEL
$$$
2 LEXINGTON AVE. (BET. 21ST & 22ND STS.)
TEL 212/475-4320 or 800/221-4038
FAX 212/505-0535
Quiet and classic, situated on a pleasant square with access to the private Gramercy Park for guests.
🛈 240 + 120 suites 🚇 6 to 23rd St. 🃏 All major cards

🏨 HOTEL METRO
$$$
45 W. 35TH ST. (BET. 5TH & 6TH AVES.)
TEL 212/947-2500 or 800/356-3870
FAX 212/279-1310
Stylish, art-deco rooms and a roof terrace with views of the Empire State Building.
🛈 155 + 20 suites 🚇 1, 2, 3, 9 to 34th St. 🅿 🃏 All major cards

RESTAURANTS

🍴 L'ACAJOU
$$$$
53 W. 19TH ST. (BET. 5TH & 6TH AVES.)
TEL 212/645-1706
French bistro often hosting regional French wine and food festivals. Solid bistro fare, dining at the bar. Have the savory tarte du jour and perhaps the calf's liver.
🍽 12 tables 🚇 1, 9 to 18th St.; F to 23rd St. 🕐 Closed Sat. L & all day Sun. 🃏 All major cards.

🍴 CHELSEA BISTRO & BAR
$$$$
358 W. 23RD ST. (BET. 8TH & 9TH AVES.)
TEL 212/727-2026
Sophisicated, contemporary French food in attractive setting. Try hot-smoked salmon and escargots.
🍽 110 🚇 C, E to 23rd St. 🕐 Closed L 🃏 All major cards

🍴 GRAMERCY TAVERN
$$$$
42 E. 20TH ST. (BET. BROADWAY & PARK AVE. S.)
TEL 212/477-0777
Well-executed, contemporary cuisine, fine wines, clubby atmosphere, with Tavern Room as a more casual option. Try the tuna tartare with sea urchin vinaigrette.
🍽 140 + 40 tavern area 🚇 6 to 23rd St. 🃏 All major cards

🍴 LES HALLES
$$$$
411 PARK AVE. S. (BET. 28TH & 29TH STS.)
TEL 212/679-4111
French butcher shop-cum-bistro with great frisée salad, boudins, merguez, tableside steak tartare, and côte de boeuf for two.
🍽 80 🚇 6 to 28th St. 🃏 All major cards

🍴 HANGAWI
$$$$
12 E. 32ND ST. (BET. 5TH & MADISON AVES.)
TEL 212/213-0077
An other-worldly Korean

PRICES

HOTELS
An indication of the cost of a double room without breakfast is given by $ signs.
$$$$$	Over $280
$$$$	$200–$280
$$$	$120–$200
$$	$80–$120
$	Under $100

RESTAURANTS
An indication of the cost of a three-course dinner without drinks is given by $ signs.
$$$$$	Over $80
$$$$	$50–$80
$$$	$35–$50
$$	$20–$35
$	Under $20

vegetarian experience: Dishes are prepared with unusual but memorable roots and greens.
🍽 60 🚇 6 to 33rd St. 🃏 All major cards

🍴 LA LUNCHONETTE
$$$$
130 10TH AVE. (AT 18TH ST.)
TEL 212/675-0342
Classic French bistro food in a hideaway. Cassoulet, rabbit stew, and skate are house specialties.
🍽 18 tables 🚇 1, 9 to 18th St.; A, C, E to 14th St. 🕐 Closed Sat. L 🃏 All major cards

🍴 MESA GRILL
$$$$
102 5TH AVE. (BET. 15TH & 16TH STS.)
TEL 212/807-7400
Chef Bobby Flay's long-running hit: upbeat Southwestern inventions in charged atmosphere. Try grilled glazed salmon or spicy tuna.
🍽 140 🚇 4, 5, 6 to Union Sq. 🃏 All major cards

🍴 I TRULLI (& ENOTECA)
$$$$
122 E. 27TH ST. (BET. LEXINGTON AVE. &

KEY 🏨 Hotel 🍴 Restaurant 🛈 No. of guest rooms 🍽 No. of seats 🚇 Subway 🕐 Closed

PARK AVE. S.)
TEL 212/481-7372
The foods and wines of Italy's Apulia region, with excellent homemade pastas, especially *bavette a funghi*, rotisserie chicken, and wood-roasted fish. Next door Enoteca is a wine bar serving casual food.
150 6 to 28th St. Closed Sat. L & all day Sun. All major cards

PATRIA
$$$$
250 PARK AVE. S. (AT 20TH ST.)
TEL 212/777-6211
Chef Andrew DiCaltado reinvented Latin cuisine *con mucho gusto* in a lively arena. Don't miss the suckling pig or seviche.
105 6 to 23rd St. Closed Sat. L & all day Sun. All major cards

PERIYALI
$$$$
35 W. 20TH ST. (BET. 5TH & 6TH AVES.)
TEL 212/463-7890
Established destination for upscale Greek food, with exquisitely simple fish and authentic dishes. Try *pikantikes salates* to start, then grilled octopus or lamb.
100 F to 23rd St. Closed Sat. L & all day Sun. All major cards

UNION SQUARE CAFÉ
$$$$
21 E. 16TH ST. (BET. 5TH AVE. & UNION SQ. W.)
TEL 212/243-4020
Award-winning and eternally successful formula of chef Michael Romano's eclectic, well-executed cuisine, great wines, and service. Signa-ture dishes include fried calamari with spicy anchovy sauce and filet mignon of tuna.
125 4, 5, 6 to Union Sq. Closed Sun. L All major cards

ADA
$$$
208 E. 58TH ST. (BET. 2ND & 3RD)
TEL 212/371-6060
Chef Rajender Rana specializes in Indian cuisine, including Garam Marsala Quails and Cochin Prawns. Waiters anticipate your every need. Reservations recommended.
100 R, W, 4, 5, 6 to 59th St. & Lexington Ave. Closed L Sat.–Sun. All major cards

BRIGHT FOOD SHOP
$$
216 8TH AVE. (BET. 21ST & 22ND STS.)
TEL 212/243-4433
Odd-sounding but good casual fare. For take-out food, try its cousin Kitchen, two doors up.
42 C, E to 23rd St. Not accepted

EL CID
$$
322 W. 15TH ST. (BET. 8TH & 9TH AVES.)
TEL 212/929-9332
Excellent tapas in jovial setting. Baby squid is best, also the shrimp in garlic sauce, and the white Sangria.
12 tables A, C, E to 14th St. Closed L & all day Mon. AE

GARDEN CAFÉ
$$
147 E. 60TH ST. (BET. LEXINGTON & 3RD ST.)
TEL 212/832-8972
Charming spot good for both business and romantic dining; try the bistro beef, meatloaf, or chicken steak.
57 4, 5, 6, N, W to 60th St. Closed Sun. Not accepted

PONGAL
$$
110 LEXINGTON AVE. (BET. 27TH & 28TH STS.)
TEL 212/696-9458
Fragrant vegetarian (kosher)

Indian menu with exceptional *thalis* and *dosai*.
45–50 6 to 28th St. Not accepted

WHEELTAPPER
$$
141 E. 44TH ST. (2 BLOCKS FROM GRAND CENTRAL)
TEL 212/351-6800
Old World Irish pub with a railroad theme. Quality pub grub, plus an authentic Irish breakfast served all day.
60 4, 5, 6, 7, S to 42nd St.-Grand Central All major cards

EISENBERG'S SANDWICH SHOP
$
174 5TH AVE. (BET. 22ND & 23RD STS.)
TEL 212/675-5096
A nice Jewish lunch counter, very New York City. Try the tuna salad on rye.
34 F to 23rd St. Closed after 5 p.m. Not accepted

ESS-A-BAGEL
$
359 1ST AVE. (AT 21ST ST.)
TEL 212/260-2252
New York's finest bagels, boiled and baked, and a mighty good whitefish salad. Who needs atmosphere? (Also in Midtown North.)
8 tables 6 to 23rd St. Closed Sun. D All major cards

MIDTOWN NORTH

HOTELS

ALGONQUIN
$$$$$
59 W. 44TH ST. (BET. 5TH & 6TH AVES.)
TEL 212/840-6800 or 800/555-8000
FAX 212/944-1618
New York's literary landmark since the 1920s. Charming, traditional rooms, nice lobby for cocktails, nice locale.
142 + 23 suites B, D,

F to 42nd St. 🍽 ⚹All
major cards

🏨 FOUR SEASONS
$$$$$
57 E. 57TH ST. (BET. PARK &
MADISON AVES.)
TEL 212/758-5700
FAX 212/758-5711
This 52-story art deco-style
monument designed by I. M.
Pei and completed in 1993
has received top ratings and
boasts the largest rooms in
the city, with accompanying
big views. Expect modernistic
furniture, giant Florentine
marble bathrooms, and
elaborate bedside push
button systems.
ⓘ 370 🚇 4, 5, 6 to 59th St.
🍽 ⚹All major cards

🏨 NEW YORK PALACE
🍴 **$$$$$**
455 MADISON AVE.
(AT 50TH ST.)
TEL 212/888-7000 or
800/697-2522
FAX 212/303-6000
Owner the Sultan of Brunei
has restored the 1882
Stanford White-designed
Villard Houses to their
original opulence, providing
the public rooms of the
hotel. The rest is an elegantly
furnished 55-story tower with
a view of St. Patrick's
Cathedral. Home of the
city's most famous French
restaurant, Le Cirque 2000
(see p. 247).
ⓘ 600 🚇 E, F to 5th Ave.;
B, D, F to Rockefeller Center
🍽 ⚹All major cards

🏨 PENINSULA
$$$$$
700 5TH AVE. (AT 55TH ST.)
TEL 212/247-2200 or
800/262-9467
FAX 212/903-3949
Turn-of-the-20th-century
beaux-arts landmark, with
views straight down Fifth
Avenue. Art nouveau
furnishings and oversized beds
and bathrooms create a grand
environment. More luxurious
trappings at the rooftop spa

and outdoor rooftop Pen-
Top Bar and Terrace,
excellent for summer-time
cocktails and city views.
ⓘ 250 🚇 E, F to 5th Ave.
or N, R to 5th Ave. 🍽 🚬
⚹All major cards

🏨 PLAZA HOTEL
$$$$$
CENTRAL PARK SOUTH
768 5TH AVE. (AT 59TH ST.)
TEL 212/759-3000 or
800/527-4727
FAX 212/759-3167
The combined forces of
fame and location of this
national landmark make
a visit to the Plaza worthwhile.
The lobby is a destination in
itself, and features the Oak Bar
for a classic New York cocktail,
or the Palm Court with
Tiffany ceiling for tea.
Rooms vary in size and
view, though all amenities
are luxurious.
ⓘ 806 🚇 N, R to 5th Ave.
🍽 ⚹All major cards

🏨 ROYALTON
$$$$$
44 W. 44TH ST. (BET. 5TH &
6TH AVES.)
TEL 212/869-4400 or
800/635-9013
FAX 212/869-8965
Phillipe Starck interiors with
high-tech modern lobby,
restaurant, bar, and lovely
rooms with slate fireplaces
and round bathtubs.
ⓘ 137 + 31 suites 🚇 1, 2,
3, 9, 7 to Times Sq. 🍽
⚹All major cards

🏨 ST. REGIS
🍴 **$$$$$**
2 E. 55TH ST. (BET. 5TH &
MADISON AVES.)
TEL 212/753-4500
FAX 212/787-3447
Elaborately restored beaux-
arts gem, with elegant yet
accessible public rooms and
the finest service and
amenities. Enjoy the riches
of Lespinasse (see p. 248),
one of New York's top
restaurants, and of the
great King Cole Bar,

dominated by the engaging
Maxfield Parrish mural of
the King himself.
ⓘ 322 🚇 E, F to 5th Ave.;
N, R to 5th Ave. 🍽 ⚹All
major cards

🏨 WALDORF-ASTORIA &
WALDORF TOWERS
$$$$$
301 PARK AVE. (AT 50TH ST.)
TEL 212/355-3000
FAX 212/872-7272
The great Waldorf-Astoria
is one of the quintessential
New York hotels. The art
deco lobby is magnificent
and the exclusive, elaborately
appointed Waldorf Towers
(floors 28–42) provide
quarters for visiting presidents,
among others. The French
restaurant, Peacock Alley, is
lavishly praised.
ⓘ 1410 🚇 6 to 51st St. or
E, F to Lexington Ave. 🍽
⚹All major cards

🏨 CARNEGIE
$$$$
229 W. 58TH ST. (BET.
BROADWAY & 7TH AVE.)
TEL 212/245-4000
FAX 212/245-6199
Nicely decorated, quiet spot
with big kitchenettes,
great location.
ⓘ 20 suites 🚇 1, 9, A, B, C,
D to Columbus Circle
⚹All major cards

🏨 CASABLANCA HOTEL
$$$$
147 W. 43RD ST. (BET. 6TH &
7TH AVE.)
TEL 212/869-1212 or
888/922-7225
FAX 212/391-7585
Moroccan-style ambience.
ⓘ 40 + 8 suites 🚇 1, 2, 3, 9,
7 to Times Sq.-42nd St. 🍽
⚹All major cards

🏨 HOTEL ELYSÉE
$$$$
60 E. 54TH ST. (BET. MADISON &
PARK AVES.)
TEL 212/753-1066 or
800/535-9733
FAX 212/980-9278
Thirties' decor, charming

rooms with antiques; small
roof terrace.
(i) 88 + 11 suites **E, F to
Lexington Ave.; 6 to 51st
St. Health club All major cards

THE MANSFIELD
$$$$
12 W. 44TH ST. (BET. 5TH
& 6TH AVES.)
TEL 212/944-6050 or
877/847-4444
FAX 212/764-4477
Former bachelors' residence
with nicely designed modern
rooms, stainless-steel sinks.
Welcoming library with
concerts and cappuccino.
(i) 103 + 26 suites B, D,
F to 42nd St.; 1, 2, 3, 9, 7 to
Times Sq. Nearby All
major cards

**SOMETHING
SPECIAL**

REGAL U.N. PLAZA
HOTEL
Staying here puts you in
the midst of global
drama, as international
diplomats and staff rush to
their seats at the United
Nations, or their offices on
the first 27 floors of the
Plaza. The award-winning
modern building rises high
above the East Side. Hotel
rooms—all with stunning
views—start at the 28th
floor. Artworks from various
nations are found
throughout the hotel. You
will want to use the excellent
sports facilities, including
indoor tennis courts. To ease
the sense of isolation, the
hotel offers free shuttle
service to other city areas
including the theater district
in the evenings.
$$$$
1 UNITED NATIONS PLAZA
(1ST AVE. AT 44TH ST.)
TEL 212/758-1234 or
800/222-8888
FAX 212/702-5051
(i) 428 4, 5, 6, 7 to
42nd St. All
major cards

THE PARAMOUNT
$$$$
235 W. 46TH ST. (BET.
BROADWAY & 8TH AVES.)
TEL 212/764-5500 or
800/225-7474
FAX 212/575-4892
Phillipe Starck-designed lobby
and playful, attractive decor.
(i) 601 + 12 suites 1, 2,
3, 9, 7 to 42nd St.-Times Sq.
Health club All major cards

THE SHOREHAM
$$$$
33 W. 55TH ST. (BET. 5TH & 6TH
AVES.)
TEL 212/247-6700 or
800/553-3347
FAX 212/765-9741
Attractive deco interior with
aluminum furniture and many
nice touches.
(i) 47 + 37 suites E, F to
5th Ave.; N, R to 5th Ave.
Nearby All major
cards

WYNDHAM HOTEL
$$$
42 W. 58TH ST. (BET. 5TH &
6TH AVES.)
TEL 212/753-3500 or
800/257-1111
FAX 212/754-5638
Spacious and attractive
rooms. A popular choice.
(i) 200 N, R to 5th Ave.
All major cards

BROADWAY BED &
BREAKFAST INN
$$
264 W. 46TH ST. (AT 8TH AVE.)
TEL 212/921 1824 or
800/826-6300
FAX 212/768-2807
Simply designed rooms in the
heart of the theater district.
(i) 41 A, C, E to 42nd
St.-Times Sq. All major
cards

RESTAURANTS

LE BERNARDIN
$$$$$
155 W. 51ST ST. (BET. 6TH &
7TH AVES.)
TEL 212/489-1762
Outstanding French seafood

cuisine, elegant, nearly flawless
service. Outstanding black
bass seviche, tuna tartare,
prix-fixe menus.
38 tables 1, 9 to
50th St. Closed Sat. L
& all day Sun. All major
cards

LA CARAVELLE
$$$$$
SHOREHAM HOTEL
33 W. 55TH ST.
(BET. 5TH & 6TH AVES.)
TEL 212/586-4252
Elegant dining, contemporary
haute French cuisine. Special-
ties include pike quenelles,
Dover sole, and roast duck.
140 E, F to 5th Ave.
Closed Sat. L & all day
Sun. All major cards

LE CIRQUE 2000
$$$$$
NEW YORK PALACE HOTEL
455 MADISON AVE. (BET. 50TH
& 51ST STS.)
TEL 212/303-7788
Dazzling Tiffany-designed
space in former Villard
mansion, with New York's
most famous host-to-the-
stars, Sirio Maccioni. Fancy
French and Italian cuisine.
110 E, F to 5th Ave.
or 6 to 51st St. All major
cards

LA COTE BASQUE
$$$$$
60 W. 55TH ST. (BET. 5TH &
6TH AVES.)
TEL 212/688-6525
One of the city's nicest
French restaurants in a lovely
setting. Specialties are
cassoulet, and roast duck.
Order frozen raspberry
soufflé when you arrive.
160 E, F to 5th Ave.
Closed Sun. L All
major cards

FELIDIA
$$$$$
243 E. 58TH ST. (BET. 2ND &
3RD AVES.)
TEL 212/758-1479
Supreme Northern Italian
cuisine by Lidia Bastianich.

HOTELS & RESTAURANTS

Wonderful pasta and risottos, and the specialties of Trieste.
🛏 90 🚊 4, 5, 6 to 59th St. 🕐 Closed Sat. L & all day Sun. 💳 All major cards

🍴 FOUR SEASONS
$$$$$
99 E. 52ND ST. (BET. LEXINGTON & PARK AVES.)
TEL 212/754-9494
Timeless design by Philip Johnson with the most professional service and classic Continental cuisine. Try the crab cakes or steak tartare.
🛏 100 🚊 6 to 51st St.; E, F to Lexington Ave. 🕐 Closed Sat. L & all day Sun. 💳 All major cards

🍴 LA GRENOUILLE
$$$$$
3 E. 52ND ST. (BET. 5TH & MADISON AVES.)
TEL 212/752-1495
Haute French cuisine in flower-filled splendor.
🛏 80 🚊 E, F to 5th Ave. 🕐 Closed Sun.–Mon. 💳 All major cards

🍴 LESPINASSE
$$$$$
ST. REGIS HOTEL, 2 E. 55TH ST. (BET. 5TH & MADISON AVES.)
TEL 212/339-6719
Sophisticated setting and some of the city's finest cuisine, mixing French techniques with Far Eastern ingredients. Try chef Gray Kunz's tasting menu.
🛏 100 🚊 E, F to 5th Ave. 🕐 Closed Sun.–Mon. 💳 All major cards

🍴 LUTÈCE
$$$$$
249 E. 50TH ST. (BET. 2ND & 3RD AVES.)
TEL 212/752-2225
Chef David Feau lightens up classic French fare. Tasting menu changes seasonally. The sautéed fois gras with dark chocolate sauce and orange marmalade, and the Dover sole filet and celery are recommended.

🛏 60 🚊 6 to 51st St. 🕐 Closed all day Sun. & Mon L 💳 All major cards

🍴 LE PÉRIGORD
$$$$$
405 E. 52ND ST. (BET. 1ST AVE. & F.D.R. DR.)
TEL 212/755-6244
Classic New York City destination serving traditional French cuisine.
🛏 120 🚊 6 to 51st St. 🕐 Closed Sat. L & all day Sun. 💳 All major cards

---

SOMETHING SPECIAL

🍴 CHINA GRILL
You know you are in NYC here: The dress code appears business or casually stylish. The atmosphere almost vibrates—it's so filled with Midtown movers and shakers, especially during weekday lunch. Film, media, and stage personalities also abound. Ideal for lunch or before or after the theater. Dining on several levels with an attractive central kitchen and two side bars. Stylishly designed, from the flower displays to the Marco Polo quotes on the floors. So is the food, a contemporary-American/ European-Asian fusion. Nearly all of the food is prepared on grills or in woks. The inventive menu features such items as grilled pork tenderloin in plum sauce and cranberry coulis. Everything served family style and you will want to try many things.
$$$$
60 W. 53RD ST.
TEL 212/333-7788
🛏 248 🚊 B, D, F to Rockefeller Center; E, F to 5th Ave. 🕐 Closed Sat. & Sun. L 💳 All major cards

---

PRICES

HOTELS
An indication of the cost of a double room without breakfast is given by $ signs.

$$$$$	Over $280
$$$$	$200–$280
$$$	$120–$200
$$	$80–$120
$	Under $100

RESTAURANTS
An indication of the cost of a three-course dinner without drinks is given by $ signs.

$$$$$	Over $80
$$$$	$50–$80
$$$	$35–$50
$$	$20–$35
$	Under $20

🍴 PETROSSIAN
$$$$$
182 W. 58TH ST. (AT 7TH AVE.)
TEL 212/245-2214
Fancy spot for the specialties that made them famous: caviar, smoked fish, champagne.
🛏 70 🚊 N, R to 57th St. 💳 All major cards

🍴 RAINBOW ROOM
$$$$$
30 ROCKEFELLER PLAZA, 65TH FLOOR (BET. 49TH & 50TH STS.)
TEL 212/632-5000
The swankiest art deco setting, with amazing views and fine Northern Italian cuisine by chef Tito Piazza. Try the carpaccio alla cipriani or the ossobuco with risotto alla Milanese.
🛏 250 🚊 A, B, C, D, E, F to Rockefeller Center 🕐 Limited, check when open to the public 💳 All major cards

🍴 AQUAVIT
$$$$
13 W. 54TH ST. (BET. 5TH & 6TH AVES.)
TEL 212/307-7311
Fancy Scandinavian fare. House specialties are gravlax, baked salmon, and Swedish meatballs.

180 ⬛ E, F to 5th Ave. ⬛ All major cards

FIREBIRD
$$$$
365 W. 46TH ST. (BET. 8TH & 9TH AVES.)
TEL 212/586-0244
Old-world, over-the-top decor presents fine backdrop for haute Russian cuisine, lounging, and exceptional caviar.
200 ⬛ A, C, E to 42nd St. 🕐 Closed Sun. L & all day Mon. ⬛ All major cards

OCEANA
$$$$
55 E. 54TH ST. (BET. MADISON & PARK AVES.)
TEL 212/759-5941
Chef Neil Gallagher does wonders with seafood. House specialties include lobster salad.
100 ⬛ 6 to 51st St. 🕐 Closed Sat. L & all day Sun. ⬛ All major cards

OSTERIA DEL CIRCO
$$$$
120 W. 55TH ST. (BET. 6TH & 7TH AVES.)
TEL 212/265-3636
Run by the sons of Le Cirque's Sirio Maccioni, and with a menu devised by their mother, this dazzling room features some fine Tuscan dishes. Don't miss the *bombolini* (fresh donuts) for dessert.
120 ⬛ N, R to 57th St. 🕐 Closed Sun. L ⬛ All major cards

PALM
$$$$
837 2ND AVE. (BET. 44TH & 45TH STS.)
TEL 212/687-2953
Sawdust on the floor, giant lobsters and steaks.
120 ⬛ 4, 5, 6 to 42nd St. 🕐 Closed Sat. L & all day Sun. ⬛ All major cards

PARK AVENUE CAFÉ
$$$$
100 E. 63RD ST. (BET.

LEXINGTON & PARK AVES.)
TEL 212/644-1900
Chef David Burke wows clientele with innovative cuisine and zany presentations. Famed for homemade pastrami salmon.
220 ⬛ 4, 5, 6 to 59th St. ⬛ All major cards

SMITH & WOLLENSKY
$$$$
797 3RD AVE. (AT 49TH ST.)
TEL 212/753-1530
One of the city's finest steakhouses.
300 ⬛ 6 to 51st St. 🕐 Closed Sat. L & all day Sun. ⬛ All major cards

SUSHISAY
$$$$
38 E. 51ST ST. (BET. MADISON & PARK AVES.)
TEL 212/755-1780
Fabulous sushi. Put yourself in the hands of the chef if you can afford it.
80 ⬛ 6 to 51st St. 🕐 Closed Sat. L & all day Sun. ⬛ All major cards

"21"
$$$$
21 W. 52ND ST. (BET. 5TH & 6TH AVES.)
TEL 212/582-7200
A New York institution, with both inventive and classic American cuisine, famous dishes of chicken hash and burgers, and great Bloody Marys.
150 ⬛ B, D, F to Rockefeller Center 🕐 Closed Sun. ⬛ All major cards

VONG
$$$$
200 E. 54TH ST. (AT 3RD AVE.)
TEL 212/486-9592
Wonderful setting and exotic Thai-French fare by Jean-Georges Vongerichten. Try house-infused liquors in cocktails.
150 ⬛ 6 to 51st St.; E, F to Lexington Ave. 🕐 Closed Sat. L & all day Sun. ⬛ All major cards

BECCO
$$$
355 W. 46TH ST. (BET. 8TH & 9TH AVES.)
TEL 212/397-7597
Lively spot with pastas from the pan and large selection of Italian wines to enjoy.
150 ⬛ A, C, E to 42nd St. ⬛ All major cards

DAWAT
$$$
210 E. 58TH ST. (BET. 2ND & 3RD AVES.)
TEL 212/355-7555
Upscale Indian cuisine. Try *bhindi masala*, okra with

BEN BENSON'S STEAK HOUSE

If you have lusty appetites and love a rollicking steakhouse atmosphere and enthusiastic beef-eaters, this is the place to go. Opened in 1982, it is one of America's top 100 independent restaurants. Here, celebrities, politicians, sports stars, and business executives, along with visitors and residents in the know, consume massive juicy steaks, huge lobsters, crab cakes, veal, and large portions of French fries and vegetables meant to be shared. Dining is on two floors, in large rooms where the feeling is warm and familiar, partly because of the colorful collection of Americana all around you. If it is for drinks only, stop in at the bar and cocktail lounge, where you will also find yourself amid faces you recognize from television and the media. Beware the bar areas can get thick with cigar smoke.

$$$
123 W. 52ND ST.
TEL 212/581-8888
175 ⬛ 1, 9 to 50th St. 🕐 Closed Sat. & Sun. L ⬛ All major cards

onions and mangos.
🎫 130 🚇 4, 5, 6 to 59th St.
🕐 Closed Sun. L 🚭 All
major cards

🍴 ESTIATORIO MILOS
$$$
125 W. 55TH ST. (BET. 6TH &
7TH AVES.)
TEL 212/245-7400
Elegant Greek seafood spot
with fish by the pound,
excellent crabs.
🎫 35 tables 🚇 E, F to 5th
Ave.; N, R to 5th Ave. 🚭 All
major cards

🍴 HANAMI
$$$
213 E. 45TH ST. (BET. 2ND &
3RD AVE.)
TEL 212/687-0127
High-quality Japanese beef
and sushi.
🎫 85 🚇 4, 5, 6 to Grand
Central 🕐 Closed Sat. L &
all Sun. 🚭 All major cards

🍴 JEZEBEL
$$$
630 9TH AVE. (AT 45TH ST.)
TEL 212/582-1045
Quasi-haute soul food like
smothered pork chops, sides
of okra and black-eyed peas,
in grand satin-and-lace setting.
🎫 125 🚇 A, C, E to 42nd
St. 🚭 AE

🍴 JUDSON GRILL
$$$
152 W. 52ND ST. (BET. 6TH &
7TH AVES.)
TEL 212/582-5252
Contemporary eclectic menu
in sleek, elegant spot.
Specializes in grilled fish.
🎫 100 🚇 1, 9 to 50th
St.; B, D, F to Rockefeller
Center 🕐 Closed Sat. &
Sun. L 🚭 All major cards

🍴 OYSTER BAR AT
GRAND CENTRAL
$$$
GRAND CENTRAL TERMINAL,
LOWER LEVEL (42ND ST. &
VANDERBILT AVE.)
TEL 212/490-6650
Classic setting in the historic
train station, with pan roasts

and raw oysters. Make sure to
ask for the lunch menu.
🎫 500 🚇 4, 5, 6, S to
42nd St.-Grand Central
🕐 Closed Sat. & Sun.
🚭 All major cards

🍴 ROSA MEXICANO
$$$
1063 1ST AVE. (AT 58TH ST.)
TEL 212/753-7407
Haute Mexican cuisine,
authentic dishes. Tableside
guacamole, pomegranate
margaritas, and *mixiote*
(lamb shanks with chilies
steamed in beer) are house
specialties.
🎫 90 🚇 4, 5, 6 to 59th St.
🕐 Closed L
🚭 All major cards

🍴 SHUN LEE PALACE
$$$
155 E. 55TH ST. (BET.
LEXINGTON & 3RD AVES.)
TEL 212/371-8844
Finest upscale Chinese
cuisine.
🎫 350 🚇 4, 5, 6 to 59th St.
🕐 Closed Mon.–Fri. L
🚭 All major cards

🍴 SOLERA
$$$
216 E. 53RD ST. (BET. 2ND &
3RD AVES.)
TEL 212/644-1166
Top Spanish cuisine and
outstanding service.
Paella, calamari, Serrano
ham, and Spanish cheeses
are specialties.
🎫 100 🚇 6 to 51st St.; E, F
to Lexington Ave. 🕐 Closed
Sun. 🚭 All major cards

🍴 ANCHE VIVOLO
$$
222 E. 58TH ST. (BET. 2ND &
3RD AVES.)
TEL 212/308-0112
Traditional Italian dishes
including penne with
tomato and basil and
chicken parmagiana.
🎫 170 🚇 4, 5, 6, R to 59th
St., N to 63rd St. 🕐 Closed
L Sat. & all Sun.
🚭 All major cards

🍴 JOE ALLEN
$$
326 W. 46TH ST. (BET. 8TH &
9TH AVES.)
TEL 212/581-6464
Things like burgers and chef's
salads make this theater-
district hangout reliable for
audience and cast.
🎫 30 tables 🚇 A, C, E to
42nd St. 🚭 MC, V

🍴 PIGALLE
$$
DAYS INN
790 8TH AVE. (AT 48TH ST.)
TEL 212/489-2233
Large portions of Parisian
food; open 24 hours.
🎫 85 🚇 C, E, N, R, W to
49th St. 🚭 All major cards

🍴 TRATTORIA DELL'ARTE
$$
900 7TH AVE. (AT 57TH ST.)
TEL 212/245-9800
Terrific antipasto and pizzas
are part of Italian menu at
this popular restaurant.
🎫 75 🚇 N, R to 57th St.
🚭 All major cards

🍴 U.N. DELEGATES'
DINING ROOM
$$
U.N. PLAZA
TEL 212/963-7626
Unusual opportunity to
sample world menus,
especially at lunch buffet,
which varies weekly.
🎫 350 🚇 4, 5, 6 to 42nd St.
🕐 Closed Sat. & Sun. D
🚭 All major cards

🍴 CARNEGIE DELI
$
854 7TH AVE. (AT 55TH ST.)
TEL 212/757-2245
New York City original
with gigantic corned beef
sandwiches and alternately
colorful or curt service.
This should be the place
where you try smoked
tongue.
🎫 50–70 🚇 N, R to 57th
St. 🚭 Not accepted

🏨 Hotel 🍴 Restaurant 🛏 No. of guest rooms 🎫 No. of seats 🚇 Subway 🕐 Closed

🍴 COSÍ SANDWICH BARS

$

61 W. 48TH ST. (5TH & 6TH AVES.)

TEL 212/588-0888

🚇 4, 5, 6 to 59th St.

165 E. 52ND ST. (BET. LEXINGTON & 3RD AVES.)

TEL 212/758-7800

🚇 6 to 51st St.

38 E. 45TH ST. (BET. MADISON & VANDERBILT AVES.)

TEL 212/949-7400

🚇 4, 5, 6 to 42nd St.

Try the delicious wood-fired flatbread sandwiches. Open for breakfast weekdays.

🍴 40–55 🕐 Closed Sat. D & all day Sun. 🚫 Not accepted

🍴 ESS-A-BAGEL

$

831 3RD AVE. (BET. 50TH & 51ST STS.)

TEL 212/980-1010

New York's finest bagels, cheerfully served. Also can be found in Midtown South at 359 First Avenue.

🍴 25 tables 🚇 6 to 51st St; E, F to Lexington Ave.

🕐 Closed Sat. & Sun. D

🚫 All major cards

🍴 GRAND SICHUAN INTERNATIONAL MIDTOWN

$

745 9TH AVE. (BET. 50TH & 51ST STS.)

TEL 212/963-7626

Emphasis on Sichuan (spicy) cuisine, plus full menu of Americanized Chinese dishes, plus some Shanghai and Canton-style dishes. Must-tries include the spicy double-cooked pork and Sichuan pickled cabbage with red oil.

🍴 125 🚇 1, 9, E, H to 50th St. 🚫 All major cards

🍴 MENCHANKO-TEI

$

43-45 W. 55TH ST. (BET. 5TH & 6TH AVES.)

TEL 212/247-1585

Casual Japanese noodle joint—a Midtown oasis.

🍴 15 tables 🚇 N, R to 57th St.; E, F to 5th Ave.

🚫 All major cards

🍴 SOUP KITCHEN INTERNATIONAL

$

259-A W. 55TH ST. (BET. 8TH AVE. & BROADWAY)

TEL 212/757-7730

Famous takeout soup spot with long lines but cult following.

🍴 No seats 🚇 1, 9, A, B, C, D to Columbus Circle-59th St. 🕐 Closed D summer

🚫 Not accepted

UPPER EAST SIDE (MUSEUM ROW)

HOTELS

SOMETHING SPECIAL

🏨 CARLYLE

🍴

$ince 1931 this gemlike hotel has welcomed the world's elite in grand European style. Rooms have antiques, Audubon prints, marble bathrooms with whirlpools, and state-of-the-art electronics. Nancy Reagan and the late President Kennedy counted among regular guests. Those who do not check in may partake of romantic dining in the Carlyle Restaurant, bistro entertainment in the Cafe Carlyle, humorous murals in the Bemelmans Bar, or tea in the Gallery, modeled after Turkey's Topkapi Palace.

$$$$$

35 E. 76TH ST.

TEL 212/744-1600 or 800-227-5737

FAX 212/717-4682

🛏 190 + 65 residential apartments 🚇 6 to 77th St. 🚫 All major cards

🏨 GRACIE INN

$$$$$

502 E. 81ST ST. (BET. YORK & EAST END AVES.)

TEL 212/628-1700

FAX 212/628-6420

Rustic-style rooms in various sizes. Good, quiet location.

🛏 12 🚇 4, 5, 6 to 86th St.

🚫 AE, MC, V

🏨 LOWELL

$$$$$

28 E. 63RD ST. (BET. PARK & MADISON AVES.)

TEL 212/838-1400 or 800/221-4444

FAX 212/319-4230

A 1920s historic landmark on a quiet street, providing tasteful, old-world charm in an intimate setting. All rooms are suites, many with working fireplaces, kitchens, and libraries.

🛏 61 🚇 4, 5, 6 to 59th St. 🏋 🚫 All major cards

🏨 THE MARK
🍴
$$$$$

25 E. 77TH ST. (BET. 5TH & MADISON AVES.)

TEL 212/744-4300 or 800/843-6275

FAX 212/744-2749

An elegant location with formal contemporary decor, large rooms with marble or Italian ceramic baths, high-quality artwork, luxurious amenities. Popular are the Mark's Bar, and the wood-paneled Mark Restaurant— for indulgent afternoon teas.

🛏 180 🚇 6 to 77th St. 🏋 🚫 All major cards

🏨 PLAZA ATHÉNÉE

$$$$$

37 E. 64TH ST. (BET. PARK & MADISON AVES.)

TEL 212/734-9100

FAX 212/772-0958

Old-world charm and Louis XVI decor star at this New York version of the Paris original, distinguished by its smaller size and location on a quiet residential block.

🛏 156 🚇 6 to 68th St. 🏋 🚫 All major cards

🏨 REGENCY

$$$$$

540 PARK AVE. (AT 61ST ST.)

TEL 212/759-4100 or 800/233-2356

FAX 212/826-5674
Named for its Regency decor, this hotel has both understated elegance and every amenity, including TVs and phones by the marble bathtubs.
🛈 288 + 74 suites
🚇 4, 5, 6 to 59th St. 🍽
⊗ All major cards

🏨 THE WESTBURY
$$$$$
15 E. 69TH ST.
(AT MADISON AVE.)
TEL 212/535-2000 or
800/321-1569
FAX 212/535-5058
A departure from others in its English style and decor, these gracious quarters come with personalized service and direct access to shopping at neighboring Madison Ave. boutiques.
🛈 231 🚇 6 to 68th St. 🍽
⊗ All major cards

🏨 THE FRANKLIN
$$$
164 E. 87TH ST. (AT LEXINGTON & 3RD AVES.)
TEL 212/369-1000 or
800/600-8787
FAX 212/369-8000
Nicely decorated rooms with canopy beds, custom furniture, and photos of the city.
🛈 53 🚇 4, 5, 6 to 86th St.
⊗ AE, MC, V

🏨 HOTEL WALES
$$$
1295 MADISON AVE.
(AT 92ND ST.)
TEL 212/876-6000 or
877/847-4444
FAX 212/860-7000
Turn-of-the-20th-century haven with spacious suites.
🛈 45 + 47 suites 🚇 6 to 96th St. ⊗ AE, MC, V

RESTAURANTS

🍴 AUREOLE
$$$$$
34 E. 61ST ST. (BET. MADISON & PARK AVES.)
TEL 212/319-1660
Charles Palmer's famous

contemporary American cuisine. Seasonal prix-fixe menu is recommended.
🍴 37 tables 🚇 4, 5, 6 to 59th St. 🕐 Closed Sat. L & all day Sun. ⊗ All major cards

🍴 DANIEL
This gastronomic palace opened in the restored Mayflower Hotel in early 1999, with a reported price tag of 10 million dollars. Chef and proprietor Daniel Boulud turned his former Restaurant Daniel at 20 East 76th Street into Café Boulud so he could open this larger, more ornate Daniel, "a Venetian-Byzantine-Deco fantasy." Boulud is New York's longest-reigning four-star chef, known also for his days at the old Le Cirque. Although his restaurant is not French in decor, his food is—founded on ancient French farmhouse recipes that he re-creates with a flair. Roasted saddle of lamb with black-truffle gnocchi, root vegetables with a satiny au jus, and other delights await those fortunate enough to get a table here.
$$$$$
60 E. 65TH ST. (BET. MADISON & PARK)
TEL 212/288-0033
🍴 100 🚇 6 to 68th St.
⊗ All major cards

🍴 BUTTERFIELD 81
$$$$
170 E. 81ST ST. (BET. LEXINGTON & 3RD AVES.)
TEL 212/288-2700
Cozy, upscale American bistro popular with young professionals. Try the avocado salad and cedar salmon, short ribs with beef barley soup.
🍴 60 🚇 6 to 77th St.
🕐 Closed L
⊗ All major cards

🍴 JO JO
$$$$
160 E. 64TH ST.
(BET. LEXINGTON & 3RD AVES.)
TEL 212/223-5656
Outstanding bistro fare by Jean-Georges Vongerichten. The lobster and the Vahlrona chocolate cake are recommended.
🛈 150 🚇 6 to 68th St.
🕐 Closed Sat. L & all day Sun. ⊗ All major cards

🍴 PAOLA'S
$$$
245 E. 84TH ST. (BET. 2ND & 3RD AVES.)
TEL 212/794-1890
An Upper East Side find, with lovely Italian cuisine, including homemade pastas.
🍴 70 + 30 outdoors 🚇 4, 5, 6 to 86th St. 🕐 Closed L
⊗ All major cards

🍴 HEIDELBERG
$$
1648 2ND AVE. (BET. 85TH & 86TH STS.)
TEL 212/628-2332
Old-world haven for oompah food: wursts and beers.
🍴 80–85 🚇 4, 5, 6 to 86th St. ⊗ All major cards

🍴 PAMIR
$$
1437 2ND AVE. (BET. 74TH & 75TH STS.)
TEL 212/734-3791
Afghani fare, specializing in chicken, lamb, and spiced pumpkin dishes. *Kormae-murgh*, a spiced chicken stew, is recommended.
🍴 70 🚇 6 to 77th St.
🕐 Closed L & all day Sun.
⊗ MC, V

🍴 SERENDIPITY 3
$$
225 E. 60TH ST. (BET. 2ND & 3RD AVES.)
TEL 212/838-3531
Over-the-top ice-cream sundaes and casual fare. Famous for frozen hot chocolate.
🍴 165 🚇 4, 5, 6 to 59th St.
⊗ All major cards

🍴 EL POLLO
$
1746 1ST AVE. (BET. 90TH & 91ST STS.)
TEL 212/996-7810
Outstanding Peruvian rotisserie chicken, especially for takeout meals (also in SoHo).
🔧 40 🚇 4, 5, 6 to 86th St.
🏧 All major cards

CENTRAL PARK

HOTELS

🏨 ESSEX HOUSE, HOTEL NIKKO NEW YORK
$$$$$
160 CENTRAL PARK S. (BET. 6TH & 7TH AVES.)
TEL 212/247-0300 or 800/645-5687
FAX 212/315-1839
Dramatic art deco setting with tasteful rooms and stunning park views.
🛏 516 + 81 suites 🚇 1, 9, A, C, B, D to Columbus Circle-59th St. 🎽 🏧 All major cards

🏨 PIERRE
$$$$$
2 E. 61ST ST. (AT 5TH AVE.)
TEL 212/838-8000 or 800/332-3442
FAX 212/825-0319
Elegance, antiques, and opulent decor charac-terize this hotel and luxury co-op building overlooking Central Park. Public rooms include the gorgeous Rotunda, where afternoon tea is served.
🛏 206 🚇 N, R to 5th Ave.
🎽 🏧 All major cards

🏨 STANHOPE
$$$$$
995 5TH AVE. (AT 81ST ST.)
TEL 212/288-5800 or 800/223-234
FAX 212/517-0088
Small and sophisticated, with a remarkable location directly across from the Metropolitan Museum of Art. Many suites are furnished with antiques

and have a Central Park view. There is a lovely sidewalk café and salon.
🛏 141 🚇 4, 5, 6 to 86th St.
🎽 🏧 All major cards

SOMETHING SPECIAL

🏨 THE MAYFLOWER
When you book, remember, the higher the floor, the better the view; a front room facing Central Park is worth the extra cost, especially around sunset when the colors can be spectacular. Proximity to Lincoln Center, the park, the theater district, and Upper West Side shopping, along with large rooms with pantries, make this a favorite with musicians and theater people. The hotel is comfortably old world—refurbished in 1996, when a fitness center was added. Chances are, if you choose to stay here, you'll keep fit by walking to the many nearby points of interest. The Conservatory Restaurant is open for all meals, including a popular Sunday brunch.
$$$$$
15 CENTRAL PARK WEST (AT 61ST ST.)
TEL 212/265-0060 or 800-223-4164
FAX 212/265-2026
🛏 377 🚇 1, 9, A, B, C, D to 59th St.-Columbus Circle 🎽 🏧 All major cards

---

RESTAURANT

🍴 TAVERN ON THE GREEN
$$$$
CENTRAL PARK W. (AT 67TH ST.)
TEL 212/873-3200
Unique setting in the park, huge, splendid decor. Mixed food reviews. Try going for jazz on Saturday nights.

🔧 700 🚇 1, 9 to 66th St.
🏧 All major cards

UPPER WEST SIDE

HOTELS

🏨 BEACON HOTEL
$$$
2130 BROADWAY (AT 75TH ST.)
TEL 212/787-1100 or 800/572-4969
FAX 212/724-0839
Generously sized rooms, somewhat faded decor, family friendly.
🛏 107 + 100 suites 🚇 1, 2, 3, 9 to 72nd St. 🎽 Nearby
🏧 All major cards

🏨 COUNTRY INN
$$$
W. 77TH ST. (BET. BROADWAY & WEST END)
TEL 212/580-4183
Nicely restored landmark town house with lovely suites. No elevator.
🛏 4 🚇 1, 9 to 79th St.

🏨 EXCELSIOR
$$$
45 W. 81ST ST. (BET. COLUMBUS AVE. & CENTRAL PARK W.)
TEL 212/362-9200 or 800/368-4575
FAX 212/721-2994
Large, comfortable rooms with traditional decor, some views.
🛏 190 🚇 1, 9 to 79th St.; C, E to 81st St. 🏧 AE, MC, V

🏨 TRUMP
🍴 INTERNATIONAL HOTEL & TOWERS
$$$$$
1 CENTRAL PARK W. (AT COLUMBUS CIRCLE)
TEL 212/299-1000 or 888/448-7867
FAX 212/299-1150
Donald Trump's megaventure at the tip of Central Park, featuring floor-to-ceiling windows and personal attachés assigned to guests to coordinate their lives in New York. Dine downstairs at Jean Georges (see p. 254),

---

🏊 Indoor swimming pool 🏊 Outdoor swimming pool 🎽 Health club 🏧 Credit cards   **KEY**

the excellent first-class restaurant, or have one of the chefs cook for you in your suite, if you prefer.
🛈 168 suites 🚇 1, 9, A, B, C, D to Columbus Circle-59th St. 🚻
🚫 All major cards

🏨 LUCERNE
$$$
201 W. 79TH ST. (AT AMSTERDAM AVE.)
TEL 212/875-1000
FAX 212/362-7257
Simple, clean rooms.
🛈 250 🚇 1, 9 to 79th St.
🚫 AE, MC, V

RESTAURANTS

🍴 JEAN GEORGES
$$$$$
TRUMP INTERNATIONAL HOTEL, 1 CENTRAL PARK W. (BET. 60TH & 61ST STS.)
TEL 212/299-3900
Top-class contemporary French-American cuisine by Jean-Georges Vongerichten. The best approach is the chef's tasting menu.
🪑 60 🚇 1, 9, A, B, C, D to Columbus Circle-59th St.
🕐 Closed Sat. L & all day Sun. 🚫 All major cards

🍴 CAFÉ DES ARTISTES
$$$$
1 W. 67TH ST. (BET. COLUMBUS AVE. & CENTRAL PARK W.)
TEL 212/877-3500
French cuisine with specialties of pot-au-feu and steak tartare, amid lovely murals and an old-world motif.
🪑 100 🚇 1, 9 to 66th St.
🚫 All major cards

🍴 CAFÉ LUXEMBOURG
$$$$
200 W. 70TH ST. (BET. AMSTERDAM & WEST END AVES.)
TEL 212/873-7411
A classic hip destination with bistro fare.
🪑 85 🚇 1, 2, 3, 9 to 72nd St. 🚫 All major cards

🍴 NOUGATINE
$$$$
TRUMP INTERNATIONAL HOTEL, 1 CENTRAL PARK W. (BET. 60TH & 61ST STS.)
TEL 212/299-3900
A more casual part of Jean-Georges restaurant. Open for breakfast except Sundays.
🪑 65–80 🚇 1, 9, A, B, C, D to Columbus Circle-59th St.
🚫 All major cards

🍴 PICHOLINE
$$$$
35 W. 64TH ST. (BET. BROADWAY & CENTRAL PARK W.)
TEL 212/724-8585
Fine Mediterranean cuisine and outstanding service, with the city's best cheese cart. Try the salmon with horseradish crust.
🪑 200 🚇 1, 9 to 66th St.
🕐 Closed Mon. L 🚫 All major cards

🍴 SHUN LEE CAFÈ
$$$$
43 W. 65TH ST. (BET. COLUMBUS AVE. & CENTRAL PARK W.)
TEL 212/769-3888
First-rate Chinese dining, some of New York's finest.
🪑 400 🚇 1, 9 to 66th St.
🚫 All major cards

🍴 OUEST
$$$
2315 BROADWAY (AT 84TH ST.)
TEL 212/580-8700
See-and-be-seen at this intimate foodie's paradise, popular among celebrities, featuring Chef Tom Valenti's distinctive boldly layered style. Don't miss his signature lamb shanks. Sunday brunch.
🪑 135 🚇 A, D to 86th St.
🕐 Closed L 🚫 All major cards

🍴 BARNEY GREENGRASS
$$
541 AMSTERDAM AVE. (BET. 86TH & 87TH STS.)
TEL 212/724-4707
Visit the "Sturgeon King" for a classic meal of smoked fish delights. Salmon and eggs and

scallion cream cheese are recommended.
🪑 55 🚇 1, 9 to 86th St.
🚫 Not accepted

🍴 SARABETH'S KITCHEN
$$
1295 MADISON (AT 92ND ST.)
TEL 212/410-7335
Baked goods and popular brunches. Open for breakfast.
🪑 80 🚇 6 to 96th St.
🚫 All major cards

HEIGHTS & HARLEM

RESTAURANTS

🍴 LONDEL'S OF STRIVERS' ROW
$$
2620 8TH AVE.. (BET. 139TH & 140TH STS.)
TEL 212/234-6114
Great Southern cooking with classic fried chicken and greens.
🪑 150 🚇 B, C, 2, 3 to 135th St. 🕐 Closed Sun. D & all day Mon. 🚫 All major cards

🍴 SYLVIA'S
$$
328 LENOX AVE. (BET. 126TH & 127TH STS.)

Well-known soul food destination with brunch on Sundays. Barbecued ribs, ham, and collard greens are recommendations.
🛏 300 🚇 2, 3 to 125th St. 🚫 All major cards

OUTER BOROUGHS

BROOKLYN

🍴 PETER LUGER'S STEAKHOUSE
$$$$
178 BROADWAY (AT DRIGGS AVE.)
TEL 718/387-7400
One of the city's finest steakhouses. No frills, just great porterhouse and creamed spinach.
🛏 150 🚇 J to Marcy Ave. 🚫 Not accepted

🍴 RIVER CAFÉ
$$$$
1 WATER ST. (BROOKLYN BRIDGE)
TEL 718/522-5200
Spectacular view of Manhattan in elegant setting—sit outdoors in summer. Lobster, lamb, and soft shells are recommended.
🛏 110 🚇 A to High St.-Brooklyn; 2, 3 to Clark St. 🚫 All major cards

🍴 BAMCAFÉ
$$
BROOKLYN ACADEMY OF MUSIC, 30 LAFAYETTE AVE.
TEL 718/636-4111
International cuisine at a cultural landmark that opens two hours before performances.
🛏 300 🚇 2, 3, 4, 5 to Atlantic Ave. 🚫 All major cards

🍴 CAFÉ TATIANA
$$
3145 BRIGHTON BEACH 4TH ST. (ON THE BOARDWALK)
TEL 718/646-7630
Fine setting in Brooklyn for Russian cuisine. Especially good are the soups and

dumplings. Open for breakfast.
🛏 100 🚇 D to Brighton Ave. 🚫 Not accepted

🍴 PRIMORSKI
$$
282 BRIGHTON BEACH AVE. (BET. 2ND & 3RD STS.)
TEL 718/891-3111
First-choice Russian restaurant, with fine casual dining or prix-fixe banquet dinners and a show. Don't miss *lavash* (bread), *pelmeni*, or *sashlik*.
🛏 150 🚇 D to Brighton Beach 🚫 Not accepted

🍴 PATSY GRIMALDI'S
$
19 OLD FULTON ST.
TEL 718/858-4300
Traditional New York-style pizza place, with juke box and red-checkered tablecloths.
🛏 50 🚇 A or C to High St. 🚫 Not accepted

QUEENS

🏨 SHERATON LAGUARDIA EAST HOTEL
$$$-$$$$
135-20 39TH AVE.
TEL 718/460-6666
Modern airport hotel near U.S. Open Tennis Center and Shea Stadium. Restaurant.
🛏 173 rooms & suites 🚇 7 to Main St., Flushing 🏋 🚫 All major cards

🏨 BEST WESTERN CITY VIEW MOTOR INN
$$$
33-17 GREENPOINT AVE., LONG ISLAND CITY
TEL 718/392-8400 or 800/248-9843
Converted 19th-century public school near Shea Stadium and U.S. Open Tennis Center. Free shuttle to and from LaGuardia.
🛏 71 rooms 🚇 7 to 40th St. 🚫 All major cards

🍴 ELIAS CORNER
$$
24-02 31ST ST. (AT 24TH AVE.)
TEL 718/932-1510
Authentic Greek seafood joint.
🛏 100 🚇 N to Astoria Boulevard 🕐 Closed L 🚫 Not accepted

🍴 JACKSON DINER
$$
37-47 74TH ST. (BET. ROOSEVELT & 37TH AVES.)
TEL 718/672-1232
Fine Indian food.
🛏 65 🚇 F, R to Roosevelt Ave., 7 to 74th St.-Broadway 🚫 Not accepted

🍴 JOE'S SHANGHAI
$$
136-21 37TH AVE. (BET. MAIN & UNION STS.)
TEL 718/539-3838
Fantastic broth-filled dumplings and other specials (also in Chinatown).
🛏 70 🚇 7 to Main St.; R to Elmhurst 🚫 Not accepted

🍴 LA BOINA ROJA
$
80-22 37TH AVE., JACKSON HEIGHTS
TEL 718/424-6711
Small Colombian steakhouse, with 23 different sauces for your beef (including one made from coffee). Chilean and Argentinian wines.
🛏 100 🚇 7 to 74th St.-Broadway 🚫 All major cards

🍴 TOURNESOL, BISTRO FRANÇAIS
$
50-12 VERNON BLVD., HUNTER'S POINT
TEL 718/472-4355
WWW.TOURNESOLNY.COM
A taste of France, including mussels in white wine, salad of lardons with poached egg, and rabbit terrine with a red onion compote. Brunch features perfect omelets.
🛏 65 🚇 7 to Vernon Blvd.-Jackson Ave. 🕐 Closed Mon. 🚫 Not accepted

SHOPPING IN NEW YORK

Everything is available in New York at both the highest and the lowest prices. Many natives spend a good portion of their lives trying to stay on one end of the spectrum by doing their homework and shopping around. Department stores are best visited weekdays mid-morning or early afternoon, some are open well into the evening. Many specialty stores do not open early in the morning. It may be worth calling specific destinations to verify hours, which can change seasonally (some places stay open later in the summer).

Although Lower Manhattan is primarily a financial district, there are some shops. Nearly all of the chain stores are represented at the South Street Seaport, so it is not included in these listings. TriBeCa is an up-and-coming shopping district, especially around Franklin St. and lower West Broadway. The Lower East Side is a fascinating area, originally Jewish but now multiethnic. Shopping there is a treat for the adventurous who will find a fascinating mixture of the oldest and the newest retail establishments. It's a great Sunday destination, since everything is open (Saturday stores are closed for the Sabbath).

The area dubbed "NoLiTa" (North of Little Italy) unofficially stretches from Houston to Spring Sts. and from Lafayette to Elizabeth Sts., and is the home to many cute boutiques. Lafayette St. contains a number of "modern vintage" furniture sources. SoHo offers a sea of shopping opportunity, but if you can go during the week, the crowds of browsers will be decidedly thinner.

In the West Village little places are tucked away here and there, and Bleecker St. and Christopher St. are good shopping locations. The East Village is the most unique neighborhood, multiethnic and ever changing. Ninth St. between Second Ave. and Ave. A is a treasure trove. Bond St., between Lafayette St. and Bowery, is a new strip of interesting old furniture stores, and the antiques zone is on 10th and 11th Sts., from University Pl. to Broadway. While Fifth Ave. is the acknowl-

edged shopping center of New York, Madison Ave. is a strip of many of the ritziest stores around. Columbus Ave. on the Upper West Side is probably the most interesting shopping strip, though Amsterdam has recently been gentrified, and Broadway is always booming, though largely with food sources.

ACCESSORIES & SHOES

Billy Martins, 220 E. 60th St., bet. 2nd & 3rd Aves., tel 212/861-3100. Subway: 4, 5, 6 to 59th St. Cowboy boots.
Dö Kham, 51 Prince St., tel 212/966-2404. Subway: N,R to Prince St.
Tibetan hats and crafts.
Harry's, 2299 Broadway, tel 212/874-2035. Subway: 1, 9 to 86th St. Closed Sun.
Durable yet fashionable shoes.
The Hat Shop, 120 Thompson St., tel 212/219-1445. Subway: C, E to Spring St. Closed a.m.
Stylish hats.
Hermés, 691 Madison Ave., at E. 62nd St, tel 212/751-3181. Subway: N, R, W to 5th Ave., 4, 5, 6 to 59th and Lexington Ave. Closed Sun.
Unique silk scarves, neckties, handbags.
Kiehl's, 109 3rd Ave., tel 212/677-3171. Subway: 6 to Astor Pl.; L to 3rd Ave. Closed Sun.
Otto Tootsi Plohound, 413 W. Broadway, tel 212/925-8931. Subway: C, E to Spring St.; 1,9 to Houston St.
The hippest shoes, with a mind-boggling selection.
Peter Fox, 105 Thompson St., tel 212/431-6359. Subway: C, E

to Spring St. Beautiful shoes.
Shoofly, 465 Amsterdam Ave., tel 212/580-4390. Subway: 1, 9 to 86th St. Closed a.m. Sun.
Children's shoes.
T. O. Dey, 9 E. 38th St., tel 212/683-6300. Subway: 4, 5, 6, 7 to 42nd St. Call for hours.
Custom shoes.

ANTIQUES

Gill & Lagodich, 108 Reade St., tel 212/619-0631. Subway: 1, 2, 3 to Chambers St. Call for hours.
Antique frames.
Manhattan Art & Antiques Center, 1050 2nd Ave. (bet. E. 55th & E. 56th Sts.), tel 212/355-4400. Subway: 4, 5, 6 to 53rd & Lexington Ave.
More than 100 galleries.
Susan Parrish Antiques, 390 Bleecker St., tel 212/645-5020. Subway: C, E to 14th St.; 1, 9 to Christopher St. Closed a.m. Tues.–Sat.; "by chance and by appointment" Sun.–Mon. American folk art.

ARTS & CRAFTS

Ceramica, 59 Thompson St., tel 212/941-1307. Subway: A, C, or E to Canal St.
Italian ceramics.
Jerry Ohlinger's, 242 W. 14th St., tel 212/989-0869. Subway: C, E to 14th St. Closed a.m. daily.
Classic and new movie stills and posters.
TriBeCa Potters, 443 Greenwich St., tel 212/431-7631. Subway: 1, 9 Canal St. Call for hours.
Ceramics studio.
Triton Gallery, 323 W. 45th St. (bet. 8th & 9th Aves.), tel 212/765-2472. Subway: A, C, E to 42nd St.
Theater-depicting posters of all sizes.
Urban Archeology, 143 Franklin St., tel 212/431-4646, Subway: 1 or 9 to Franklin St. Closed Sun.
Amazing array of architectural elements as well as new fixtures.

BAGS & HANDBAGS

Altman Luggage, 135 Orchard St., tel 212/254-7275. Subway: F to Houston St. Closed Sat.
Well-priced bags, backpacks, and pens.
Big Drop, 174 Spring St., tel 212/966-4299. Subway: C or E to Spring St.
Bags and trendy clothing.
Il Bisonte, 120 Sullivan St., tel 212/966-8773. Subway: C, E to Spring St.; A, C, E to Canal St. Closed a.m.
Leather goods and bags.
Gucci, 685 5th Ave., tel 212/826-2600. Subway: E, F to 5th Ave. Closed a.m. Sun.
Expensive designer goods.
Jutta Neumann, 158 Allen St., tel 212/982-7048. Subway: 6 to Astor Pl. Closed a.m. and Sun. Leather designs.
Kate Spade, 454 Broom St., tel 212/274-1991. Subway: C, E to Spring St.
Chic handbags.

BOOKS

Biography Bookshop, 400 Bleecker St., tel 212/807-8655. Subway: C, E to 14th St. Closed a.m. Mon.–Sat.
Many lives.
Gotham, 41 W. 47th St., tel 212/719-4448. Subway: B, D, F to Rockefeller Center. Closed Sun.
Out of print books and first editions.
Kitchen Arts & Letters, 1435 Lexington Ave., tel 212/876-5550. Subway: 4, 5, 6 to 86th St.; 6 to 96th St. Closed Sun. & a.m. Mon.
Outstanding cookbook collection.
Pageant Books & Prints, 114 W. Houston St., tel 212/674-5296. Subway: 1, 9 to Houston St. Closed a.m. and Sun.–Mon.
Old books and an amazing print collection.
Rizzoli, 31 W. 57th St. (bet. 5th & 6th Aves.), tel 212/765-2472. Subway: N, R to 57th St.
Books and magazines in a distinguished environment.
Strand, 828 Broadway, tel 212/473-1452. Subway: 4, 5, 6 to 14th St.-Union Sq. Closed early a.m. Sun.
Ultimate used bookstore.
Traveler's Bookstore, 22 W. 52nd St. (in Time Warner Building), tel 212/664-0995. Subway: B, D, F to Rockefeller Center. Closed Sun.
Books on travel.
Used Book Café, 126 Crosby St., tel 212/334-3324. Subway: B, D, F to Broadway-Lafayette St. Closed a.m. Sun.
Comfortable shop for book lovers and lounging; benefits people living with AIDS.
Weitz Weitz & Coleman, 1377 Lexington Ave., tel 212/831-2213. Subway: 4, 5, 6 to 86th St.; 6 to 96th St. Closed a.m. Sat. & Sun. or by appointment.
Interesting shop with chatty owner.
West Sider, 2246 Broadway (bet. W. 80th & W. 81st Sts.), tel 212/362-0706. Subway: 1 to 79th St. A close, yet variety-filled space of rare art and fiction books.

CLOTHES

A/X: Armani Exchange, 568 Broadway (at Prince St.), tel 212/431-6000. Subway: N, R to Prince St.
The Armani name at an affordable price: T-shirts, jeans, jackets, and more.
Agnès B., 116 Prince St., tel 212/925-4649. Subway: N or R to Prince St.
Designer clothing.
Anna Sui, 113 Greene St., tel 212/941-8406. Subway: N, R to Prince St.
Women's designer clothing.
April Cornell, 487 Columbus Ave., tel 212/799-4342. Subway: 1, 9 to 86th St.
Indian fabrics used in clothes and linens.
Atomic Passion, 430 E. 9th St., tel 212/533-0718. Subway: 6 to Astor Place-8th St. Closed until 2 p.m. Vintage clothing and objets d'art.
Bebe, 100 5th Ave., tel 212/675-2323. Subway: 4, 5, 6 to 14th St.-Union Sq.
Well-priced knock-offs of trendy clothing.
Ben Freedman, 137 Orchard St., tel 212/674-0854. Subway: F to Delancey-Essex Sts.
"Gents furnishings" with discounted London Fog coats.
Brooks Brothers, 346 Madison Ave., tel 212/682-8800. Subway: 6 to 33rd St.
Menswear and furnishings.
Calvin Klein, 654 Madison Ave., tel 212/292-9000. Subway: N, R to 5th Ave.; 4, 5, 6, to 59th St. Closed a.m. Sun.
American chic for men, women, and home.
Camouflage, 141 8th Ave., tel 212/691-1750. Subway: 1, 9 to 18th St. Closed a.m. Mon.–Fri. and Sun. Men's clothing.
Canal Jean Co., 504 Broadway, tel 212/226-1130. Subway: 6 to Spring St.; N, R to Prince St.
New and old street clothes.
Century 21, 22 Cortlandt St., tel 212/227-9092. Subway: C, E to World Trade Center; 1, 9, N, R to Cortlandt St.
Discount clothing.
Chanel, 5 E. 57th St., tel 212/355-5050. Subway: N, R to 5th Ave. Closed Sun.
Designer wear.
Comme des Garçons, 520 W. 22nd St., tel 212/604-9200. Subway: C, E to 23rd St.
Designer clothing.
DNKY, 655 Madison Ave. (at E. 60th St.), tel 212/223-3569. Subway: M, R, W to 5t Ave.
Wearables and nonwearables ensuring a very unique look.
Diesel, 770 Lexington Ave., tel 212/308-0055. Subway: 4, 5, 6 to 59th St.
Hip Italian fashion.
Gianni Versace, 815 Madison Ave., tel 212/744-6868, closed Sun. Subway: 6 to 68th St.
Italian glitz.
Gucci, 685 5th Ave. (bet. E. 53rd & E. 54th Sts.), tel 212/826-2600. Subway: E to 53rd St.
Hot and cool styles for every occasion.
INA, 101 Thompson St., tel 212/941-4757. Subway: C, E to

Spring St. Closed a.m.
Gently worn designer clothing.
Infinity, 1116 Madison Ave., tel
212/517-4232. Subway: 4, 5, 6 to
86th St. Closed a.m. Sat. & Sun.
Junior girls' clothes and
accessories paradise.
**Irvington Institute Thrift
Store,** 1534 2nd Ave., tel
212/879-4555. Subway: 6 to 77th
St. Closed a.m. Sun.
Some fine, gently worn wear
from swanky closets.
Lilliput, 265 Lafayette St., tel
212/965-9567. Subway: B, D, F to
Broadway-Lafayette St.; 6 to
Bleecker St.
Children's clothes.
NY Firefighter's Friend, 263
Lafayette St., tel 212/226-3142.
Subway: 6 to Spring St.
Closed Sun.
Fire-related clothes and toys.
Original Levi's Store, 750
Lexington Ave., tel 212/826-
5957. Subway: 4, 5, 6 to 59th St.
Closed a.m. Sun.
Flagship store with all models
(even custom) of jeans.
Patricia Field, 382 W.
Broadway, tel 212/254-1699.
Subway: 6 to Astor Pl.
Closed a.m.
Established destination for wild
clothing and accessories.
Paul Smith, 108 5th Ave.,
tel 212/627-9770. Subway: 4, 5, 6
to Union Sq.-14th St.
Closed a.m. Sun.
Tasteful menswear.
Peanut Butter & Jane, 617
Hudson St., tel 212/620-7952.
Subway: C, E to 14th St. Closed
a.m. Sun.
Toys, vintage and new
children's clothes.
Pop Shop, 292 Lafayette St.,
tel 212/219-2784. Subway: B, D, P
to Bleecker-Lafayette Sts.
Closed Mon.
Keith Haring designs.
Resurrection Vintage,
217 Mott St., tel 212/625-1374.
Subway: 6 to Spring St.
Closed a.m.
Antique and vintage clothing.
Ritz Thrift Store, 107 W. 57th
St., tel 212/265-4559. Subway: 4,
5, 6, 7, to 42nd St. Closed Sun.
The place for used furs.
Todd Oldham, 123 Wooster

St., tel 212/925-8931. Subway: N,
R to Prince St.
Trend-setting urban fashions.
TG-170, 170 Ludlow St., tel
212/995-8660. Subway: F to
Essex-Delancey Sts. Closed a.m.
Women's clothing.
Yohji Yamamoto, 103 Grand
St., tel 212/966-9066. Subway: A,
C, E to Canal St.
Designer clothing in
large premises.
Yu, 151 Ludlow St., tel 212/979-
9370. Subway: F to Delancey-
Essex Sts. Closed a.m.
Designer consignment.

DEPARTMENT STORES

Barney's, 660 Madison Ave., tel
212/593-7800 or 212/826-8900.
Subway: N,R to 5th Ave.; 4, 5, 6
to 59th St. Closed a.m. Sun.
Upscale department store with
fashions, cosmetics, housewares.
Popular with the trendy crowd.
Bergdorf Goodman, 754 5th
Ave. at 57th St., tel 212/753-
7300. Subway: N, R to 5th Ave.;
E, F to 5th Ave. Closed Sun.
Elegant fashions.
Bergdorf Goodman Men,
745 5th Ave., tel 212/753-7300.
Subway: N, R to 5th Ave.; E, F to
5th Ave. Closed Sun.
High-end men's fashion.
Bloomingdale's, 1000 3rd
Ave., tel 212/705-2000. Subway:
4, 5, 6 to 59th St.
Flagship department store.
Henri Bendel, 712 5th Ave., tel
212/247-1100. Subway: N, R to
5th Ave.; E, F to 5th Ave. Closed
a.m. Sun.
Boutique department store.
Lord & Taylor's, 424 5th Ave.,
tel 212/391-3344. Subway: B, D, F
to 42nd St.; 7 to 5th Ave.
Classic department store
specializing in women's wear
and dresses.
Macy's, 151 W. 34th St., tel
212/695-4400. Subway: 1, 2, 3
to 34th St.
NYC's biggest, with everything.
Saks Fifth Avenue, 611 5th
Ave., tel 212/753-4000. Subway:
B, D, F to Rockefeller Center; E,
F to 5th Ave. Closed a.m. Sun.

Flagship store of fashion.
Shanghai Tang, 714 Madison
Ave., tel 212/888-0111. Subway:
N,R to 5th Ave.; 4, 5, 6 to 59th
St. Closed a.m. Sun.
Chinese luxury
department store.
Takashimaya, 693 5th Ave., tel
212/350-0100. Subway: B, D, F to
Rockefeller Center; E, F to 5th
Ave. Closed Sun.
Fabulous Japanese department
store with new and old.

FOOD STORES

Angelica's Herb, 147 1st Ave.,
tel 212/677-1549. Subway: C to
1st Ave.; 6 to Astor Pl. Closed
a.m. Sun.
Herbal remedies and herbs.
Balducci's, 424 6th Ave., tel
212/673-2600. Subway: A, B, C,
D, E, F to W. 4th St.
Lovely gourmet food and house-
brand pastas.
Dean & Deluca, 560
Broadway, tel 212/226-6800.
Subway: N, R to Prince St.
Where food is fashion.
Economy Candy, 108
Rivington St., tel 212/254-1531.
Subway: Essex St.-Delancey St.
Chocolates, candies, nuts.
**International Grocery and
International Food,** 529 &
543 9th Ave., tel 212/279-5514.
Subway: A, C, E to 42nd St.
Closed Sun.
Amazing spice and dried goods
selection, Greek dips and
cheeses (uptown store).
Kalustyan's, 123 Lexington
Ave., tel 212/685-3451. Subway:
6 to 28th St.
The best spices, Indian foods.
Kam-man, 200 Canal St. (at
Mott St.), tel 212-571-0300.
Subway: 6, M, R to Canal St.
Edibles from beneath the sea,
including dried squid and
shark fins.
Li-lac Chocolates, 120
Christopher St., tel 212/242-
7374. Subway: 1, 9 to Christo-
pher St. Closed a.m. Sun.
Handmade chocolates.
McNulty's, 109 Christopher
St., tel 212/242-5351. Subway:
1, 9 to Christopher St.

Teas and coffees.
Murray's Cheese Shop, 257
Bleecker St., tel 212/243-3289.
Subway: A, B, C, D, E, F to
W. 4th St.
Great selection served by a
knowledgeable staff.
Myer's of Keswick, 634
Hudson St., tel 212/691-4194.
Subway: C, E to 14th St. Closed
a.m. Sun.
British foods.
Payard, 1032 Lexington Ave
(bet. 73rd & E. 7th Sts.), tel
212/717-5252. Closed Sun.
Subway: 6 to 68th St.
Bistro with delectable pastries
and celebrated chocolates.
Russ & Daughters, 179
E. Houston St., tel 212/475-4880.
Subway: F to Houston St.
Some of NYC's best smoked fish
and caviar.
Sullivan St. Bakery, 73
Sullivan St., tel 212/334-9435.
Subway: C, E to Spring St.
Great breads and snacks.
T Salon & Emporium, 11 E.
20th St., tel 212/358-0506.
Subway: 6 to 23rd St.
150 varieties of tea
and accessories.
Veniero's Pasticceria & Cafe,
342 E. 11th St., tel 212/674 7264.
Subway: C to 1st Ave.; 6 to
Astor Pl. Closed p.m.
Italian pastries.
Vinegar Factory, 431 E. 91st
St. (bet. York & 1st Aves.), tel
212/987-0885. Subway: 4, 5, 6 at
86th or 96th Sts.
Vast selection of vinegar and
oils, produce and cheese, and
weekend brunch.
Zabar's, 2245 Broadway,
tel 212/787-2000. Subway: 1, 9 to
79th St.
Gourmet foods and housewares.

FURNITURE: ANTIQUE & MODERN

280 Modern, 123 Crosby St.,
tel 212/941-5825. Subway: B, D, F
to Broadway-Lafayette St. Call
for Sun. hours.
Vintage modern furniture.
**Art & Industrial Design
Shop,** 399 Lafayette St.,
tel 212/477-0116. Subway: B, D, F

to Broadway-Lafayette St.
Closed Sun.
Vintage 20th-century furniture.
Cathers & Dembrosky, 43 E.
10th St., tel 212/353-1244.
Subway: Astor Pl.
Mission furniture.
Crate & Barrel, 650 Madison
Ave. (at E. 59th St.), tel 212/308-
0011. Subway: 4, 5, 6, N, R to
59th St. and Lexington Ave.)
Cheery store offering simple
furniture to kitchen essentials.
Pantry and Hearth, 121
E. 35th St., tel 212/889-0026.
Subway: 6 to 33rd St. Call for
hours or appointment.
18th-century American furniture
and china.
Wyeth's, 315 Spring St., tel
212/243-3661. Subway: 1, 9 to
Franklin St. Closed Sun.
Modern and refurbished
furniture, lighting, ceramics.

HOUSEHOLD

ABC Carpet & Home, 888
Broadway, tel 212/473-3000.
Subway: 6 to 23rd St.; 4, 5, 6
to 14th St.
Unbelievable emporium of
absolutely everything for the
home, gifts, antiques, etc.
Bridge Kitchenware, 214
E. 52nd St., tel 212/688-4220.
Subway: E to 53rd St.-Lexington
St.; 6 to 53rd St. Closed Sun.
Very NYC, funky
kitchenware store.
Felissimo, 10 W. 56th St.,
tel 212/247-5656. Subway: N, R
to 5th Ave. Closed Sat.–Sun.
Unique goods for the table.
JB Prince, 36 E. 31st St., 11th
floor, tel 212/683-3553. Subway:
33rd St. Closed Sat.–Sun.
Knives and kitchen gadgets.
Kam Man, 200 Canal St.,
tel 212/571-0330. Subway: 6 to
Canal St.; N, R to Canal St.
Chinese food and housewares
emporium.
Le Fanion, 299 W. 4th St., tel
212/463-8760. Subway: 1, 9 to
Christopher St. Closed a.m.
& Sun.
French ceramics old and new.
Mxyplyzyk, 123 Greenwich
Ave., tel 212/989-4300. Subway:

C, E to 14th St.-8th Ave. Closed
a.m. Sun.
Housewares and gadgets of the
most modern design.
Porthault, 829 Madison Ave.,
tel 212/688-1660. Subway: 6 to
68th St. Closed Sun.
French luxury linens.
Pratesi, 829 Madison Ave.,
tel 212/288-2315. Subway: 6 to
68th St. Closed Sun.
Italian linens.
Shabby Chic, 83 Wooster St.
(bet. Spring & Broome Sts.), tel
212/274-9842. Subway: N, R to
Prince St./F to Broadway,
Lafayette.
Furnishings with
multifaceted fabrics.
Waterworks, 225 E. 57th St.
(bet. 2nd & 3rd Aves.), tel
212/371-9266, closed Sun.
Subway: 4, 5, 6, N, R to 59th St.
More than just a faucet shop.
Woodrow-Greenstein, 506
E. 74th St., tel 212/988-2906.
Subway: 6 to 77th St. Closed
Sun. & Sat.; by appointment only.
Painted American country
antiques, quilts.

JEWELRY

Cartier, 653 5th Ave. (near 52nd
St.), tel 212/753-0111. Closed Sun.
Subway: E, V to 53rd St.
Old favorites to new
design jewelry.
David Baruch, 36 W. 47th St.,
tel 212/719-2884. Subway:
B, D, F to Rockefeller Center.
Closed Fri.–Sun.
Brand name silver.
Fortunoff, 681 5th Ave., tel
212/758-6660. Subway: B, D, F to
Rockefeller Center. Closed Sun.
Gold and silver jewelry, both
new and antique.
Fairly good value.
Fred Leighton, 773 Madison
Ave., tel 212/288-1872. Subway:
6 to 68th St. Closed Sun.
Antique jewelry.
Gold Standard, 21 W. 47th St.,
6th fl., tel 212/719-5656. Subway:
B, D, F to Rockefeller Center.
Closed Sat.–Sun.
Gold jewelry and objets d'art.
Jean's Silversmiths, 16 W.
45th St., tel 212/575-0723.

Subway: B, D, F to Rockefeller Center. Closed Sat.–Sun.
Antique silverware and objects.
Jewelry Exchange, 15 W. 47th St., Subway: B, D, F to Rockefeller Center.
Dizzying array of jewelers' booths and shops.
Mark Jewelry, 32 W. 47th St., tel 212/391-4279. Subway: B, D, F to Rockefeller Center. Closed Sat.–Sun.
Silver jewelry.
Robert Lee Morris, 400 W. Broadway, tel 212/431-3630. Subway: C, E to 6th Ave.; 1, 9 to Houston St.; N, R to Prince St. Closed Sun. a.m.
Original gold jewelry design.
Tiffany, 727 5th Ave., tel 212/755-8000. Subway: N, R to 5th Ave. Closed Sun.
Jewelry, tabletop, and other fancy items. No breakfast.

TOYS: BIG KIDS, LITTLE KIDS

Big City Kites, 1210 Lexington Ave., tel 212/472-2623. Subway: 4, 5, 6 to 86th St. Call for hours.
Kites and darts.
Chess Forum, 219 Thompson St., tel 212/475-2369. Subway: A. B, C, D, E, F to W. 4th St.
Dinosaur Hill, 306 E. 9th St. (bet. 1st & 2nd Aves.), tel 212/473-5850. Subway: 6 to Astor Pl.
Siimple, precious classics, including marionettes to craft kits.
Enchanted Forest, 85 Mercer St., tel 212/925-6677. Subway: N, R to Prince St. Closed Sun a.m.
Fantasy toy store.
FAO Schwartz, 767 5th Ave., tel 212/644-9400. Subway: N, R to 5th Ave.
Open since the mid-19th century. Toys, toys, toys.
Geppetto's Toy Box, 10 Christopher St. (at Greenwich Ave.), tel 212/620-7511. Subway: 1, A, C, D, E, F, G to W. 4th St.
Dolls to rubber duckies— most are handmade.
Pokémon Center, 10 Rockefeller Plaza (at 48th St.),

tel 212/307-0900. Subway: B, D, F, V to Rockefeller Plaza.
Go animated with trading cards or in the video game room.

MARKETS

Chelsea Antiques Fair and Market, 6th Ave. Subway: F to 23rd St.; 1, 9 to 23rd St. Closed Mon.–Fri.
Outdoor flea market with some of everything. Sunday is biggest. Arrive early if you're serious.
Chelsea Market, 75 9th Ave. Subway: A, C, E to 14th St.
Indoor food shopping in attractive setting.
Flea Market, corner of Broadway and Grand St. Subway: 6 to Canal St.-Broadway. Closed Mon.–Fri.
Flea Market at P.S. 183, 419 E. 67th St. Subway: 6 to 68th St. Closed Sun.–Fri.
Union Square Greenmarket, Uptown side of Union Sq. Subway: 4, 5, 6 to Union Sq. Closed Tues., Thurs., and Sun.
Local farmers sell their produce, cheeses, and ciders. Especially amazing selection in midsummer and fall with lots of foodies and special events.

RECORDS, CDS

Academy Records & CD's, 12 W. 18th St., tel 212/242-3000. Subway: 1, 9 to 18th St.
Used items, specializing in classical music.

PHOTOGRAPHY

Well-priced photo equipment.
B & H, 420 9th Ave., tel 212/444-6615. Subway: A, C, E to 34th St. Call for hours.
Photo equipment.

THIS & THAT

The Art of Shaving, 141 E. 62nd St., tel 212/317-8436. Subway: 4, 5, 6 to 59th St. Closed Sun.
Supplies or a shave.
E.A.T., 1064 Madison Ave., tel 212/772-0022. Subway: 6 to 77th St. Closed a.m. Sun.
Gifts for all ages.
Fountain Pen Hospital, 10 Warren St., tel 212/964-0580. Subway: A, C to Chambers St. Closed Sat.–Sun.
Well-priced vintage and new pens.
Kate's Paperie, 561 Broadway, tel 212/941-9816. Subway: N, R to Prince St.
Lovely paper and stationery.
Leo Kaplan Ltd., 114 E. 57th St., tel 212/355-7212. Subway: 6 to 77th St. Closed Sun.
Impressive antique and new paperweight collection.
The Pop Shop, 292 Lafayette St. (bet. Prince & Jersey Sts.), tel 212/219-2784. Subway: N, R to Prince and Broadway; 6 to Bleeker St.
Creative Keith Haring paraphernalia.

ENTERTAINMENT

Oh, can you be entertained in New York City! The questions are how, and for how much? Just as with eating and shopping, there are options across the spectrum. Perhaps the most interesting time can be had by carefully scheduling anything you really have your heart set on doing, then leaving the rest to last-minute inspirations and serendipity. The real magic of the city often presents itself right on the street and out of the blue, and it is that element of exquisite randomness that native New Yorkers most enjoy talking about at the end of the day.

GENERAL ENTERTAINMENT INFORMATION

New York Convention & Visitors Bureau, 229 W. 42nd St. (7th–8th Aves.), tel 800/NYC-VISIT. Literature on various forms of entertainment mailed to you, or speak to an agent (tel 212/484-1222 or website: www.nyc visit.com). Free tickets to concerts and TV tapings sometimes offered in person.

NYC/On Stage, tel 212/768-1818 or 800/STAGE-NY. Recorded information on theater, performances, dance, music, with transfer to ticket-buying service.

Theater Development Fund, 1501 Broadway (43rd–44th Sts.), tel 212/221-0885. Show your passport or out-of-state driver's license to buy four vouchers for $28, good for admission at Off-off Broadway theater, dance, and music events. Cash or travelers' checks only.

USEFUL PUBLICATIONS

Check out the *New York Times,* particularly Friday's Weekend section and Sunday's Arts and Leisure section; *The New Yorker, New York Magazine, The New York Observer,* the *Village Voice, Time Out New York,* and *Paper* (monthly).

USEFUL WEBSITES

www.nytimes.com The *New York Times,* strong on cultural events.
www.newyorkmag.com *New York Magazine* site with Cue section.
www.timeout.com/newyork *Time Out* listings and city guide.

THEATER

Theater, like other forms of entertainment in New York, runs the gamut from mainstream blockbusters on Broadway to the most experimental skits in some East Village cellar. No one can say which you will find most appealing, but neither should be written off. Off-off Broadway can mean less expensive but can still be soul-nurturing, while wily ticket buyers can end up spending the same to see world-class productions. There are officially 38 Broadway theaters, about 20 Off-Broadway (most under 500 seats), and about 300 Off-off Broadway venues (most under 100 seats).

SOURCES OF INFORMATION

It's always worth checking with the box office of the theater showing what you'd like to see. There may be house seats available, single seats, or cancel-lations. They are generally open from 10 a.m. until after the performance begins, and you can call them.

TKTS booths For 25–50% savings on Broadway and Off-Broadway tickets, try your luck here. The Lower Manhattan Center is located at the South Street Seaport, 199 Water St. Matinee tickets must be purchased the day before from this site. Hours are 11 a.m.–6 p.m. Mon.–Sat. and 11 a.m.–3:30 p.m. Sun. The main branch is in the heart of the Theater District at 47th St. and Broadway, Duffy Sq. It is open daily 3 p.m. to 8 p.m. for evening performances, 10 a.m.–2 p.m. Wednesday and Saturday for matinees, and 11 a.m.–7 p.m. Sunday for all performances. They accept cash or travelers' checks only and there is a small surcharge. Come armed with your theater-review magazines.

Association for a Better New York, tel 212/370-5800. Good information on smaller productions, and for investigating by venue versus show title.

Broadway Line, tel 212/563-2929. Current show information; you can be transferred to buy tickets.

New York Shakespeare Festival, tel 212/539-8500. Free at Delacorte Theater in Central Park in summertime, but you will need a ticket.

Telecharge, tel 212/239-6200 or 800/432-7250. Ticket agency to reserve seats for Broadway and Off-Broadway by credit card for a small handling fee.

Ticketmaster, tel 212/307-4100 or 800/755-4000. Same as above. Buy tickets on their website, www.ticketmaster.com.

Prestige Entertainment, tel 212/697-7788. Independent agent who may be able to find that seat.

BROADWAY VENUES

See pp. 114–115 for listings.
New Amsterdam, 214 W. 42nd St. (bet. 7th & 8th Aves), tel 212/282-2907. Subway: 1, 9, N, R to Times Square. Acclaimed performances and outstanding productions. Tours available.

OFF-BROADWAY VENUES

Astor Place Theater, 434 Lafayette St., tel 212/254-4370. Home of long-running Blue Man Group's *Tubes.*
Brooklyn Academy of Music, 30 Lafayette Ave., Brooklyn, tel 718/636-4100. Established destination for innovative works.

Classic Stage Company, 136 E. 13th St. (bet. 3rd & 4th Aves.), tel 212/239-6200. Subway: L, N. R, 4, 5, 6 to 14th St.
Past works find influence again in today's audiences.
De la Guarda, Union Square E. (at 15th St.), tel 212/239-6200. Subway: 6, N, R to 23rd St.
Joining performances of theater and circus.
Lincoln Center Theater, 150 W. 65th St., tel 212/239-6200.
Top productions on two stages.
La Mama E.T.C., 74A E. 4th St., tel 212/475-7710.
The mama of Off-Broadway groundbreakers.
Manhattan Theatre Club, 131 W. 55th St., tel 212/581-1212.
Two theaters, one for new and established playwrights, the other for readings, workshops.
New York Theater Workshop, 79 E. 4th St., tel 212/460-5475.
New plays by young directors, including Rent.
The Public Theater, 425 Lafayette St., tel 212/239-6200.
One of the finest theaters in New York, founded by Joseph Papp.

OFF-OFF BROADWAY VENUES & COMPANIES
Bowerie Lane Theater, 330 Bowery at Bond St., tel 212/677-0060.
Home of Jean Cocteau Theater Company, retakes of classics.
Irish Repertory Theater, 132 W. 22nd St., tel 212/727-2737.
Classic and contemporary Irish playwrights.

DANCE

At the Music and Dance Booth in Bryant Park, half-price, day-of-performance tickets can be available to certain dance events. Also try TKTS (see p. 261).

BALLET
The American Ballet Theater, Metropolitan Opera House, 19th and Broadway, tel 212/477-3030.
Classics and works created in traditional style by founder Michael Mordkin. Large theater, so top tiers are far from stage. Also for visiting foreign ballet companies.
New York City Ballet, New York State Theater, Broadway at 63rd St., tel 212/870-5570.
Works by founder George Balanchine, founding choreographer Jerome Robbins, and present director Peter Martins. Two seasons: Just before Thanksgiving to the beginning of March, featuring one month of Nutcracker performances; then beginning late April/May for 8 weeks.

CONTEMPORARY DANCE
Brooklyn Academy of Music, 30 Lafayette Ave., Brooklyn, tel 718/636-4100.
Excellent modern dance companies, lovely stage, Next Wave festival every autumn featuring renowned artists and experimental dance, and other festivals featuring many dance forms.
City Center, 131 W. 55th St., tel 212/247-0430.
Regular performances by famous, lesser known, and visiting troupes.
Joyce, 175 8th Ave. at 19th St., tel 212/242-0800.
One of the best dance destinations with great variety and an emphasis on newer artists.

OTHER TROUPES & VENUES
Dance Theater Workshop, 219 W. 19th St., tel 212/924-0077.
Relaxing atmosphere for alternative dance performances.
Dance Theater of Harlem, 466 W. 152nd St., tel 212/690-2800.
Rarely in town, catch them if you can.
Julliard Theater, 155 W. 65th St, tel 212/769-7406.
The Julliard School performs at the Julliard Theater.
The Kitchen, 512 W. 19th St., tel 212/255-5793.
Experimental works.

Merce Cunningham Studio, 55 Bethune St., tel 212/691-9751. Various works.
Movement Research, 537 Broadway, tel 212/598-0551.
Free Monday night dance series since 60s.
P.S. 122, 150 1st Ave., tel 212/477-5288.
Unconventional works.

OUTDOOR SUMMER DANCE EVENTS
Central Park Summerstage, Rumsey Playfield at 72nd St., tel 212/360-2777.
Free dance program Fridays in July and the beginning of August.
Out of Doors Lincoln Center, 70 Lincoln Plaza, 212/875-5108.
Free dance events on plaza.

MUSIC

Tickets are available directly from venues, or can be booked through Ticketmaster for a fee, tel 212/307-4100.
Another option, for discounted same day tickets, is TKTS (see p. 261).

CLASSICAL MUSIC
Alice Tully Hall, tel 212/721-6500.
Home of Chamber Music Society.
Avery Fisher Hall, tel 212/875-5030.
Home of the New York Philharmonic.
Bargemusic, Fulton Ferry Landing, Brooklyn, tel 718/624-4061.
Concerts on Thursdays and Sundays on a barge with an awesome view of Manhattan.
Brooklyn Academy of Music, 30 Lafayette Ave., Brooklyn, tel 718/636-4100.
Home of Brooklyn Philharmonic Orchestra, specializing in contemporary classical composers.
Carnegie Hall, 881 7th Ave., tel 212/247-7800.
One of the world's greatest.
Damrosch Park, tel 212/721-6500.

Free outdoor concerts
in summer.
Julliard School of Music,
tel 212/799-5000.
Many free recitals.
Kaufmann Concert Hall,
92nd St. YMCA, 1395 Lexington
Ave., tel 212/415-5440.
Great acoustics and
interesting series.
Lincoln Center, 55 W. 65th St.,
tel 212/875-5000.
**Metropolitan Museum of
Art,** 5th Ave. at 82nd St.,
tel 212/535-7710.
Chamber music
in various locations.

OTHER CLASSICAL
MUSIC VENUES
**Cathedral of St. John the
Divine,** Amsterdam Ave. at
112th St., tel 212/662-2133.
Central Park Summerstage,
tel 212/360-3444.
Summertime concerts—many
are free.
**Church of St. Ignatius
Loyola,** 980 Park Ave.,
tel 212/288-2520.
Church of the Ascension, 5th
Ave. (at W. 10th St.), tel 212/254-
8620. Subway: N, R to 5th Ave.
The Cloisters, Fort Tryon
Park, Inwood, tel 212/650-2290.
Subway: A to 190th St.
World Financial Center,
West St. to the Hudson River,
tel 212/945-0505.

OPERA
**Amato Opera Theater
Intimate,** 319 Bowery at 2nd
St., tel 212/228-8200.
City Center, 130 W. 55th St.
(bet. 6th & 7th Aves.), tel
212/581-1212. Subway: N, R, Q,
W to 57th St.
Julliard Opera Center,
Lincoln Center, tel 212/769-
7406. Students' productions.
Metropolitan Opera House,
Lincoln Center,
tel 212/362-6000.
Has its own company and
visiting performers, world-class
productions.
New York State Theater,
Lincoln Center,
tel 212/870-5570.
Variety of productions.

MUSIC VENUES
Many of these venues do not
accept credit cards.
Apollo Theater, 253 W. 125th
St., tel 212/749-5838.
Variety of African-American
musical acts, especially on
amateur night (Wednesday).
Beacon Theater, 2124
Broadway (at 74th St.), tel
212/496-7070.
Good bet for mainstream
groups.
Bitter End, 147 Bleecker St.,
tel 212/673-7030.
Small singer-songwriter joint.
CBGB's, 315 E. Bowery,
tel 212/982-4052.
Down and dirty legendary
punk venue.
Central Park Summerstage,
tel 212/360-2777.
Variety of acts.
Fez, (under Time Café) 380
Lafayette St., tel 212/533-2680.
Variety of acts.
Irving Plaza, 17 Irving Pl.,
tel 212/777-6800.
Mid-level nearly big-time acts.
Jones Beach, Long Island,
tel 516/221-1000.
Summertime open amphitheater
for top performances.
Knitting Factory, 74 Leonard
St., tel 212/219-3055.
Progressive rock, experimental
music, etc.
Madison Square Garden,
7th Ave. at 33rd St.,
tel 212/465-6741.
Biggest rock acts.
Meadowlands, 50 Route 120,
East Rutherford, N.J.,
tel 201/935-3900.
Big, big acts.
Mercury Lounge, 217 E.
Houston St., tel 212/260-4700.
Hip spot for new bands.
Nassau Coliseum, 1255
Hempstead Turnpike, Uniondale,
N.Y., tel 516/794-9303.
Biggest rock acts.
Paddy Reilly's, 519 2nd Ave.,
tel 212/686-1210.
Irish rock.
Radio City Music Hall, 50th
St. at 6th Ave., tel 212/632-4000.
Art deco hall with huge acts.
Roseland, 239 W. 52nd St., tel
212/247-0200.
Major acts.

Shea Stadium, 126th St. at
Roosevelt Ave., Queens,
tel 718/507-8499.
The biggest rock concerts.
Sin'e, 122 St. Mark's Pl.,
tel 212/982-0370.
Modern Irish folk.
S.O.B's, 200 Varick St.,
tel 212/243-4940.
Premier world music venue.
Webster Hall, 125 E. 11th St.,
tel 212/353-1600.
Big downtown dance bar.

JAZZ & BLUES
Birdland, 315 W. 44th St.,
tel 212/581-3080.
A classier spot for top jazz.
Blue Note, 131 W. 3rd St.,
tel 212/475-8592.
Big names.
Iridium, 1615 Broadway,
tel 212/582-2121.
Top performers.
Jazz Standard, 116 E. 27th St.,
tel 212/576-2232.
Restaurant/jazz club combo.
Knickerbocker, 74 Leonard St.
(bet. Broadway & Church St.), tel
212/219-3055. Subway: N, R to
Astor Pl.
Good lineups of blues players.
Lenox Lounge, 288 Malcolm X
Blvd. (bet. W. 124th & W. 125th
Sts.), tel 212/427-0253. Subway:
2, 3 to 125th St.
Dating from the 1930s, its Zebra
Room hosts blues acts and jam
sessions.
Manny's Carwash, 1558 3rd
Ave., tel 212/369-2583.
Local and national blues acts.
Smalls, 183 W. 10th St.,
tel 212/929-7565.
Emerging artists in a casual all-
night spot.
Village Vanguard, 178 7th
Ave., tel 212/255-4037.
A basement club, and one
of the best.
Zinc Bar, 90 W. Houston St
(bet. Thompson St. & LaGuardia
Pl.), tel 212/477-8337. Subway: 1,
9 to Houston St.
Brazilian jazz on weekends,
Cuban rifts during the week.

CABARET

Bemelmans Bar, Carlyle Hotel, 35 E. 76th St., Tel 212/570-7189. A less expensive alternative, with fine pianists.

Café Carlyle, 35 E. 76th St., tel 212/744-1600. Classic shows by Bobby Short, Eartha Kitt, and others (Woody Allen plays Dixieland Mondays).

Danny's Skylight Room, 346 W. 46th St. (bet. 8th & 9th Aves.), tel 212/265-8133. Subway: L to 8th Ave. Located on Restaurant Row, with a variety of musical performances including jazz.

Don't Tell Mama, 343 W. 46th St., tel 212/757-0788. Variety of emerging acts, revues.

Joe's Pub, 425 Lafayette St. (bet. E. 4th St. & Astor Pl.), tel 212/539-8770. Subway: 6 to Astor Pl. Italian menu available at night.

The Oak Room, Algonquin Hotel, 59 W. 44th St., tel 212/840-6800. Great performers.

Supper Club, 240 W. 47th St., tel 212/921-1940. Restored ballroom with big bands and dancing.

View, 151 E. 50th St., tel 212/753-1144. Supper club with fancy dress featuring various acts.

COMEDY

Caroline's Comedy Club, 1626 Broadway at 49th St., tel 212/757-4100.

Comedy Cellar, 117 MacDougal St., tel 212/254-3480.

Comic Strip, 1568 2nd Ave., tel 212/861-9386.

Dangerfield's, 1118 1st Ave., tel 212/593-1650.

Gotham Comedy Club, 34 W. 22nd St., tel 212/367-9000. Top performers.

New York Comedy Club, 241 E. 24th St., tel 212/696-5233.

The Original Improv, 422 W. 34th St., tel 212/279-3446.

New and established acts.

Stand Up NY, 236 W. 78th St., tel 212/595-0850. Small venue for up-and-coming as well as established acts.

FILM

In addition to regular Hollywood fare, the city offers an unparalleled selection of films unavailable in other locales, from small independent premieres, to classic films shown to the tune of live organ music, to outdoor movies in Bryant Park in the summer months. A number of museums also sponsor film festivals and for those inclined to research, there are fine collections open to the public in libraries and museums. If your interest is in filmmaking, some of the world's best programs and schools are here as well.

MovieFone, tel 212/777-FILM, has recorded information on all films showing, nearest locations, ticket-buying system ($1.50 surcharge), helpful for popular shows at popular times.

The New York Film Festival, tel 212/875-5600, presented by the Film Society of Lincoln Center, begins in late September and consists of two weeks of new American and foreign films.

FOREIGN & INDEPENDENT FILM HOUSES

Angelika Film Center, 8 W. Houston St., tel 212/995-2000.

Asia Society 725 Park Ave., tel 212/517-2742.

Carnegie Hall Cinema, 7th Ave. at 56th St., tel 212/265-2520.

Cinema Village, 22 E. 12th St., tel 212/924-3363.

Film Forum, 209 W. Houston St., tel 212/727-8110.

French Institute, 55 E. 59th St. tel 212/355-6160.

Lincoln Plaza Cinema, 30 Lincoln Plaza, tel 212/757-2280.

Quad Cinema, 34 W. 13th St. tel 212/255-8800.

68th St. Playhouse, 3rd Ave.

at 68th St., tel 212/734-0302.

Paris Theater, 4 W. 58th St., tel 212/688-3800.

Walter Reade Theater, 70 Lincoln Center Plaza, tel 212/875-5600. Home of the Film Society of Lincoln Center.

CLASSIC FILM VENUES

American Museum of the Moving Image, 35th Ave. at 36th St., Long Island City, tel 718/784-0077.

Anthology Film Archives, 32 2nd Ave., tel 212/505-5110.

Film Forum, 209 W. Houston St., tel 212/727-8110.

Museum of Modern Art, showings current held at Gramercy Theatre, 127 E. 23rd St. (off Lexington Ave.).

Museum of Television and Radio, 25 W. 52nd St., tel 212/621-6600.

Public Theater, 425 Lafayette St., tel 212/539-8500.

Whitney Museum of Art, 945 Madison Ave., tel 212/570-3600.

ULTRA MOVIE EXPERIENCES

The Ziegfeld, 141 W. 54th St., tel 212/765-7600. 1,400-seat, velvet-seated palace. A throwback and a classic venue, no matter what's playing.

Sony IMAX Theater, 1992 Broadway, tel 212/336-5000. Monstrous screen with 3-D offerings. Short subjects.

CHILDREN'S CINEMA

Guild Theater, 33 W. 50th St., tel 212/757-2406. Lovely old theater often offering Disney, near Rockefeller Center.

Imax Theater, at the American Museum of Natural History, Central Park W. at 79th St., tel 212/769-5100. Nature movies on a huge screen.

Walter Reade Theater/Film Society of Lincoln Center, 70 Lincoln Center Plaza, tel 212/875-5600. Saturday morning children's series.

ILLUSTRATIONS CREDITS

Abbreviations for terms appearing below: (t) top; (b) bottom; (l) left; (r) right.

Cover, (tl, tr), Image Bank; (bl), Tony Stone Images; (br), Kelly Mooney Photog.

1, Pictor. 2/3, Dallas & John Heaton/CORBIS. 4, Pix. 9, Telegraph Colour Library. 11, Kelly Mooney Photog. 12/13, Photo Researchers Inc. 14/15, Pix. 16/17, Steve McCurry. 18/19, AKG. 21, The Bridgeman Art Library. 22, Fraunces Tavern Museum. 23, Art Resource. 24/25, Metropolitan Museum of Art. 26, NASA. 27, Kelly Mooney Photog. 28/9, Karen Kasmauski. 30, Joe McNally. 33, Kelly Mooney. 34/5, Jodi Cobb. 36, FPG. 39, Nathan Benn. 40, Peter Arnold Inc. 41, Esto Photographics. 42/3, Keith Meyers/The New York Times. 45(t), Royalty-Free/CORBIS; 45(b), Reuters NewMedia Inc./CORBIS. 47, AA Photo Library/Clive Sawyer. 50, Photo Researchers Inc. 51(t), Pix.; artwork Matlings. 52, Kelly Mooney Photog. 53, AA Photo Library/Douglas Corrance. 54/55, Kelly Mooney Photog. 56(t), Corbis; 56(b), The Bridgeman Art Library. 57, Photo Researchers Inc. 58, Kelly Mooney Photog. 59, Kelly Mooney Photog. 61, AA Photo Library/R. Elliott. 62, Kelly Mooney Photog. 63, Pix. 64, Kelly Mooney Photog. 65, FPG 67, Photo Researchers Inc. 68/69 Kelly Mooney Photog. 71, Steve McCurry. 72, Mary Ann Lynch. 73, Mary Ann Lynch. 74, Gamma. 75, Pix. 78/79, FPG. 80, Mary Ann Lynch. 81, AA Photo Library/Ellen Rooney. 83(t), Tamiment Institute Library, New York University; 83(bl), Tamiment Institute Library, New York University; 83(br) Archives of American Art, Smithsonian Institution. 84, Pix. 85, Esto Photographics. 86, Steve McCurry. 87, FPG. 90, Pix. 91(t) Steve McCurry. 91(b) Pix. 92, Pix. 93, FPG. 95, Kelly Mooney Photog. 96, Kelly Mooney Photog. 97, Bob Sacha. 98, Joe McNally. 100, Kelly Mooney Photog. 101, FPG. 104, The St. Regis. 104/5, FPG. 106, The Stock Market Photo Agency Inc. 107, Photo Researchers Inc. 109, Pix. 110, Photo Researchers Inc. 111, The Royalton Hotel. 112/3, FPG. 114, Pix. 115, The Image Bank, Getty

Images, 116, Pix. 117, Esto Photographics. 119, Telegraph Colour Library. 120, FPG. 121(t), SuperStock; 121(b), AA Photo Library/Doug Corrance. 122/3, Courtesy MoMA. 124/5, Courtesy MoMA. 126, Michael Moran. 127, Norman McGrath, 2000. 129, FPG. 130, Photo Researchers Inc. 131, Colorific. 134, The Frick Collection. 135, The Frick Collection. 136, AA Photo Library/Richard Elliott. 138, art-work Maltings. 139, AA Photo Library/Doug Corrance. 140/1, Joe McNally. 142, The Bridgeman Art Library. 142/3, Gamma. 144, Photo Researchers. 145, Joe McNally. 146/7, Joe McNally. 148/9, Joe McNally. 149, Colorific. 150, Joe McNally. 151, Pix. 152, Colorific. 154, Art Resource. 154/5, Esto Photographics. 155, Jewish Museum. 156, ICP/David Spear. 157, Sofika (L Zielyk). 158, Courtesy of the Museum of the City of New York. 159, The Bridgeman Art Library. 160(t), Karl Peterson; 160(b), Karl Peterson. 161, Abigail Adams Smith Museum. 162, Pix. 163, AA Photo Library/Richard Elliott. 164/5, Whitney Museum of American Art, New York. 165, Steve McCurry. 166, J Allan Cash Ltd. 167, José Azel. 170/1, Photo Researchers Inc. 172, Telegraph Colour Library. 173, FPG. 176/7, Photo Researchers Inc. 177, Kelly Mooney Photog. 178, Kelly Mooney Photog. 179(t), FPG; 179(b), St Tammaus. 182, Historical Society. 183, The Bridgeman Art Library. 184, Craig Chesek. 185, Pix. 186, AMNH/D. Finnin. 187, AA Photo Library/Doug Corrance. 188(t), Childrens Museum of Manhattan; 188(b), Nicholas Roerich Museum. 189, Colorific. 192, Photo Researchers Inc. 193, Photo Researchers Inc. 194, Photo Researchers Inc. 195, Pix. 196, Photo Researchers Inc. 197, Kelly Mooney Photog. 198, David Alan Harvey. 199, Photo Researchers Inc. 200, Corbis/Library of Congress. 201(tr), Culver Pictures; 201(bl), Corbis/Bettmann; 201(br), Culver Pictures. 202, The Bridgeman Art Library. 203, National Geographic Society. 207, SuperStock. 208, Pix. 209, Pix. 210/11, The Bridgeman Art Library. 211, The Bridgeman Art Library. 213, John Calabrese. 214, AA Photo Library/Richard Elliott. 215, FPG. 216, Pix. 217, Pix. 218, Jacques Marchais Museum of

Tibetan Art. 219, Steve Crandall & Associates. 220, Pix. 221, Wildlife Conservation Society. 222, Wave Hill. 223, FPG. 224, AA Photo Library/Paul Kenward. 225, AA Photo Library/Richard Elliott. 226(t), Pix; 226(b), Courtesy Museum for African Art. 230/1, SuperStock. 232, SuperStock. 233, SuperStock. 234, SuperStock. 235, Telegraph Colour Library.

The world's largest nonprofit scientific and educational organization, the National Geographic Society was founded in 1888 "for the increase and diffusion of geographic knowledge." Since then it has supported scientific exploration and spread information to its more than nine million members worldwide.

The National Geographic Society educates and inspires millions every day through magazines, books, television programs, videos, maps and atlases, research grants, the National Geography Bee, teacher workshops, and innovative classroom materials.

The Society is supported through membership dues, charitable gifts, and income from the sale of its educational products. Members receive NATIONAL GEOGRAPHIC magazine—the Society's official journal—discounts on Society products, and other benefits.

For more information about the National Geographic Society, its educational programs, publications, or how to support its work, call 1-800-NGS-LINE (647-5463), or write to: National Geographic Society, 1145 17th Street, N.W., Washington, D.C. 20036 U.S.A.

Printed in the U.S.A.

Published by the National Geographic Society
John M. Fahey, Jr., *President and Chief Executive Officer*
Gilbert M. Grosvenor, *Chairman of the Board*
Nina D. Hoffman, *Executive Vice President,*
President, Books and School Publishing
Kevin Mulroy, *Vice President and Editor-in-Chief*
Marianne Koszorus, *Design Director*
Charles Kogod, *Director of Photography*
Elizabeth L. Newhouse, *Director of Travel Publishing*
Barbara A. Noe, *Senior Editor and Series Editor*
Cinda Rose, *Art Director*
Caroline Hickey, *Senior Researcher*
Carl Mehler, *Director of Maps*
R. Gary Colbert, *Production Director*
Richard S. Wain, *Production Project Manager*

2003 edition
Mary Ann Lynch, *Consultant*
Sharon Kocsis Berry, *Picture Editor*
The M Factory, *Map Research and Production*
Nicolette Costantino, Clio Pakenham, *Contributors*

Edited and designed by AA Publishing (a trading name of Automobile Association Developments Limited, whose registered office is Norfolk House, Priestley Road, Basingstoke, Hampshire, England RG24 9NY. Registered number: 1878835).
Betty Sheldrick, *Project Manager*
David Austin, *Senior Art Editor*
Marilynne Lanng, *Editor*
Phil Barfoot, Nick Otway, *Designers*
Simon Mumford, *Senior Cartographic Editor*
Nicky Barker-Dix, Helen Beever, *Cartographers*
Richard Firth, *Production Director*
Picture Research by Poppy Owen, Image Select International Limited
Map art by Chris Orr Associates, Southampton, England
Cutaway illustrations drawn by Maltings Partnership, Derby, England

Updated 2001, 2003.

Library of Congress Cataloging-in-Publication Data
The National geographic traveler. New York.
    p. cm.
    Includes index.
    ISBN 0-7922-7430-X (alk. paper)
    1. New York (N.Y.)—Guidebooks. 1. National Geographic Society (U.S.) 11. Title: New York.
    F128.18.N28   1999
    917.47'10443—dc21   99-11701
                              CIP

Printed and bound by R.R. Donnelley & Sons, Willard, Ohio; Color separations by Leo Reprographics, Hong Kong; Cover separations by L.C. Repro, Aldermaston, U.K.; Cover printed by Miken Inc., Cheektowaga, New York.
Visit the society's Web site at http:/www.nationalgeographic.com

The information in this book has been carefully checked and to the best of our knowledge is accurate. However, details are subject to change, and the National Geographic Society cannot be responsible for such changes or for errors or omissions. Assessments of sites, hotels, and restaurants are based on the author's subjective opinion. The publisher cannot be responsible for any consequences arising from the use of this book.

NATIONAL GEOGRAPHIC
TRAVELER
Arizona

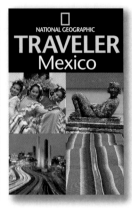

NATIONAL GEOGRAPHIC
TRAVELER
Mexico

NATIONAL GEOGRAPHIC
TRAVELER
Venice

NATIONAL GEOGRAPHIC
TRAVELER
A Century of Travel Expertise in Every Guide

- **Amsterdam** ISBN: 0-7922-7900-X
- **Arizona** ISBN: 0-7922-7899-2
- **Australia** ISBN: 0-7922-7431-8
- **Barcelona** ISBN: 0-7922-7902-6
- **Boston & Environs** ISBN: 0-7922-7926-3
- **California** ISBN: 0-7922-7564-0
- **Canada** ISBN: 0-7922-7427-X
- **The Caribbean** ISBN: 0-7922-7434-2
- **China** ISBN: 0-7922-7921-2
- **Costa Rica** ISBN: 0-7922-7946-8
- **Cuba** ISBN: 0-7922-6931-4
- **Egypt** ISBN: 0-7922-7896-8
- **Florence & Tuscany** ISBN: 0-7922-7924-7
- **Florida** ISBN: 0-7922-7432-6
- **France** ISBN: 0-7922-7426-1
- **Great Britain** ISBN: 0-7922-7425-3
- **Greece** ISBN: 0-7922-7923-9
- **Hawaii** ISBN: 0-7922-7944-1
- **Hong Kong** ISBN: 0-7922-7901-8

- **India** ISBN: 0-7922-7898-4
- **Italy** ISBN: 0-7922-7562-4
- **Japan** ISBN: 0-7922-7563-2
- **London** ISBN: 0-7922-7428-8
- **Los Angeles** ISBN: 0-7922-7947-6
- **Mexico** ISBN: 0-7922-7897-6
- **Miami and the Keys** ISBN: 0-7922-7433-4
- **New Orleans** ISBN: 0-7922-7948-4
- **New York** ISBN: 0-7922-7430-X
- **Paris** ISBN: 0-7922-7429-6
- **Rome** ISBN: 0-7922-7566-7
- **San Diego** ISBN: 0-7922-6933-0
- **San Francisco** ISBN: 0-7922-7565-9
- **Spain** ISBN: 0-7922-7922-0
- **Sydney** ISBN: 0-7922-7435-0
- **Thailand** ISBN: 0-7922-7943-3
- **Venice** ISBN: 0-7922-7917-4
- **Washington, D.C.** ISBN: 0-7922-7903-4

AVAILABLE WHEREVER BOOKS ARE SOLD